AN ATLAS OF ROMAN
RURAL SETTLEMENT
IN ENGLAND

AN ATLAS OF ROMAN RURAL SETTLEMENT IN ENGLAND

Jeremy Taylor

CBA Research Report 151
Council for British Archaeology
2007

Published 2007 by the Council for British Archaeology
St Mary's House, 66 Bootham, York YO30 7BZ

British Library Cataloguing in Publication Data

A catalogue record for this book is available from the British Library

ISBN: 978 1 902771 66 3

Cover designed by BP Design, York
Typeset by Carnegie Book Production, Lancaster
Printed by The Alden Press, Oxford

The publisher acknowledges with gratitude a grant from English Heritage towards the cost of publication

Front cover illustration: A Roman nucleated settlement on
the fen edge at Camp Ground, Earith, Cambridgeshire
(© Cambridge Archaeological Unit)

Contents

List of Figures

Chapter 7

List of Tables

Acknowledgements

This book presents the results of a project sponsored by English Heritage and the Leverhulme Trust, subsequently developed by the author into the characterisation, mapping, and assessment of late prehistoric and Roman rural settlement across the whole of England. My thanks go to all those at both organisations who have helped in the often painful process of bringing this work to fruition. I would especially like to thank Martin Millett, Deborah Porter, and Graham Fairclough for their patience.

This project has utilised evidence from every Sites and Monuments Record in the country and a host of other published and unpublished material, and has necessarily drawn on the help and experience of an enormous number of people. I would like to thank all those local authority staff who provided data for the project and much useful advice on how to make sense of it. Especial thanks also to staff in the National Mapping Programme at English Heritage and to Chris Gerrard, Richard Jones, Pete Liddle, and Steve Parry for providing unpublished survey data.

In the publication of this work I have often relied on the support of a number of colleagues in the School of Archaeology and Ancient History at the University of Leicester, but particular gratitude to Mark Gillings, for coffee, encouragement, and GIS advice, and Simon James, for reading drafts, liaison with the CBA, and the occasional kick up the backside.

Finally I would like to thank staff at the CBA and especially Catrina Appleby and Jane Thorniley-Walker for helping to pull together my manuscript into some semblance of order.

Abbreviations

AOD	Above Ordnance Datum
ASUD	Archaeological Services, University of Durham
HBMCE	Historic Buildings and Monuments Commission for England
HLC	Historic Landscape Characterisation
HMSO	Her Majesty's Stationery Office
MCD	Monument Class Description
MORPH2	Morphological classification system used by English Heritage to record systematically aerial photographic evidence
MPP	Monuments Protection Programme
NMP	National Mapping Programme
NMR	National Monuments Record
RCHME	Royal Commission on the Historical Monuments of England
SMR*	Sites and Monuments Record
SPTA	Salisbury Plain Training Area

*Since the research for this project was carried out, the term Sites and Monuments Record has been replaced by the term Historic Environment Record (HER)

Summary

This volume presents the results of a project sponsored by English Heritage and the Leverhulme Trust into the characterisation, mapping, and assessment of late prehistoric and Roman rural settlement across the whole of England. Utilising evidence from every local authority archive in the country and a host of other published and unpublished material, it outlines an integrated framework for the evaluation of Iron Age and Roman rural settlement, and highlights directions for future research. The challenges of researching, understanding, and managing this enormous archaeological resource, a key area of academic and public concern, are discussed in relation to a national review of the literature and current recording practice.

Rural landscapes, where the great majority of the population lived, were a key arena of social change in Roman Britain, yet past approaches to research have tended to focus on a few settlement categories such as villas that account for only a fraction of the recognised forms. This has led to major biases and gaps in our understanding of the complex rural societies of the period. It has also created problems by applying an understanding of rural settlement commonly based on detailed excavation to the more fragmentary survey-based data typical of the majority of sites. This book looks at how, through the use of a wider range of material evidence, it is possible to develop a better understanding of the whole resource and its potential significance for the wider study of Roman Britain.

Mapping the information from a systematic national survey of the evidence, this volume provides a guide to major regional and chronological trends in rural settlement pattern, form, and function. Together, the results provide a national overview of research strengths and weaknesses in the subject, and patterns of regionality in Roman rural settlement, land allotment, and land use. Wider dissemination of this information is fundamental to the establishment of future priorities in the study of Roman rural society, and will significantly enhance our understanding of Roman Britain as a whole. It will also provide guidance for characterisation and management of recorded settlements at a regional and national level.

The book first explores the background to the project, the nature of the data available, and the strengths and limitations of the approach used; it then goes on to discuss the main results of this work. The initial national survey of archival evidence indicates a marked regional difference between rural landscapes of mixed enclosed, enclosure complex, and open settlements in the south and east of the country and those of overwhelmingly enclosed settlement in the north and west. These differences in basic settlement morphology appear to relate to different patterns in overall settlement size and the relationship of settlements to wider patterns of rural land allotment. A region by region overview of the evidence for field systems and other evidence of land allotment shows the extraordinary variety of systems of land use developed across the country. Within this notable diversity, however, can be seen major regional differences between areas, characterised predominantly by open, partially or locally enclosed landscapes and those in which large tracts or the entire rural landscape appear to have been demarcated by field boundaries, trackways, and roads.

Assessment of the excavated evidence and the results of a series of local case studies of aerial photographic data confirms that the regions of mixed settlement morphology were also those that saw the development of marked differentiation in rural settlement size. Here the rural landscapes of the Roman period incorporated both small farmsteads and a range of nucleated 'hamlets' and 'villages'. These patterns were locally diverse and complex, with some areas experiencing a greater degree of settlement nucleation than others. Most areas of mixed settlement morphology, however, also saw the rise of significant settlement hierarchy during the Roman period with a proportion of both dispersed and nucleated settlements developing into villas. In the west and north of the country, by contrast, dispersed settlement in enclosed farmsteads or smaller 'hamlets' was the norm and evidence for obvious settlement hierarchy in the form of villas was rare or entirely absent.

Analysis of a range of aerial photographic, field-walking, and excavation-based case studies suggested that in some cases the pattern of mixed dispersed and nucleated settlement in the south and east of the country was established by the Late Iron Age. In other parts of the south and east, however, it represented a generally gradual shift towards a more nucleated pattern during the 2nd to 4th centuries AD. This was in stark contrast to the patterns further west and north where dispersed settlement in farmsteads remained the overwhelming norm throughout the Roman period.

The concluding sections of the book draw together these diverse strands of evidence in order to outline the major differences in the character of rural settlement across that part of Roman Britain that lay within the boundaries of modern England. Whilst not intended to be a detailed treatise on the reasons for the diversity seen, it shows how there appear to be at least two Roman Britains. In the first, rural life is transformed with the development of a rural landscape characterised by a settlement hierarchy defined by both size and apparent wealth. These changes appear to be closely related to wider rural land use, with extensively farmed and demarcated landscapes linked to communications networks that enabled the produce of these lands to be mobilised. It is no surprise to see that these regions also develop major rural industries such as pottery, iron, and salt manufacturing as well as a network of secondary market centres. In the second Britain there is far less evidence for marked differentiation within patterns of rural settlement. Whilst far from static, rural life here changes in ways that appear to bear little resemblance to the patterns seen to the south and east. Rural industry is either dispersed or on a small scale or, in the case of some of the extractive industries, seemingly under close military oversight. The wider reasons for these differences and the impact they have on the development of the Roman province go beyond the scope of this book but it is hoped the evidence gathered together here will help to raise the profile of rural settlement in future debates on the subject.

Résumé

Ce volume est consacré aux résultats d'un programme mené sous l'égide de English Heritage et le Leverhulme Trust, qui avait comme objectif la caractérisation, la cartographie et l'évaluation de l'habitat rural de la fin de la protohistoire et de la période romaine dans l'Angleterre. Utilisant des données tirés de toutes les archives municipales du pays et d'un très grand nombre de documents publiés et inédits, ce volume esquisse dans ses grandes lignes un cadre intégré pour évaluer l'occupation du sol à de l'âge du fer et à l'époque romaine, et propose d'éventuelles directions pour la recherche future. Les difficultés éprouvées dans la recherche, la compréhension et la gestion de cette immense ressource archéologique – également une préoccupation des universitaires et du grand publique – sont traités ici dans le contexte d'un bilan national de la documentation et des pratiques courantes d'enregistrement.

Les paysages ruraux, où vivait l'écrasante majorité de la population, constituaient une arène clé de l'évolution sociale dans la Grande-Bretagne à l'époque romaine, mais la plupart des recherches antérieures se sont concentré sur certaines catégories de site, telles que les villas, qui ne représentent qu'une faible proportion des types reconnus. Il en résulte d'importants préjugés et lacunes dans nos connaissances des sociétés rurales complexes de cette période. D'autres problèmes sont dûs à l'application des modèles de l'habitat rural fondés sur les résultats des fouilles, aux données plus partielles issues de la prospection et typiques de la majorité des sites. Ce livre examine la manière dont, par l'utilisation d'une gamme plus large d'informations matérielles, il est possible d'augmenter notre compréhension de la ressource archéologique dans sa totalité et de sa signification potentielle pour l'étude générale de la période romaine en Grande-Bretagne.

Dressant la carte des informations obtenues d'un dépouillement systématique de la documentation au niveau national, ce volume présente un sommaire des principales tendances régionales et chronologiques concernant l'habitat rural, sa forme et sa fonction. Pris dans leur ensemble, les résultats fournissent un aperçu des forces et des faiblesses de la recherche actuelle, et mettent au jour de tendances régionales dans l'habitat rural romain, le morcellement des terres et l'exploitation du terrain. Une diffusion plus large de ces informations est indispensable pour la mise en place d'un futur schéma de recherche dans le domaine de la société romaine rurale. Elle améliorera de façon significative notre compréhension de la Grande-Bretagne à l'époque romaine. En plus elle facilitera la caractérisation et la gestion des sites reconnus au niveau national ainsi que régional.

Cet œuvre commence par explorer le contexte du projet, le caractère des données disponibles, et les atouts ainsi que les limitations de la méthodologie choisie; il se poursuit par la présentation des principaux résultats de ce travail. Le relevé préliminaire des archives indique une différence régionale marquée entre les paysages du Sud et de l'Est – jouxtant des établissements enclos, des groupements d'enclos et des habitats ouverts – et ceux du Nord et de l'Ouest dominés par des enclos. Ces tendances morphologiques semblent se rattacher aux différences dans la taille générale des sites et aux rapports entre les habitats et l'occupation du terrain. Un bilan, région par région, des parcellaires et d'autres témoins de la division des terres montre la grande diversité des systèmes d'exploitation du terrain le long du pays. Au sein de cette remarquable diversité, on constate néanmoins d'importantes différences régionales entre des zones caractérisées par des paysages ouverts, partiellement ou localement encloses, et celles dans lesquelles une grande partie du terrain – sinon le paysage entier – semble avoir été délimitée par les parcellaires, les chemins et les routes.

Une évaluation des données de fouilles et d'une série d'études détaillées locales des photographies aériennes confirme que les régions présentant une structure d'habitat mixte étaient également celles où la différenciation en taille des habitats est bien marquée. Ici, les paysages ruraux de l'époque romaine incorporaient à la fois les petites fermes et toute une gamme de 'villages' et de 'hameaux'. Ces tendances étaient complexes et variables au niveau local; certaines zones connaissant un plus haut degré d'agglomération que d'autres. La plupart des zones présentant une structure d'habitat mixte avaient toutefois également subi une hiérarchisation d'habitat significative au cours de la période romaine, un bon nombre de sites – soit dispersés soit groupés – se transformant en villa. En revanche, dans l'Ouest et le Nord, les habitats dispersés – fermes encloses ou petits 'hameaux' – constituaient la norme, et les témoins d'une hiérarchie d'habitat sous la forme de villas étaient rares ou faisaient totalement défaut.

Plusieurs études particulières utilisant la photographie aérienne, et les résultats de la prospection et des fouilles, suggéraient que, dans certains cas, le système d'habitat mixte (sites à la fois dispersés et groupés inclus) dans le Sud et l'Est existait déjà à la fin de l'âge du fer. Toutefois, ailleurs dans la même zone, il y avait une transition généralement graduelle vers la nucléation au cours du 2ème au 4ème siècle. Ceci présentait un contraste très net avec la situation dans l'Ouest et le Nord, où une structure d'habitat de fermes dispersées restait la norme pendant toute la période romaine.

La conclusion rassemble les divers enchaînements de données afin de souligner les plus importantes différences dans l'occupation du sol dans la partie de la province romaine qui se situe au sein des limites de l'Angleterre. Bien que ce livre ne soit pas conçu pour expliquer en détaille les causes de la diversité observée, il montre néanmoins qu'il semble y avoir au moins deux Grande-Bretagnes romaines. Dans la première, la vie rurale a été transformée par le développement d'un paysage rural caractérisé par une hiérarchie de sites basée à la fois sur la taille et la richesse des habitats. Ces changements semblent être étroitement liés à l'exploitation du terrain, où des paysages majoritairement agricoles et délimités étaient liés à des réseaux de communication qui permettaient de mobiliser les produits de ces terres. Il n'est guère surprenant de constater que c'est dans ces régions également que se sont développées d'importantes industries rurales, telles que celles de la céramique, du fer et du sel ainsi qu'un réseau d'agglomérations secondaires. Dans la deuxième Grande-Bretagne romaine, l'habitat rural témoigne moins de différenciation sur le plan de l'habitat. Bien que loin d'être statique, la vie rurale ici change de manière qui semble n'avoir guère de ressemblances avec les développements vus au Sud et à l'Est. Ici, l'industrie rurale est soit dispersée soit à petite échelle, ou bien, dans le cas de certaines des industries d'exploitation minière, sous une surveillance militaire étroite. L'analyse des causes plus profondes de ces différences et leur influence sur le développement de la province romaine dépassent la portée de ce livre mais on espère que les données rassemblées ici aideront à mettre en valeur l'habitat rural lors de futurs débats à ce sujet.

Zusammenfassung

Dieser Band faßt die Resultate eines Projektes zusammen, daß von English Heritage und dem Leverhulme Trust finanziert wurde. Es hat zum Thema, die ländliche Siedlungsstruktur der späten Vorgeschichte und Römerzeit für ganz England zu charakterisieren, kartieren und bewerten. Dazu wurden Informationen aus den Archiven der jeweiligen Denkmalbehörden und eine Vielzahl von anderen veröffentlichten und unveröffentlichten Quellen herangezogen. Das Resultat ist ein integriertes Rahmenwerk zur Studie von ländlichen Siedlungen aus der späten Eisenzeit und Römerzeit, das es ermöglicht Forschungsschwerpunkte für die Zukunft zu bestimmen. Herausforderungen für die Forschung, das Verständnis und das Management dieses großen archäologischen Bestandes, ein besonderer Schwerpunkt des akademischen und öffentlichen Interesses, werden im Zusammenhang mit einer Literaturrevision und aktueller Aufzeichnungspraxis diskutiert.

Das Land, wo der Großteil der Bevölkerung lebte, war ein Schauplatz von sozialer Entwicklung im römischen Britannien, dennoch haben sich die meisten Forschungsprojekte auf spezielle Siedlungskategorien gestützt, wie zum Beispiel Villen, die nur einen kleinen Teil des Gesamtbestandes ausmachen. Das hat zu Vorurteilen und Lücken in unserem Verständnis der komplexen ländlichen Bevölkerungsstruktur dieser Periode geführt. Probleme bei der Interpretation entstehen, wenn Kenntnisse, die aus detaillierten Ausgrabungen stammen, mit dem lückenhaften Datenbestand, der aus Geländearbeit stammt, verglichen werden. In diesem Buch wird untersucht, wie man durch den Gebrauch von einer Vielfalt von materiellen Beweisstücken den archäologischen Gesamtbestand besser erfassen und dessen Signifikanz für das Verständnis Britanniens in der Römerzeit beurteilen kann.

Die Informationen aus einer systematischen landesweiten Quellenstudie werden kartiert und in diesem Band zusammengefasst. Sie dienen als Nachschlagewerk zu den regionalen und chronologischen Trends im Verbreitungsmuster, Form und Funktion der ländlichen Besiedlung. Die Ergebnisse ergeben eine landesweite Bilanz von Forschungsschwerpunkten und Schwächen zu diesem Thema und legen regionale Siedlungsmuster der römischen ländlichen Siedlungen, Landverteilung und Bodennutzung dar. Die Verbreitung dieser Information soll dazu beitragen, zukünftige Forschungsschwerpunkte in der Studie der römischen Gesellschaftsstruktur auf dem Lande zu definieren, und liefert dadurch einen wichtigen Beitrag zum Verständnis der Geschichte Britanniens während der Römerzeit. Es soll auch als Leitfaden dienen, um die Aufzeichnung und das Pflege dieser Siedlungen auf regionaler und nationaler Ebene zu vereinheitlichen.

Dieses Buch untersucht als Erstes den Hintergrund dieses Projekts, die Beschaffenheit der aufgezeichneten Daten und die Stärken und Schwächen der angewandten Methoden; darauf folgt die Diskussion der Hauptresultate dieser Forschungsarbeit. Die ursprüngliche landesweite Archivstudie wies einen markanten regionalen Unterschied der Landschaft nach, mit gemischten eingefriedeten und offenen Siedlungen im Süden und Osten des Landes und überwiegend eingefriedeten im Norden und Westen. Diese Unterschiede in der grundlegenden Morphologie stehen in direktem Verhältnis mit der Größe der Siedlungen und deren Beziehung zur Landverteilung. Eine regionale Studie der Flursysteme und Landverteilung ergab eine landesweite Vielfalt von Systemen der Landnutzung. In dieser Vielfalt sind jedoch regionale Unterschiede zu erkennen, zum einen offene sowie teilweise bzw. lokal eingezäunte Landstriche, und zum anderen Landschaften die zum grössten Teil bzw. in seiner Gesamtheit aus mit Hecken, Wegen und Straßen eingegrenzten Feldern besteht.

Die Auswertung von Ausgrabungsfunden und Luftfotographien bestätigen, dass in den Regionen, wo eine gemischte Siedlungsmorphologie vorherrscht, die Größe der Siedlungen differenzierter war. Hier bestand die römische Siedlungslandschaft aus sowohl kleinen Gehöften als auch einer Reihe von ‚Weilern' und ‚Dörfern'. Diese Muster waren örtlich verschieden und komplex, in einigen Gebieten gab es stärker ausgeprägte Zentralisierung der Siedlungen als in anderen. In Gebieten mit gemischter Siedlungsmorphologie kann man während der Römerzeit eine zunehmende Siedlungshierarchie beobachten, wobei ein Teil der Einzelhöfe und Kerndörfer in römische Gutshöfe umgewandelt wurde. Im Gegensatz dazu waren im Norden und Westen verstreute Einzelhöfe oder kleinere ‚Weiler' die Norm und Hinweise auf eine Siedlungshierarchie in der Form von römischen Gutshöfen sind selten bzw. gar nicht vorhanden.

Datenanalyse aus Luftfotographien, Geländeuntersuchungen und Ausgrabungen zeigt, dass das Muster der Einzelhöfe und Kerndörfer im Süden und Osten in einigen Gegenden schon in der späten Eisenzeit etabliert war, in anderen sah man eine schrittweise Dorfbildung während des 2. bis 4. Jahrhunderts n. Chr. Im Gegensatz dazu waren Einzelhöfe im Norden und Westen während der gesamten Römerzeit die Norm.

Im Schlusskapitel werden die verschiedenen Beweise zusammengefasst und die verschiedenen Dorfstrukturen aus der Römerzeit innerhalb der modernen Grenzen von England beschrieben. Zwar soll hier keine wissenschaftliche Abhandlung über die Gründe für die verschiedenartigen Veränderungen geschrieben werden, es wird aber deutlich dargestellt, dass es anscheinend mindestens zwei Strukturtypen im römischen Britannien gab. Im Ersten wird das ländliche Leben durch die Entwicklung einer Siedlungshierarchie, die durch Größe und Wohlstand definiert wird, grundlegend verändert. Diese Veränderungen stehen im Verhältnis zu der Bodennutzung, wobei Gegenden mit intensiver Nutzung und Flurverteilung ein entwickeltes Straßennetz haben, das die Verbreitung der Produkte dieser Gebiete ermöglichte. Es ist kein Zufall, dass sich in diesen Regionen Industrien im ländlichen Bereich auch etablierten, wie zum Beispiel Keramik, Eisen- und Salzherstellung und die Entwicklung von sekundären Marktzentren. Im Zweiten Strukturtyp gibt es nur wenige Belege für eine starke Differenzierung innerhalb ländlicher Besiedlungsmuster. Der Fortschritt steht zwar nicht still, aber das ländliche Leben hat hier nur wenig mit den Veränderungen im Süden und Osten gemeinsam. Handwerk ist verstreut oder nur von geringer Intensität und der Abbau von Rohmaterialien scheint nur unter militärischer Aufsicht stattzufinden. Die Gründe für diese Differenzierungen sind außerhalb der Grenzen dieser Abhandlung, aber es wird erhofft, dass das hier vorgestellte Material dazu beitragen wird, dass in zukünftigen Diskussionen die ländliche Besiedlung einen wichtigen Platz einnimmt.

Chapter 1
Introduction

Rural landscapes were a key arena of social change in Roman Britain. They were, after all, where the great majority of the population lived, yet past approaches have tended to focus on a few settlement categories, such as villas, that account for only a fraction of the observed variation in recognised forms. This has led to major biases and gaps in our understanding of the complex rural societies of the period. It has also created problems in interpretation, as researchers have attempted to apply understandings of rural settlement commonly based on detailed excavation or earthwork information to the more fragmentary survey-based data typical of the majority of sites. This book looks at how, through the use of a wider range of material evidence, it is possible to develop a better understanding of the whole archaeological resource and its potential significance for the wider study of Roman Britain.

This volume maps the information yielded by a systematic national survey of the evidence and provides a guide to major regional and chronological trends in rural settlement pattern, form, and function. The system of classification used here is both informed by current academic debate and adaptable to the nature of the available evidence, and the results of the project are intended to encourage, inform, and frame debate on the importance of regional diversity in the historic development of Roman Britain.

Moreover, the book provides a national context for evaluating research strengths and weaknesses in the subject and identifying patterns of regionality in Roman rural settlement, land allotment, and land use. The wider dissemination of this information may prove invaluable in the establishment of future priorities in the study of Roman rural society and will significantly enhance our understanding of Roman Britain as a whole, providing a context for the ongoing detailed analysis of rural settlement at a regional and national level.

Characterising rural settlement in later prehistory and the Roman period: a potted history

Studies of change in Britain during the Roman period have long emphasised those spheres of social activity popular with students of the heart of the Classical world: in particular, the economy, urbanism, the role of the military and to some extent the nature of religious belief. This has been detrimental to our understanding of agrarian communities, and is a bias which has frequently been commented upon (eg Jones and Miles 1979; Miles 1989; Hingley 1989; 1991; 2004; Reece 1988), but, with a few notable exceptions, such comment does not seem to have appreciably shifted the emphasis of study. Instead, in rural archaeology over the last twenty years we have seen a continuing focus on the collection of an impressive array of information within something of a conceptual vacuum, a situation compounded and accelerated by fieldwork related to the advent of Planning Policy Guidance 16 (PPG16).

In particular, Roman archaeology in Britain has a long and well-developed tradition of landscape survey of rural settlement. This has created an enormous body of empirical evidence, many local studies, and a number of summaries of changing patterns of rural settlement (eg Phillips 1970; Gaffney and Tingle 1989; papers in Parker Pearson and Schadla-Hall 1994; Rippon 1997). These studies, along with similar surveys in the Mediterranean, have seen many methodological advances, and are often characterised by high standards of recording and primary analysis. That said, they have rarely contributed to wider synthetic studies of the province on anything other than an illustrative level, and their potential value for investigations of the wider impact of Roman conquest on the great mass of the population continues to go untapped. Furthermore, frustratingly few of these surveys have been fully published and consequently much of this evidence does not yet contribute to wider debates about the regional history of the province or the significance of rural society to the development of the empire.

It is unsurprising that broader theoretical developments have frequently failed to keep pace with this empirical work. Where research aims in rural archaeology have been made explicit they have tended to recapitulate a perspective of Roman Britain developed during the early 20th century that has been the subject of much critical debate (eg Hingley 1991; 2000; Freeman 1993; Barrett 1997; Grahame 1998). Part of this debate has recognised that Roman archaeology in Britain has seen a broad shift away from an early 20th-century perspective, in which classically orientated text-dominated views of the countryside focused on the villa as a symbol of successful Romanisation (*cf* Hingley 2000), to a situation in which attempts were made to redress this imbalance by recovering the archaeology of native non-elite society (eg Millett 1990; Hingley 1989; Webster 1996; Nevell 1999). Despite this shift, much of the debate over the impact of Roman occupation still focused on a rigid dichotomy between Roman/Imperialist and British/Native identities. Although there are clearly exceptions to this rule, one of the main consequences has been a tendency for the mass of such work to focus on largely descriptive, typological studies interpreted (if at all) in the same Roman/native terms (Collingwood and Richmond 1969; Hingley 1989; Dark and Dark 1997).

The study of Roman rural settlement, in particular, has been characterised by largely descriptive overviews of the mass of empirical evidence collected in an area, summarised in a local or regional synthetic study. This reluctance to develop explicitly defined theories is best exemplified by the lengthy list of overviews which incorporate sections on the countryside or rural settlement (eg Webster 1991; Ramm 1978; Branigan 1985; Miles 1989; Todd 1991; Corney 2000). These works are often structured around a limited range of theoretical assumptions that are rarely stated explicitly, yet together comprise so potent an orthodoxy as to remain largely unchallenged. It is difficult here to do justice to the history of this approach, but two major lines of enquiry seem to typify much of it: typological studies and socio-economic approaches.

Typological studies which concentrate on the description and classification of settlements and house types, commonly according to their excavated plans, have been characteristic of Roman archaeology in Britain. This work, initially culture-historical in outlook, provided the foundations for our understanding of the chronological development and geographical extent of particular forms of material evidence (eg Collingwood and Richmond 1969; Applebaum 1972; Hingley 1989). Authors such as these also, however, tended to use assumptions about cultural change, such as acculturation or social emulation, that were rarely considered to be in need of explanation or justification. Particular innovations were deemed to be understandable in terms of the supposed practical advantages or the comforts of Romanisation. Furthermore, as I have noted elsewhere (Taylor 2001, 49), there has been a tendency towards a kind of object fetishism in which the subject of study, such as the description and classification of building or settlement plans and the details of their evolution, becomes the object, thus avoiding an analysis of the social context of their construction and use. While it is arguable that this approach was justifiable in a first attempt to better understand the diverse range of evidence being recorded, it is disappointing that after several decades the subject does not seem to have moved on.

More systemic economic approaches to rural settlement in Roman Britain have developed since the 1970s. Influenced by the broader development of processual approaches to archaeology and by the work of economic historians (eg Jones 1974; Duncan-Jones 1982; Garnsey and Saller 1987), this work had the considerable benefit of returning the archaeology of settlements to a consideration of their material and social context. In Britain, these new approaches focused primarily on the impact of the Roman conquest and subsequent establishment of the province, and on changing economic conditions in the countryside (eg Todd 1978; Branigan 1977; 1985; Miles 1982; Branigan and Miles 1988; Fulford 1989). The analysis of evidence for the economy of villas and for villa estates as indicators of wealth and status became a recurring theme in considerations of rural society. Related studies of plant and animal remains, and, in particular, artefactual assemblages, revolutionised our understanding of agricultural practice and craft production in rural contexts (eg King 1984; Grant 1989; van der Veen 1992; Swan 1984; Millett 1990). The basic tenet of these approaches, however, was that new developments in rural settlement, agriculture or craft production were considered to be largely due to the influence of new economic factors in the aftermath of the conquest. In rural archaeology the classic example was the relating of the presence of villas to the development of Roman methods of wealth accumulation and status display linked to the establishment of taxation, expanding landed estates, and urban markets (Branigan and Miles 1988). Problems with such approaches have been discussed in recent reviews of the subject (eg Taylor 2001; Hingley 2004) and do not need reiterating here, but not least amongst them is the tendency which these approaches have to assume a straightforward relationship between the presence of particular forms of material evidence and wealth, so that the absence of such 'Roman' forms of wealth accumulation and display indicates poverty. In practice, however, choices of material expression are decisions that are specific to each social context, and thus should be a matter of investigation, not assumption (*cf* Taylor 2001; Haselgrove 2004).

During the course of the 1990s, a shift is apparent in Roman rural archaeology in Britain, with attempts to analyse rural social organisation at a local scale through the medium of rural settlement architecture. Hingley (1991) noted that earlier scholars' implicit acceptance of emulation or social evolution had tended to inhibit work in this direction, but some notable attempts have been made to build social models from the evidence (Stevens 1966; Smith 1978; 1987). Hingley (1990), Smith (1997) and a number of others (eg Scott 1990; Samson 1990a; 1990b; Clarke 1990; 1998; 1999; Scott 1995; 2000) attempted to realise the potential of such approaches for the study of social diversity in the development of rural communities in Roman Britain. Hingley (1989) and Clarke (1998), for example, highlighted the role potentially played by settlement layout and form in social status, organisation, and communication at a communal and intercommunal scale. Much of this work drew on a realisation of the need to study how architectural and wider geographical space was incorporated within the relations between people, and the uses to which such spaces were put. Clarke (1999, 37–9), for example, pointed out the most basic but striking distinctions between the architecture and layout of the Roman settlement at Newstead and contemporaneous rural settlements in the area. In the former, buildings were without exception rectangular and the settlement was laid out in relation to key elements of the fort's built environment, such as roads, while in the latter we see a similarly near-absolute adherence to roundhouse architecture and a topographically and environmentally influenced approach to the location and layout of settlements. Similar work in the Mediterranean world, especially in the study of Roman towns (eg Wallace-Hadrill 1994; Laurence 1994; Cornell and Lomas 1994; Revell 1999), the countryside (Purcell 1994) and travel (Witcher 1998; Laurence 1999; Adams and Laurence 2001), have also ably demonstrated the ideological and symbolic significance to Roman society in Italy and elsewhere of urban architecture, villas, and roads.

Such work led to the realisation that if we wish to study the significance of settlement and the wider landscape in the development of society in Britain it is important that we recognise and study the complexity and diversity of rural settlements in their spatial and chronological context. To understand why forms of settlement and patterns of land use were adopted in particular places at particular times and whether they constituted a radical change in social organisation, we need to understand how architecture was structured and how the resultant spaces related to particular forms of use (see Barrett 1999 for a wider discussion of these themes).

However, the fact that much of this work, especially since the advent of PPG16, has been largely site-specific has meant that with some notable exceptions (eg Williamson 1984; Gaffney and Tingle 1989; Bewley 1994; Fowler 2000) few attempts have been made to interpret the wider significance of developments in rural settlement and landscapes. In particular, analytical, rather than descriptive, approaches to the wider landscape have been rare and field systems have not been a focus of study in the Roman period. This is especially surprising (as well as a saddening reflection of an academic divide in British archaeology) given the excellent range of such detailed studies available for prehistoric periods in Britain (eg Fleming 1988; Barrett *et al* 1991; Bradley *et al* 1994).

Thanks to the extensive use of remote sensing techniques in Britain and the ongoing transcription and mapping of the results, we have an astonishing quantity of information about the layout and extent of the architecture of settlement and the wider landscape in later prehistory and the Roman period. Unfortunately, little of this information has been used as a research resource in its own right, despite attempts by those involved to alert a wider audience to its potential (eg Riley 1980; Palmer 1984; Stoertz 1997; Bewley 1998). A number of highly distinctive field systems and settlement networks have been recorded within Britain through such work (compare, for example, the evidence presented in Stoertz 1997 with that in Taylor 1999, or Riley and Wilson-North 2001 with McOmish *et al* 2002), but all too often we have satisfied ourselves by simply noting their form or recording the presence or absence of villas and towns.

This is a great pity given the realisation that access to, and the arrangement of, land use both for agricultural production and in mediating the wider relationships of rural communities is likely to have been very significant to the development of later Iron Age and Roman society. This lesson, as noted above, has clearly been learnt in prehistoric studies, but is still scarcely applied within archaeological studies of the Roman period in Britain. Happily, there is now an expanding body of work, such as that in Nottinghamshire and South Yorkshire (Chadwick 1999) and the Vale of Pickering (Powlesland 1998), that may yet remedy this situation.

Recently, landscape studies covering both the later Iron Age and Roman periods have developed interesting approaches that focus on theoretically explicit interpretations of the role of settlement and material culture in understanding the significance of local and regional diversity in rural society (such as Willis 1999; Hingley 2004; papers in Haselgrove and Moore 2007). These studies have begun to show how rural society in later Iron Age and Roman Britain followed distinctive local and regional social traditions that may well have been a major factor in influencing the make-up of Roman society. Such approaches, which recognise the great diversity that is apparent in local and regional social development, are implicit in the present study and are discussed further below (Chapters 4 and 5). Before addressing the evidence for this regional diversity, however, it is useful to have an understanding of the original context of the development of the rural settlement project and its biases (Chapter 3).

Chapter 2
Background and aims of the project

Background to the project

The background to the current project lay within the work of English Heritage's Monuments Protection Programme (MPP). The MPP was established in 1986 to speed up the rate at which statutory protection was extended to nationally important ancient monuments. Its principal objectives were to evaluate existing information held in local authority Sites and Monuments Records (SMRs) in order to identify sites of national importance; to recommend to the Secretary of State which sites should be protected; and to use the MPP's national perspective to help produce an improved response to the problem of managing poorly understood areas of the archaeological record. One key method of evaluating the evidence used by the MPP was the creation of Monument Class Descriptions (MCDs). Based on a synthesis of then current knowledge about the subject, the descriptions were an attempt to categorise the wide variety of evidence into comparable classes that could be assessed on the basis of their rarity, archaeological potential, and vulnerability.

The Single Monument Class evaluation stage of the Monuments Protection Programme produced a number of MCDs for Roman rural settlement which were influenced by wider developments within Roman archaeology. These were based on a synthesis of published information and led in 1990 to the creation of a range of classes, including Major and Minor Roman Villas, Aggregate Villages, Linear Villages, and Roman Farmsteads. A number of other related classes, such as Roman religious sites, *mansiones*, and *vici*, were also defined. Criteria for the evaluation of these classes of site were then developed, which gave the greatest archaeological potential to well-preserved earthwork sites. Cropmark and soilmark sites were to be considered under a separate national project reviewing the role of aerial photography in conjunction with the then Royal Commission on the Historical Monuments of England (RCHME) through the National Mapping Programme (NMP) (Bewley 1995). Most English counties were then asked to carry out desk-based evaluations using the MCD definitions and the scoring criteria to assign monuments to classes. As a result of this exercise records for 16 major villas, 390 minor villas, 196 aggregate villages, 77 linear villages, and 1125 farmsteads were produced.

When, however, a paper was produced which tried to assess sites of national importance (Porter 1995), it became clear that there were a number of limitations to any exercise that attempted to base scheduling policy on these existing MCDs. First, the descriptions were too closely specified, requiring a level of information simply not available in the majority of cases. The level of prior detail required to classify a site as a major or minor villa, for example, meant that only sites previously subject to excavation and with good aerial photographic or geophysical survey coverage could be considered. Part of the description of major villas noted that they should be defined as 'a large and well appointed building comprising a series of more or less rectangular courtyards', but that the class should exclude 'those minor villas which may appear, at first glance, to have a rectangular courtyard plan' (English Heritage MCD description document). This level of detail led to the potential exclusion of many probable villas but also meant that, as a consequence of the kind of information needed, the great majority of less well-known but potentially far better-preserved settlements were left unclassified.

Second, the reliance on a range of very detailed terms that were derived from long-term usage within the subject led to the creation of a fragmented and not always internally consistent methodology being applied to rural settlement classification as a whole. Thus, while the MCD for Farmsteads was based on defining a discrete group of not more than four domestic buildings, settlements with a known distinctive regional distribution and within local prehistoric building traditions were excluded, even if known to be occupied in the Roman period. When applied nationally this meant that the selected sites did not appear to represent anything like the full range of forms that Roman rural settlements were known to take. Local or regional colloquial terms such as rounds, banjo enclosures, and courtyard house settlements tended to be excluded by such an approach. While these sites could be assessed under their own MCDs, this fragmentation created many opportunities for settlements to be counted twice or to fall between the gaps in defining the different rural settlement forms.

Third, the decision to focus primarily on sites of which there was a high level of prior knowledge, usually as a result of excavation or their survival as earthworks, meant that the distribution of assessed monuments did not reflect the real distribution of sites. Instead, the resultant pattern clearly reflected modern patterns of archaeological survival and patterns of past archaeological research. Thus the totals from County Durham (with 172 listed sites) and Northumberland (with 126), where a high proportion of all recorded sites survive as earthworks in upland areas, constituted 26% of all Farmsteads recorded by the survey. This compares with just four recorded in Buckinghamshire and three in Staffordshire.

Fourth, variability in the quality of the SMRs themselves meant that much information on settlement held by them was recorded under simple terms such as 'settlement' or 'occupation', categories that simply could not be evaluated under the existing MCDs. This problem was exacerbated by the decision to exclude sites known only as cropmarks and artefact scatters in the original survey. These clearly represented the vast majority of settlements recorded within SMRs and remain our main sources of evidence for rural settlement nationally.

Finally, the chronological range assigned to the MCDs was too restricted to allow for settlement continuity from later prehistory and into the early medieval period. Some of the descriptions, as noted above, tended to exclude sites known to be based on local prehistoric architectural traditions that 'made no concessions to Roman influences' (Porter 1995). This limitation of the original MPP work highlights the fact that the Roman period in Britain represents a complex cultural process as much as it does a strict chronological horizon. In south-eastern England Roman material culture entered British society to a significant degree before the Claudian conquest and was quickly abundant in its aftermath (eg Haselgrove 1997; Willis 2000). In parts of northern and western England, however, the adoption of datable Roman material culture was frequently limited, with traditions of settlement and portable material culture use reflecting patterns developed through the Iron Age. Thus, while it is possible to argue for the Roman period as beginning in the aftermath of the Caesarian invasion or at least during the Augustan period in the south-east (Creighton 2000), it is equally possible to question whether rural societies were, in parts of the north and west, ever really Roman. In the context of the MPP survey, this meant that settlements in those areas with marked continuity of material form and location through both the Iron Age and Roman periods were frequently excluded from the survey, as they could not be securely 'fixed' to the Roman period in the absence of excavation. This constituted a particular problem in areas of western and south-western England, where rural settlement forms were stable over long periods of time and where the vast majority of sites are known only through aerial or ground-based survey.

Consequently, proposals were developed that aimed to tackle the problems described above in order to provide a new national approach to the characterisation of Roman rural settlement. At the outset it was clear that any programme would need to tackle three major issues. In the light of the experiences of the original MPP review, it was obvious that the project would first need to assess settlement over a broader chronological horizon than that of the 1st to 4th centuries AD. Consequently, the project extended its horizons to consider how to incorporate both probable later Iron Age and Roman settlement (Chapter 3). It was also clear at an early stage that the subject was handicapped by the limited understanding of even the basic size and nature of the resource as recorded in SMRs nationally, especially given the use of methods of classification that were hard, if not impossible, to apply to many sites. The project therefore needed to develop an approach that would at least attempt to systematically analyse the nature of the resource nationally. Finally, it was critical to devise a methodology that was both analytically useful (investigating aspects of settlement diversity that were informative) and practically applicable to the immense variety of the available evidence. With these points in mind the initial phase of the project began.

From the beginning, the project had three staged objectives (Taylor 2004). The first of these was to carry out a review of the evidence available through regional syntheses and recent research for perspectives on the nature and significance of forms of rural settlement across the country. Few national syntheses on the subject have been attempted for Roman Britain and it was clear at the outset that there was little sense of a concerted direction to research into rural settlement of this period. In this respect Roman archaeology contrasted markedly with research into the later prehistoric and medieval periods, which have notable traditions of large-scale synthetic studies of the nature, extent, and diversity of settlement and landscape regionally and nationally (eg Cunliffe 1991; Palmer 1984; Roberts and Wrathmell 2000; Lewis *et al* 1996). A preliminary aim, therefore, was to study the available literature and seek the opinions of interested parties to identify possible themes for research into rural settlement and landscapes in later prehistory and the Roman period. Once complete, the information from this could then be used to inform the process of selecting criteria considered useful to the evaluation of the significance of particular settlements at regional and national level.

The second stage of the project was intended to provide a far better basic understanding of the quantity, quality, and diversity of evidence for settlements of this period than was available at the outset (Chapter 3). If sensible strategies for the assessment, protection, and future research of rural settlements were to be developed, it was important to have some basic idea of the scale and form of the resource. Mapping this information and showing the spectrum of evidence across the country would allow us to judge better the representativeness of any detailed patterns of rural settlement diversity. Such a search provided a control against which to judge future analyses of settlement in any particular area, and also a national context in which to place the plethora of published detailed local studies already available.

A third stage was then designed to develop methodologies for characterising Roman rural settlement diversity and to apply these to recorded SMR data across the country. This approach had two advantages. First, it would provide a systematically assessed national group of settlements for further assessment by the MPP. Second, it would constitute a test of the methodology's applicability and flexibility for research in the face of real data sets. The results of this stage of the work provided the first systematically recorded national overview of the form and variability of rural settlement in Roman Britain (see Chapter 4). Based on an explicitly defined set of archaeological criteria for form, diversity, and potential significance, it represented an authoritative first restructuring of the way in which Roman rural settlement has been defined and studied in England.

The final stage was to carry out several local case studies, based primarily on aerial photographic and fieldwalking data, to check the applicability of the method to research of different landscapes across the country and to help build up a clearer picture of the nature of late Iron Age and Roman rural settlement archaeology in England. The results of this analysis within the context of the MPP were then presented in two reports in 2000 and 2004. It is these studies that form the basis of the current volume.

Past and present understandings of the archaeological resource: some lines of enquiry

Given this context, an important starting point for the study was to attempt to select potentially useful avenues for research into the characterisation of rural settlement diversity that were appropriate to the current levels of knowledge about the resource. While many such approaches were being developed within the discipline, some of which were clearly of great interest to our wider understanding of the subject of rural settlement and society in Roman Britain, some were never likely to be applicable to the investigation of wider regional and national patterns because of the detailed levels of information which they generally required. Owing to the need to provide a national context within which to consider other areas of social change in Roman Britain, only those approaches that might be applied even when detailed information was limited were deemed useful. Consequently, the following headings summarise areas of study that it was felt might elucidate some key trends in rural social change in Roman Britain, with the proviso that they should also be applicable to the less than perfect data sets covering the larger regions with which such a national survey was inevitably concerned.

Settlement dispersion, nucleation and urbanism

The period considered here is one that marks the rise of settlements of urban character alongside marked changes in patterns of rural settlement nucleation and dispersal (Burnham *et al* 2001). Debates over the urban/non-urban characteristics of many nucleated settlements have led to a realisation of the complex non-agricultural roles of many nucleated settlements and the somewhat ambiguous position occupied by settlements usually referred to as small towns or *vici* (*cf* Burnham *et al* 2001; Millett 2001). It is clear, however, that there was great variability in the extent and nature of these changes in settlement form, and that such basic demographic and social developments must have had a marked impact on the nature of agricultural societies. Progress on mapping and synthesising these patterns has, however, been limited beyond a local scale. Consequently, there has been little agreement on common terms to describe or analyse the nature and form of distinctive rural settlements, apart from the recognition of certain architectural traditions, such as villas, and the acceptance into wider debate of local terms such as ladder settlements, rounds, and scooped settlements, without significant consideration of their definition or the historical or social significance of such classifications. This issue is clearly reflected in the diversity and seeming confusion in the way SMRs record settlements of the period.

Some progress has been achieved at a national level, with the terms used by the NMR and the systematic approach to the classification of settlement morphology adopted by the NMP, and at a local level, with the adoption of certain criteria considered useful in the recording of survey or metal detecting data, for example in individual SMRs. This increasingly complete and impressive patchwork of approaches, however, has rarely been discussed or considered within an academic context, and the implications of the emerging geographical and chronological validity of some of its results are yet to be synthesised. Thus long-suspected intuitive impressions about nascent rural settlement nucleation in the Iron Age of south-eastern England, the southerly and easterly bias in the development of villas, and the gross morphological differences in settlement form between the north and west and south and east remain to be demonstrated within any explicitly defined and systematically studied framework.

Settlement patterns: continuity and change

One obvious characteristic of the period is the variable and often dramatic degree to which rural settlement location changed or remained stable through time in relation to marked changes in the organisation of rural society. Examples are common, but range from the sometimes dramatic change apparent around the emerging towns of the South East and East Midlands during the later Iron Age and early Roman period to the relative longevity and stability of many rural settlements in Cornwall up to the 5th and 6th centuries AD. Understanding the location, timing, and extent of these changes is critical to recognising the diverse trajectories taken in rural settlement and society in late Iron Age and Roman Britain.

The strong empirical tradition noted above (Chapter 1) has provided many local field surveys of rural settlement, but these tend to be infrequently published and are often largely descriptive rather than analytical. In areas of extensive excavation there has often been a tendency to treat settlements individually, rather than as part of local comparative studies in which patterns of settlement colonisation, continuity, shift or abandonment are key concerns. Despite this, local case studies and largely impressionistic overviews suggest rural settlement dynamics varied considerably from area to area through the period.

In order to analyse these dynamics a minimum level of chronological information is required to be able to break down settlement patterns through time. This is usually possible at a basic level from fieldwalking data and commonly in Britain a threefold division of Iron Age, earlier Roman and later Roman is achievable. By doing this, it is at least feasible to identify broad patterns of continuity and discontinuity in settlement patterns through time and space. This has a number of important implications for studying rural development during the broad period covered here, and potentially affects the numbers of settlements that need to be studied in any area in order to comprehend its settlement history. Unfortunately, there has been little debate about these issues in the study of Roman Britain and, as a consequence, little agreement has been reached about useful ways to proceed at anything above the local level or beyond very superficial national treatments.

Status, architecture, and the spatial organisation of rural settlement

Much interest has been shown in understanding the nature and role of architectural traditions in rural society. Initially, this focused heavily on forms that approximated to Classical parallels (especially the villas and rural temples) but by the 1980s and 1990s a shift in interest became apparent, with researchers beginning to analyse the development of domestic architecture more generally and even starting to consider the significance of wider settlement space. It is still true to say, however, that it is only villa-type buildings which have received larger-scale systematic attempts at synthesis, in the works of J T Smith (1997) amongst others. We have only a sketchy overview of the nature of other common (indeed, often dominant) architectural traditions such as aisled buildings (eg Hadman 1978) or roundhouses (Hingley 1989; 1990; though see Pope forthcoming).

Domestic architecture and wider settlement space are now widely seen as being fundamental arenas in rural social life in later prehistory (eg Hill 1995; 1999) and the medieval periods (eg Johnson 1993; Hamerow 2002), and it was surely no less so in the Roman period, which saw widespread developments in the use of a dramatic range of architectural styles in rural social discourse. These developments have long been noted in the various spheres of public display and administration in towns (largely outside the scope of this survey), but rural vernacular architecture and the planning and layout of settlements also changed dramatically and varied widely from region to region (*cf* Taylor 2001). Regional and local traditions in housing culture, and their development through time, are thus very important in defining local social traditions in rural society during the later Iron Age and Roman period. As was noted above, there has long been a strong tradition of such work on the more obviously classicising forms, but these still tend to be studied in isolation, hindering an understanding of any wider housing culture and the local and regional context in which the more distinctively 'Roman' buildings developed.

It is particularly important that we also note that the potential significance of architectural development should be extended to the structure and organisation of whole settlements. The use of a range of structures to order and delimit space across settlements in particular ways may also express important social and functional changes in rural communities in this period that are at least as significant as changes in the architecture of domestic buildings. In this regard it is important that we remember not to confuse the study of the two, as has tended to happen in the past. All too often in the study of Roman Britain examinations of the villa have conflated the analysis and recognition of a building of a particular form with the wider settlement of which it is a part. While considerable progress has been made in recent years with the systematic recording and classification of settlement forms (in, for example, the work of the NMP – Stoertz 1997; Bewley 1998), this has tended to occur in something of a conceptual and theoretical vacuum. Thankfully, a number of recent authors, especially Richard Hingley, have started to try to address this issue and flag its potential importance.

Landscapes of production

A number of recent reviews of the evidence for both agricultural practice and craft/industrial activity have stressed that the later Iron Age and Roman periods in Britain see a dramatic rise in specialisation, at the scale of both individual settlements and specific landscapes (eg van der Veen and O'Connor 1998; Dobney 2001). Unfortunately, the level and quality of botanical and zoological data required means that agricultural practice cannot be used to characterise unexcavated settlements, which constitute by far the majority of those known. Some forms of craft activity, such as metalworking and pottery and salt production, however, leave more durable traces that are more commonly recognisable, and numerous detailed local or regional studies have been carried out (eg Lyne and Jefferies 1979; Young 1977; Wilson 1989; Cleere and Crossley 1985; Woodiwiss 1992; Bell *et al* 1999; Schrufer-Kolb 2004). Though clearly only an aspect of the economic life of rural settlements, these industries are nevertheless a critical part of the changes some areas of rural society underwent in later Iron Age and Roman Britain. Consequently it is imperative that particularly significant sites and, importantly, landscapes of more intensive or specialised production are recognised and assessed as one of the criteria in judging the significant variability of rural settlement nationally and its potential significance to the economic and social development of the province.

Cosmology, ritual, and belief

The last twenty years have seen the acceptance in both Iron Age and Roman studies of the deep significance of ritual practice and burial rites within the traditions of agricultural communities. For a long time Roman archaeologists tended to concentrate on architecturally well-defined, spatially distinct places of worship – shrines or temples – but the last ten years has seen a gradual shift towards an interest in broader ritual practices in agricultural life. Such work is still at a relatively early stage, however, and often requires detailed information from excavation to allow interpretation. At a wider regional and national level assessment of rural religious practice is limited to the longer-established and easily recognisable forms noted above (*cf* Pearce *et al* 2000). Shrines, mausolea, and cemeteries often form important components of rural settlements and, rather than attempting to treat them as separate monuments, it is probably better to incorporate them within a wider appreciation of the role of settlement and ritual in rural life. In this respect any criteria used for the assessment of rural settlement would benefit from incorporating information on those sites where the presence of particular religious foci may represent their most important attribute. This is particularly true of those areas and periods in the country where earlier studies, such as those by Whimster (1981), Wait (1985) and Philpott (1991), have recognised distinctive rites.

Military and civilian communities

The study of military occupation is largely outside the scope of the present project, but is it important to mention one aspect of it here. After many years in which civilian and military life were treated as wholly separate worlds within Romano-British archaeology there is now a developing realisation that settlements closely associated with military sites (the *vici*) deserve study within the context of their neighbouring rural landscapes (Taylor 2001; James 2001). For this reason the current survey did incorporate some consideration of military *vici* by recording examples in the same way as neighbouring rural sites. In many respects the *vici* differ little from other roadside settlements elsewhere in the province and it seems wise in future to ensure that any attempt to preserve the rural landscapes of the frontier regions takes these sites into account.

An emerging methodology?

It is perhaps inevitable that this project summary offers a limited selection of the possible approaches that could have been taken. Despite this, the recording and analysis of information about the six main aspects of Roman rural settlement described above were thought to provide the best initial solution to the problem of characterising the diversity of rural settlement and society at a national scale. The following chapters show how these criteria were turned into a simple national methodology, and how this approach fared in the face of the great complexity, variability, and sheer scale of the archaeological evidence available for the period.

Chapter 3
Sources and methods

The methodology used here in recording, classifying, and mapping rural settlement and other evidence had to take into account the factors noted in Chapter 2. First, it had to deal with the limitations of the information about rural settlements as it was recorded in archives nationally, and particularly the variability in the quality of recorded information available from local authority SMRs across the country which resulted from the complex and varied histories of recording within SMRs. Second, it had to be applicable to sites known largely or solely through survey-based data. This is because it was clear at the outset of the project that good-quality excavated data was available for only a tiny fraction of the likely population of rural settlements. If the project was to avoid repeating previously published overviews largely based upon such evidence then a wider range of evidence would need to be considered. Third, the method of recording had to be simple enough to be systematically applicable to the enormous number of sites suspected to be held in these archives, thus allowing recording in a form that was comparable from region to region. Finally, and most critically, it had to encapsulate as much important information as possible about the nature of each rural settlement and thus record patterns of genuine significance in the range and diversity of rural settlement across Roman Britain that would be valuable to research.

As a first step the project assessed the nature of the resource as it appears today. Our previous heavy reliance on the very small proportion of sites that have been extensively excavated, and their pre-eminent role in the literature of the subject, have been noted above, so here it was important to map, according to its form, the enormous range of survey-based information that is potentially available (eg earthwork survey, fieldwalking, aerial photography). By mapping the sources of the information we have about each site it was possible to explore the nature of the currently available archaeological resource. It also provided the opportunity to get a better idea of the potential role of survey data in helping to bring a broader landscape-based perspective to the study of rural society. Consequently, a national survey of regional and national trends in the basic form, density, variety, and survival of settlement evidence of the period was carried out, and the results are discussed below. The diversity of recording strategies encountered and the need for a consistent and considered approach to the characterisation of Roman settlement based on material evidence soon becomes evident when this information is assessed. This discussion is then followed by an account of the simple methodology used by the survey and the rationale behind it. While far from ideal, it provided an approach to the evidence that was both flexible enough to cope with the limitations of the available data and yet still capable of demonstrating some important characteristics of late prehistoric and Roman rural archaeology that have wider implications for the subject.

Source critique

An initial aim of the project was to record, map, and evaluate patterns in the distribution of the recorded form of the evidence for each potential settlement. The results of this process act as a fairly straightforward guide to how we know about particular settlements and, to a degree, to differences in their level of preservation. This is key because such differences affect what can be said about the settlement record for any area and the directions in which future characterisation work on the majority of settlements (not just well-understood, primarily excavated sites) should go. In the following section the evidence from the survey is used to show how this simple tool proved to be a very powerful aid in considering the regionality of settlement evidence and likely patterns of preservation.

Table 3.1 Terms for the forms of evidence used by SMRs in the north of England

Northumberland	Durham	Cleveland	Cumbria	Lancashire	N Yorks	Humberside
Exc	Exc feature	Exc	Building foundation	Exc	Excavated site	Exc
Earthwork	Earthwork	Earthwork	Earthwork	Earthwork	Earthwork	Ewk
AP	Cropmark	Cropmark/AP	Cropmark	Cropmark/AP site/Soilmark	Cropmark	CM
Pot Scat	Finds	Pottery scatter	Finds	Finds	Fieldwalking	Find
	Documentary	Documentary	Documentary		Documentary	Doc
Geophysics	Building foundation	Obs	Circumstantial		Geophysical	Geo
	Circumstantial				Stray find	MD
					Foundations	

The survey used certain headings to summarise the different forms of evidence for settlements. SMRs vary in the specific terms they use (see the individual regional summaries in Chapter 4 for specific cases); Table 3.1, for example, shows the terms used by authorities in the North East and North West of England and reflects much of the variability found nationally, in that the separate recording of geophysical survey, metal detecting, rescue observation, and documentary evidence were inconsistently used. Summary assessment of the proportions of settlements within each authority known from these sources clearly indicated marked variation in distribution, although it was not altogether clear to what degree this reflected SMR practices or was a genuine reflection of the evidence. Earthworks, finds scatters, excavations, cropmarks, and soilmarks were generally much more consistently recorded, however, and acted as the basis for the sites subsequently mapped by the survey.

Mapping the survey evidence by recorded form clearly demonstrated significant real patterns in the nature of the evidence, which can best be seen in Figure 3.1. There are clearly many locally significant variations in the nature of the evidence mapped but here there is only space to summarise the major trends that are apparent (further local patterns are discussed in the individual regional summaries). Evidence for settlements recorded as earthworks (Fig 3.2) shows that the best-preserved settlements appear to be heavily biased towards the northern and western upland regions of England as well as (although in smaller numbers) towards some of the chalkland landscapes and coastal wetland margins. Though this distribution matches that which might be expected given the overviews already available, the map clearly demonstrates the sheer scale and weighting of this bias in the surviving archaeological record, with some 83% of all recorded examples coming from the North East, North West, West Midlands, and South West regions.

Earthwork sites provide primarily morphological evidence for settlement study and are complemented nationally by aerial photographs of cropmarks and soilmarks which, as Figure 3.3 shows, are distributed densely over much of the country, especially on permeable geologies in areas where land is now under arable

Table 3.2 The recorded form of evidence for rural settlements in England by region (figures in brackets represent the percentage for each region)

	North East	North West	Yorks	East Midlands	West Midlands	East	South East	South West	Total
Earthwork	521 (34)	1242 (47)	88 (2)	110 (3)	259 (7)	149 (4)	312 (7)	929 (23)	3610 (13)
Cropmarks	679 (46)	1091 (42)	2525 (59)	1563 (43)	2346 (66)	1455 (38)	985 (23)	1584 (38)	12228 (44)
Other	334 (20)	287 (11)	1686 (39)	1963 (54)	957 (27)	2195 (58)	3039 (70)	1603 (39)	12064 (43)
Total	1534	2620	4299	3636	3562	3799	4336	4116	27902

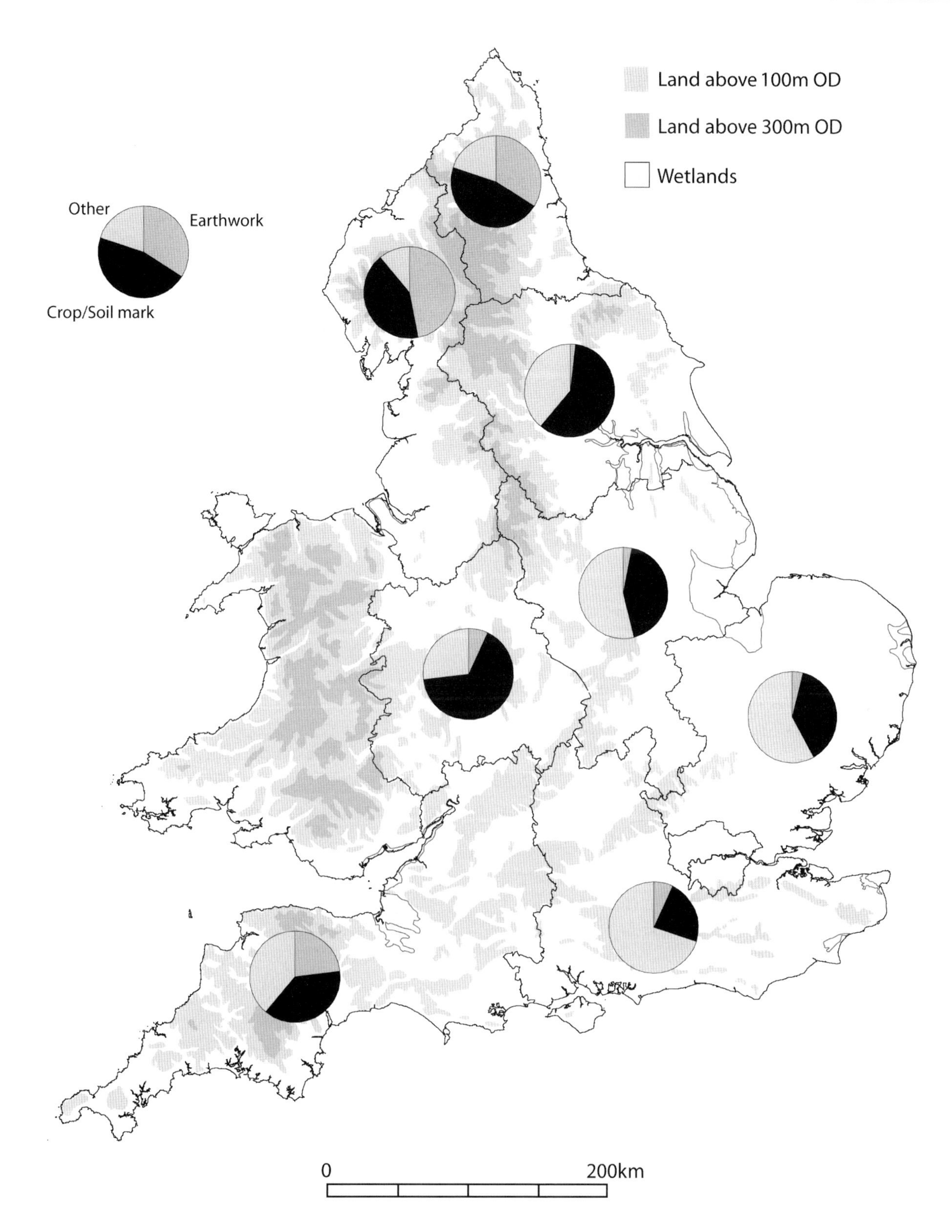

Figure 3.1 The proportion by region of sites recorded as earthworks, cropmarks or soilmarks, and through other means

farming. Some variations in density are due to the uneven recording of cropmark sites by some SMRs, but the comparative absence of examples recorded in parts of North West England and the South East are a reflection of the presence of large urban conurbations and largely unreceptive impermeable soils.

Together the earthwork and aerial photographic evidence provided the project's single biggest resource for the study of settlement and thus biases in their combined distribution inevitably affected the ability of the survey to characterise settlement accurately. Regions such as the South East, with relatively low proportions of settlements recorded through these means, suffered correspondingly (Table 3.2; Fig 3.1),

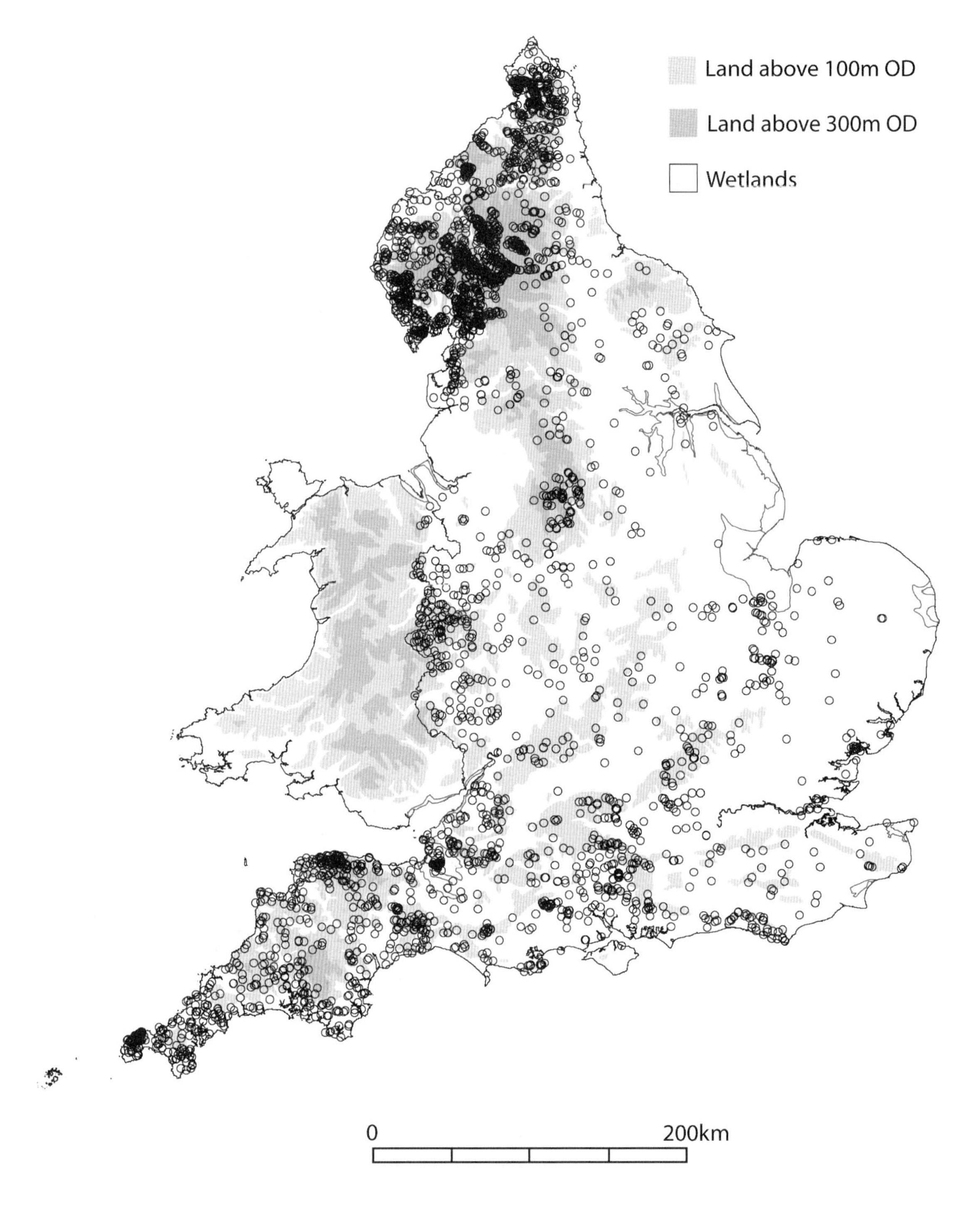

Figure 3.2 Distribution map of settlements recorded as earthworks

although in this particular area this problem was partly offset by the higher numbers of settlements known through excavation.

The next most abundant source of evidence was finds scatters or groups, which constituted approximately 28% of recorded examples nationally. The distribution of these sites is heavily biased towards central and southern districts of England where arable land use and modern development have been at their most intense. Figure 3.4, however, also shows how long-noted variability in the past use of portable material culture in the period is reflected in the recorded evidence. Significant areas of the South West, the West Midlands, and the North that are extensively cultivated still do not prove particularly receptive to fieldwalking even where settlements are suspected through other means. Finds groups are a minor part of the archaeological resource north and west of the Tees valley, for example, even though the distribution of cropmarks shows that there are extensive areas of arable cultivation that might be expected to bring material to the surface.

Other sources of evidence, such as documentary evidence and geophysical surveys, are, as has been noted, too infrequently and inconsistently recorded to be of real help, but the distribution of sites with excavated evidence is generally very instructive of patterns of past and present archaeological interest (Fig 3.5). Here, it is possible to see the overwhelming impact of a long history of excavation related to modern development in the most densely settled parts of modern England, as well as those areas that have been particularly prone to extensive surface mineral extraction. Dense bands of excavated sites along the major river valleys and modern communications routes tell their own story but it is important to note the way in which this has been augmented by a long history of local archaeological research in various parts of the country.

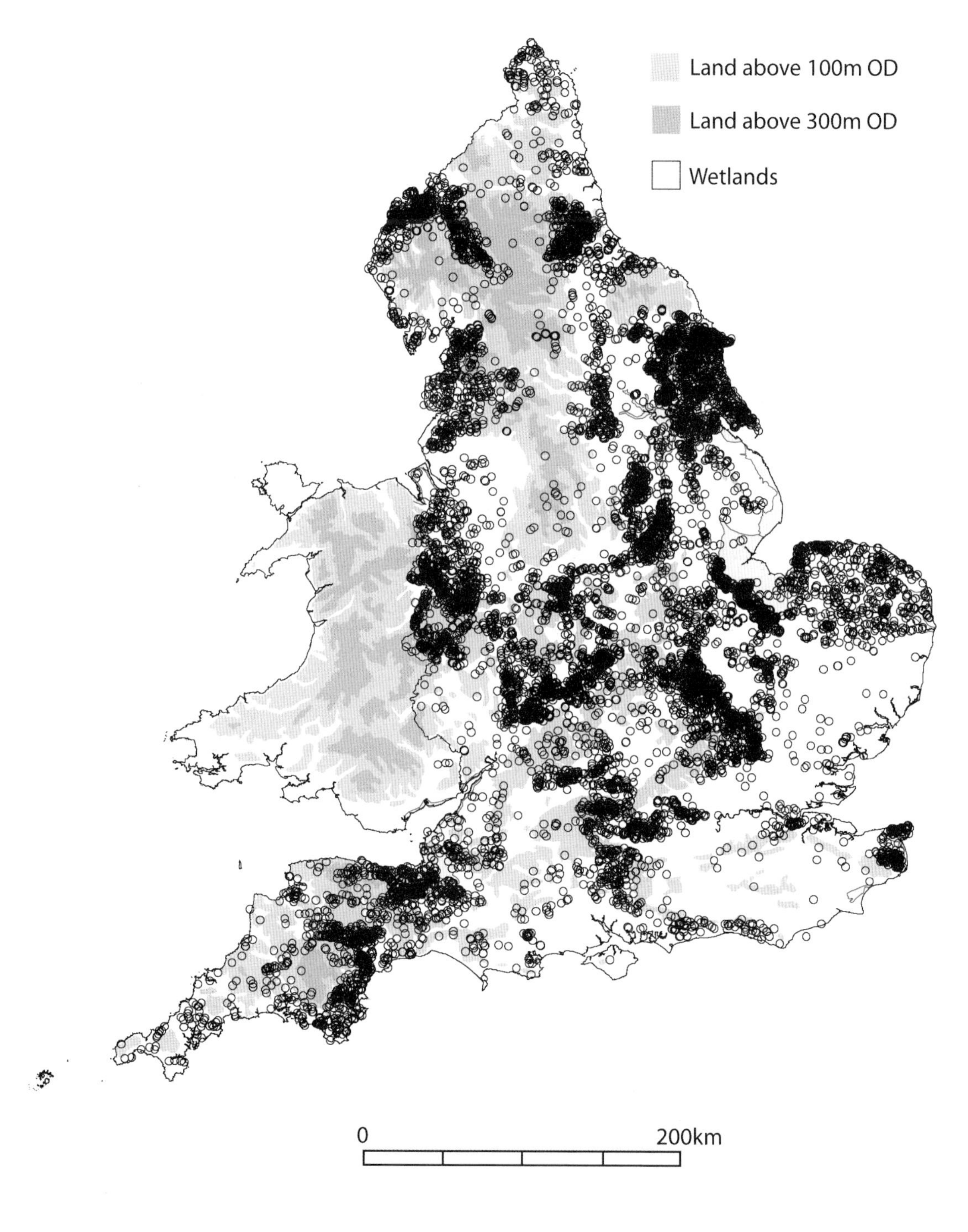

Figure 3.3 Distribution map of settlements recorded as cropmarks and soilmarks

Figure 3.4 Distribution map of all settlements recorded through finds scatters, metal detecting, and as finds groups

Until comparatively recently it has been these programmes of research and local amateur investigation that have provided the bulk of examples in many less densely settled districts, such as West Cornwall and Northumberland. Figure 3.5 only partly reflects the activity of archaeologists of the Roman period in different parts of the country because excavations of military and urban sites were under-represented in the survey as they were not specifically searched for within the SMR data. Consequently, the scarcity of excavation seen in the North West and South West, for example, reflects the way in which Roman rural settlement has been somewhat neglected in excavation-based research by archaeologists working in these regions.

It was rapidly apparent that there was a series of additional problems in attempting to use SMR data for an evaluation at a national scale. A number of recurring

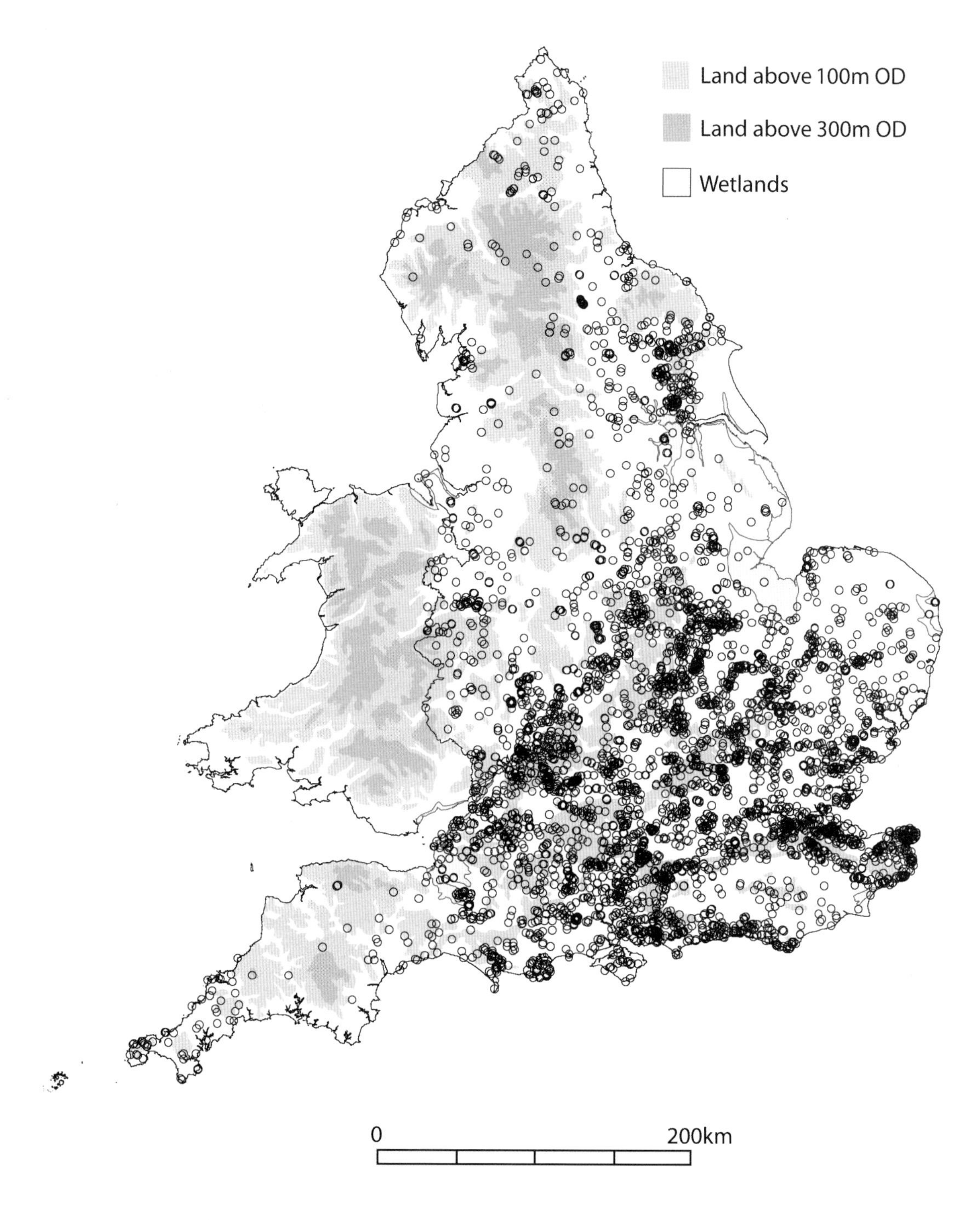

Figure 3.5 Distribution map of settlements recorded through excavation, evaluation, and rescue observation

problems, and the implications of these, were readily seen during the project. First, local authority resourcing of SMRs has been highly variable and partly as a consequence of this many were at very different stages in the development of computerised archives at the time of the survey. Although the project database was established to be able to cope with any common digital format, a number of SMRs were not themselves set up to do this at the time. Even where computerised archives existed some had not transferred records from the paper originals. In these situations the length of time required to input the data into the project database would have been prohibitive and the data therefore had to be excluded (although some have subsequently been recorded in a limited follow-up survey in 2003 and are included in the maps that follow). Some authorities, though possessing computerised SMRs, provided the data in hard copy, which then had to be painstakingly edited and keyed into the database. The organisation of SMRs and the availability of information technology support to them were further complicated during the survey by the effects of local government reorganisation. A number of authorities were being reconstituted in different forms at the time of the SMR visits and this consequently led to obvious problems in acquiring information. Though a significant problem for the current project, it did not constitute a continuing issue once the reorganisation had bedded down. Where these problems created specific caveats in the survey database they have been discussed in the individual regional summaries, but it is important to note here that while for much of the country the maps provide a good approximation of our current state of knowledge there are areas (parts of North Yorkshire and Lancashire, to name two) where there is certainly more information to be added.

The survey methodology and some limitations

In the light of the findings of the review and a pilot study of data from five authorities, a methodology was devised which incorporated information that would be useful in developing our understanding of the research themes noted in Chapter 2, while being able to cope with the limitations and biases likely in the data (outlined above).

Each local authority SMR was contacted and subsequently visited with a set of broadly defined search criteria to be used in drawing together all potential settlements of the period. This process was designed to be deliberately inclusive in order to gain a clearer idea of the whole of the probable resource, rather than risk excluding potentially important sites at the outset, as had tended to be the consequence of the existing approach. Therefore, sites that were of probable Roman date, based on local analogy of form or structure, were included alongside sites of known Roman date. It was obvious that the database would incorporate some sites of earlier and later date and of dubious veracity but, on the whole, discussion with the local authority archaeologists suggested that most sites ascribed a probable Roman date would indeed be Late Iron Age and/or Roman. The sheer size of the survey meant that it was imperative wherever possible to receive output in digital format in order for there to be sufficient time to evaluate, edit, prepare, and map the data within the project Geographical Information System (GIS). If the data could successfully be incorporated within the database it would also then be possible to manipulate and analyse the data far more effectively, as well as provide an easily accessible resource for future use.

Recording criteria

Six key sets of data were recorded. The intention was simply to summarise, compare, and map the basic resource as it was recorded by the SMRs and to assess regional and national patterns in settlement form and simple character. In order to do this, each record in the survey noted the SMR no. (or Primary Record Number (PRN)), the Ordnance Survey grid reference, the nature of any sources of information about the site (its recorded rather than present physical Form), any characterisation criteria or categories (Types) that could be retrieved from the SMR entry, the site's probable extent (Size), and its suggested date (Period).

The Primary Record Number

The PRN was recorded in order to provide a point of cross-reference between the survey and each original entry as recorded by the SMR. In the database each record received an additional unique identifier (in order to prevent any repetition in the identifier used for two sites from separate authorities); this number is used to identify any settlement within the project GIS.

Grid references

OS grid references, with a six-figure reference or better, were recorded for every site. Sites with less specific references were held to be too poorly located to be reliably assessed in future stages of the project and were thus rejected. The reference for each site was then converted to a national twelve-figure reference that would locate every site within the national map bases used by the project GIS.

Form

The Form data were recorded for each site by use of a system of codes. These codes described the nature of the record held by the local authority, and were: Source Unknown, Excavation, Finds Scatter, Finds Group (finds recorded but not from fieldwalking), Cropmark/Soilmark, Topographic Survey/Earthwork,

Geophysics, Documentary, Observation, Metal Detecting. Although the use of such descriptors varied significantly between authorities, they were held to provide the most reliable available guide as to how potential settlements were known within the archaeological records for any area. The Form data gave a useful, if brief, indication of a site's likely state of preservation and documentation. It also provided a limited proxy guide to the major impacts on the preservation of monuments of the period at a regional and national scale.

Type

Potential settlements were originally identified in the SMRs using a list of keywords devised for the survey that were intended to help characterise settlements and evidence for their associated function(s). In part, these terms were known to be used by the SMRs themselves, but the list included a series of widely applicable non-specific terms (such as enclosure, settlement or site) that were designed to capture potential sites systematically across authority and regional boundaries. Quantifying and mapping these terms helped to draw out particular biases in the way common class descriptions were assigned by local authorities.

The selected records were then systematically searched for supporting information that would allow them to be recategorised using standard terms chosen for the current survey. These standardised amended records were used for the final survey to provide systematically recorded categories that could be mapped and compared nationally. It is these systematically amended and categorised records that were used for the final regional and national maps published here. Potential settlements that could not be further assessed remained as unclassified records in need of further analysis and were quantified and mapped only as a control to identify areas where settlement characterisation using the survey methodology was more or less effective.

The primary criterion used for categorisation was a settlement's basic morphology. This was an admittedly limited first step in summarising the complex patterns that settlements can take, and was done by recording the elementary structural relationships of the main boundary divisions and their apparent basic layout. The available terms used were similar to those adopted by the NMP, but were simplified in order to allow rapid characterisation of settlements at this simple level. Three basic forms were chosen: enclosed settlements (Fig 3.6a), unenclosed settlements (Fig 3.6b, used for sites defined only by a single non-enclosing linear boundary or by none at all), and linear system settlements (Fig 3.6c). Some effort was also made to incorporate further aspects of shape and form into the records. These, however, were not part of the initial programme of work and await analysis at a later stage.

Most of the terms used above are fairly self-explanatory, but they were found useful in summarising key differences in settlement complexity, usually but not always associated with size. The term 'unenclosed settlement' usually referred to simple farmsteads with a single cluster of buildings, but occasionally included larger settlements of house clusters, usually of later Iron Age date. Enclosed settlements included both simple farmsteads and hillforts, as well as enclosed types associated with various Roman rural settlements. The simple morphological characteristics alone did not always draw out distinctions between hillforts and farms but, when combined with size and period information, they represented a simple but powerful tool for settlement mapping. In order to be able to check this, traditional terms such as hillfort were not removed from the original site records and could be checked against size and morphology records.

'Linear system settlement' referred to all those forms of settlement defined by complex groups of enclosures, compounds or other spaces defined by multiple boundaries. This heading incorporated a wide range of rural settlement types, from small but complex farmsteads up to and including *vici* and other larger nucleated settlements. Again, without the use of additional shape and form criteria or the addition of size or period criteria this term was a relatively simple tool, but it still provided a good initial guide to variability in settlement plan for the purposes of large-scale mapping.

A series of additional criteria was also then recorded for each site, wherever available. The first of these was the architecture of buildings within rural settlements. Here the aim was to record systematically the main types of building styles known in Iron Age and Roman Britain. The database used a fixed set of types taken from the literature review that was felt to summarise current practice best and which should be applicable to relatively simple data sets. In the outline of results below these types are grouped into well-established traditions in order to simplify the maps for the purposes of interpretation but, in the future, the database could be used to interrogate these in more detail.

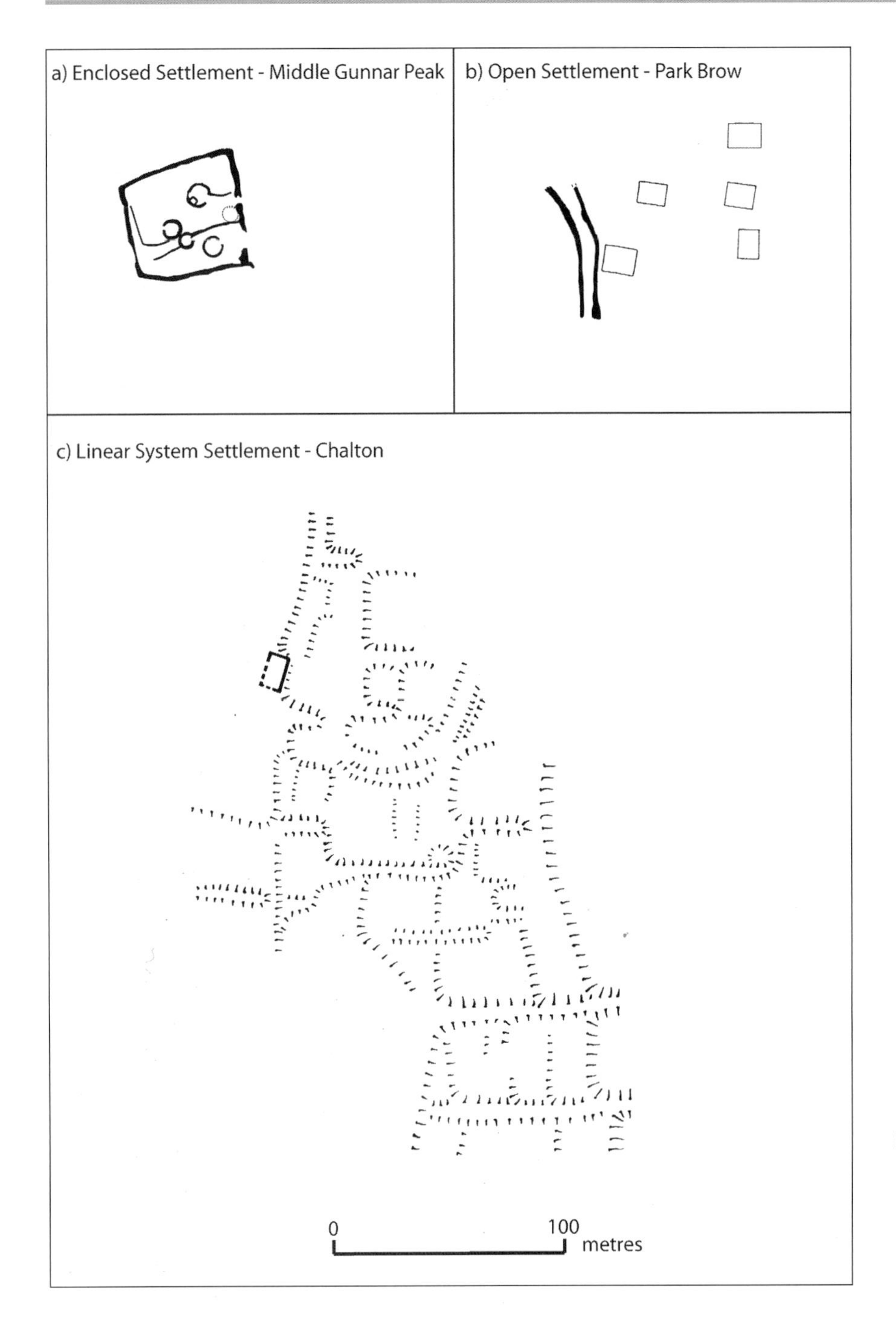

Figure 3.6 Examples of the three main morphological forms of settlement recorded for the national survey: enclosed settlements, linear system settlements and open or unenclosed settlements

Given the need, noted above, to consider specialised landscapes or settlements focusing on craft production, the database was designed to record the presence and date of craft activities. More detailed approaches that attempted to quantify or better characterise the specifics of production were found to be too unwieldy and were thus omitted after the pilot stage. Each field was designed to record the date and form of the evidence in order to be able to map important differences in the location and distribution of, for example, iron smelting across the country.

In developing brief records for the presence and distribution of burial and ceremonial evidence from settlements, initial attempts to develop more sophisticated criteria were again found to be too time-consuming and restrictive in application. Consequently, a simple distinction was made between evidence for individual burials and for formal cemeteries and where possible the form of disposal (inhumation or cremation) was also recorded.

The presence of evidence for military activity on settlements was also recorded, as it was deemed important to recognise, for example, probable military *vici* that in other respects may have appeared similar to other forms of nucleated linear system settlement.

Though the results from any one site tend to be limited, the impression from the project is that, when put together, they accurately recorded key differences in settlement form, architecture, and activity through time and space. This information was then used to build a picture of regional patterns of settlement form and change during the Iron Age and Roman periods.

Size

Where possible, evidence for a settlement's extent (size) was recorded as a proxy guide to the degree and extent of settlement nucleation or dispersal. One of the problems with the original MPP MCDs was that although they recorded both nucleated (village, large villa) and dispersed (farmstead, small villa) settlements, the detail required to do so was greater than that possessed by the majority of known sites. Research by the author as part of the pilot study showed that at a simple level a distinction between such settlements could be made by recording the broad extent of settlement area. Sites that were less than 2ha in size generally constituted single farmsteads or clusters of two or three farmsteads (small 'hamlets', for want of a better word) and were considered to be dispersed settlements. Those greater than 2ha constituted settlements of intermediate to large size, such as hillforts, larger 'hamlets', and the 'village' type settlements of the Roman period, as well as the large settlements associated with some villas, and were termed nucleated settlements. The upper end of this range (above *c* 8ha) included settlements often referred to as *vici*, possible small towns or roadside settlements.

Period

Finally, the periods of occupation given for each site in the SMR entries were recorded in order to identify trends in the chronology of settlement. To simplify any subsequent analysis, the varied expressions used by the SMRs to describe the same basic chronological horizons were edited into single project terms. Thus systematic chronological searches of the entire database could be made on a regional and national basis. It was hoped that these data, simple though they were, would be able to provide a basic guide to chronological change in the distribution and character of Iron Age and Roman settlement.

Some limitations

One issue intrinsic to the chosen methodology of the survey was the inevitable limitations created by the forms of information held about sites across the country. In order to characterise settlements by their layout even at a simple level, for example, some form of earthwork, aerial photographic, geophysical survey or excavated evidence would be required. Probable settlements known only from fieldwalking, metal detecting, trial trenching or finds groups recovered through salvage work could not often be used to characterise settlements in this form. Clearly, the balance between these two groups of evidence affects the degree to which settlement layout can be characterised. The impact of this issue is amply demonstrated in Table 3.3, where it is clear that a significant proportion of all settlements could not be characterised by plan form; however, it should not be forgotten that the project was still able to assess a very much higher proportion of settlements than had been achieved previously.

Similarly, sites known only through earthwork, geophysical or aerial photographic survey frequently provide little chronological information or evidence for domestic architecture or function. Commonly, cropmark settlement sites were recorded by SMRs as Iron Age/Roman or Unknown Prehistoric. The impact of these issues is discussed in more detail below.

Even where chronological information was available through excavation or artefact assemblages there was marked variation in the degree of precision with which most SMRs record the dates of sites. Many use only a general period classification – 'Iron Age' or 'Roman' – and provide insufficient additional comment to allow any finer division. In part this is understandable,

Table 3.3 The number of settlements recorded that could be characterised by plan form

	North East	North West	Yorks	East Midlands	West Midlands	East	South East	South West
Settlements characterised	674	1100	2639	1560	1812	1322	1104	2414
Unclassified	860	1520	1660	2075	1730	2477	3232	1712
Total	1534	2620	4299	3635	3542	3799	4336	4126

given the general planning and control role of SMRs; in this context, such information is deemed unnecessary within the main entries. It is clear from the survey, however, that this difficulty is exacerbated in the case of fieldwalked and metal-detected evidence by the often limited level of the original recording. This issue, alongside the failure to publish many local field surveys, is a continuing problem for broader-scale assessments of continuity and change in settlement patterns. Consequently, for most areas in the survey the chronological definition of sites was too broad within the period, or simply non-specific, and could not be used in detailed mapping. The possibilities of promising results in the characterisation of settlement dynamics from even simple analysis of this material are discussed in the field survey case studies (Chapter 6) that were carried out as part of the wider project.

A further concern arose in relation to the ability of the SMR records to provide regular and consistent information on the likely extent of individual settlements. Size was recognised as an important and useful, if crude, guide to the degree of nucleation or dispersal of settlements and was an integral part of the six MCDs devised at the start of the project. Where settlement boundaries were easily recognised, as was often the case with sites of simple enclosed form, recording of size was often reliable. The sizes of complex linear system settlements and especially open settlements, however, were rarely recorded within SMR entries. Surprisingly, this was also often the case with fieldwalking surveys, where extent would be one of the few simple criteria that one might expect to be considered. Consequently, systematic national mapping of settlements by size was not often possible within the resources of the main project, though in each of the subsequent case studies involving aerial photographic and fieldwalking data it has proved to be a simple and very valuable tool in assessing settlement diversity and hierarchy (see Chapter 6).

A more detailed discussion of the results of all these points is reserved for Chapter 4, where mapping and summary statistics have provided the opportunity to make a series of comments about biases and problems in the present record for specific parts of the country. As a separate part of the project, several recent aerial photographic and fieldwalking surveys were chosen as detailed case studies in order to assess some of the settlement characterisation and chronological issues raised by the main survey. The results of these studies are incorporated in Chapter 6.

Chapter 4
Settlement pattern and settlement form

This chapter, the first focusing on the results of the project, maps and analyses patterns in Roman rural settlement density, nucleation, layout, and form at a regional scale across the country. In the process, it becomes possible to compare, at national and regional scales, aspects of the character and changing form of Roman rural settlement, such as:

- the significance and extent of differing patterns of dispersed and nucleated rural settlement;
- the patterns and interrelationships between different forms of settlement space, comparing enclosed, open, and complex bounded traditions of settlement;
- the nature of regionality and its influence on Roman rural settlement form, and the study of this interaction;
- the role of terrain, hydrology, coastal margins, and wetlands in influencing patterns of settlement.

Despite the limitations noted in Chapter 3, the survey successfully recorded *c* 28,000 probable and definite rural settlements nationally (Fig 4.1), out of an original resource of some 117,000 possible sites. While only 45% of these could be further characterised on morphological grounds, the project has produced a systematically recorded database of rural settlement for the period on a scale that has not been previously possible. While simplistic and containing a number of obvious weaknesses it is still comfortably the best overview of this under-studied area of Roman Britain yet available. In the sections that follow, some of the results of this work are discussed in order to provide a guide to the emerging character of the rural settlement landscapes of England in the later Iron Age and Roman period.

National overview

Patterns of settlement layout (morphology)

This part of the survey focused on assessing the nature and form of the rural settlements by summarising the evidence recorded from the SMRs under the thematic headings suggested after the literature review and described above. Table 3.3 highlights the way in which confusion between SMRs over what criteria to record has been reflected in the proportion of sites that could be further characterised in each region. Although the various SMRs tended to use different terms it was possible during the survey to reassess much of the data and thus create a more consistent format with criteria for basic settlement morphology and the presence or absence of evidence for settlement architecture, ritual activity, industry, and military associations. The size of probable settlements was often too inconsistently or infrequently recorded to be analysed at this stage,

Table 4.1 Numbers of rural settlements recorded by region for each main morphological class

	North East	North West	Yorks	East Midlands	West Midlands	East	South East	South West	Total
Enclosed	610	1006	2279	1167	1699	1174	885	2182	11002
Linear system	23	13	117	333	109	129	173	117	1014
Open	41	81	163	57	4	19	46	115	526

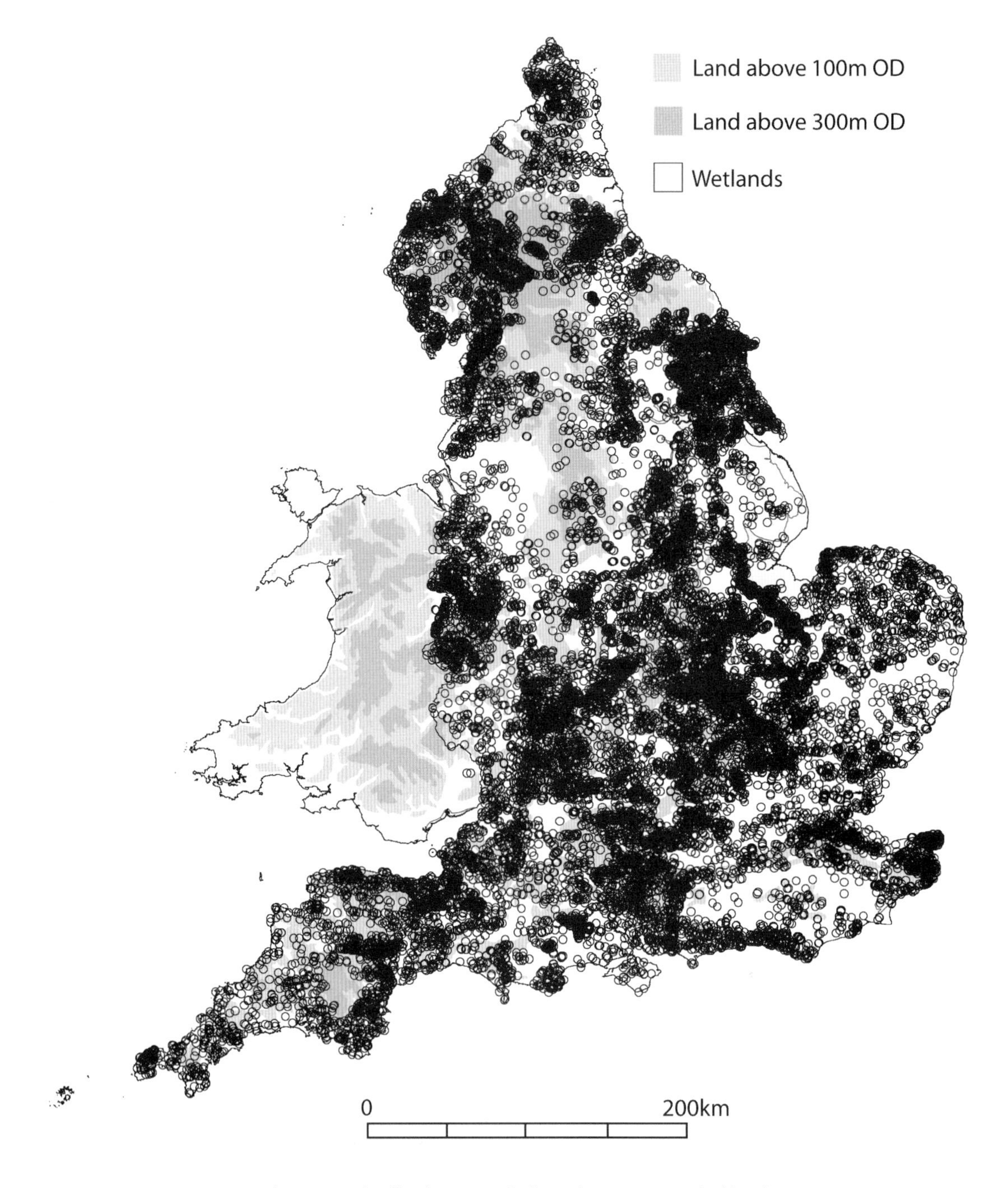

Figure 4.1 Distribution map of all settlements recorded by the survey

although the majority of the evidence, in the form of earthwork and cropmark sites, fieldwalked scatters, and excavations, indicates that this kind of analysis should be achievable with further study (*cf* the case studies in Chapter 6).

Figures 4.2, 4.3, and 4.4 and Table 4.1 illustrate the results obtained by the simple characterisation of rural settlement according to the morphological criteria. Dispersed and nucleated enclosed settlements (Fig 4.2) are the most easily distinguishable archaeologically and were generally abundant or common across the country. In general, the high densities of enclosed settlement (see Table 4.1) reflect their high visibility in areas with good earthwork survival or cropmark formation and the ease with which they are recorded (see Figs 3.2 and 3.3). They represent the overwhelmingly dominant form in the north of England, the West Midlands, and, in the South West, in Somerset, Devon, and Cornwall. They are also very densely recorded across the major river valleys and permeable geologies of much of central and southern England. Interestingly, they were comparatively scarce in much of Lincolnshire and parts of the South East, such as Essex, the Thames estuary, Surrey, Kent, and East Sussex. This is despite the fact that several of these areas display good conditions for cropmark recovery and otherwise good levels of SMR detail on settlement form.

Complex linear systems of settlement (Fig 4.3) are less common, partly due to the fact that, although easily identified as earthworks or cropmarks, they are often not well defined. There has been little general agreement about what to call such complex sites, and they are often simply termed 'enclosure complex', 'settlement complex' or 'cropmark complex' in archive records. An attempt was made to examine the SMR descriptions further in order to identify whether the sites concerned were in fact linear system settlements, but this was frequently not possible and consequently they are quite likely to be generally under-represented in the survey, with many examples currently recorded under unclassified settlement. Despite this, analysis of their distribution shows a clear national pattern. Rare north of the Vale of Pickering and west of the Pennines

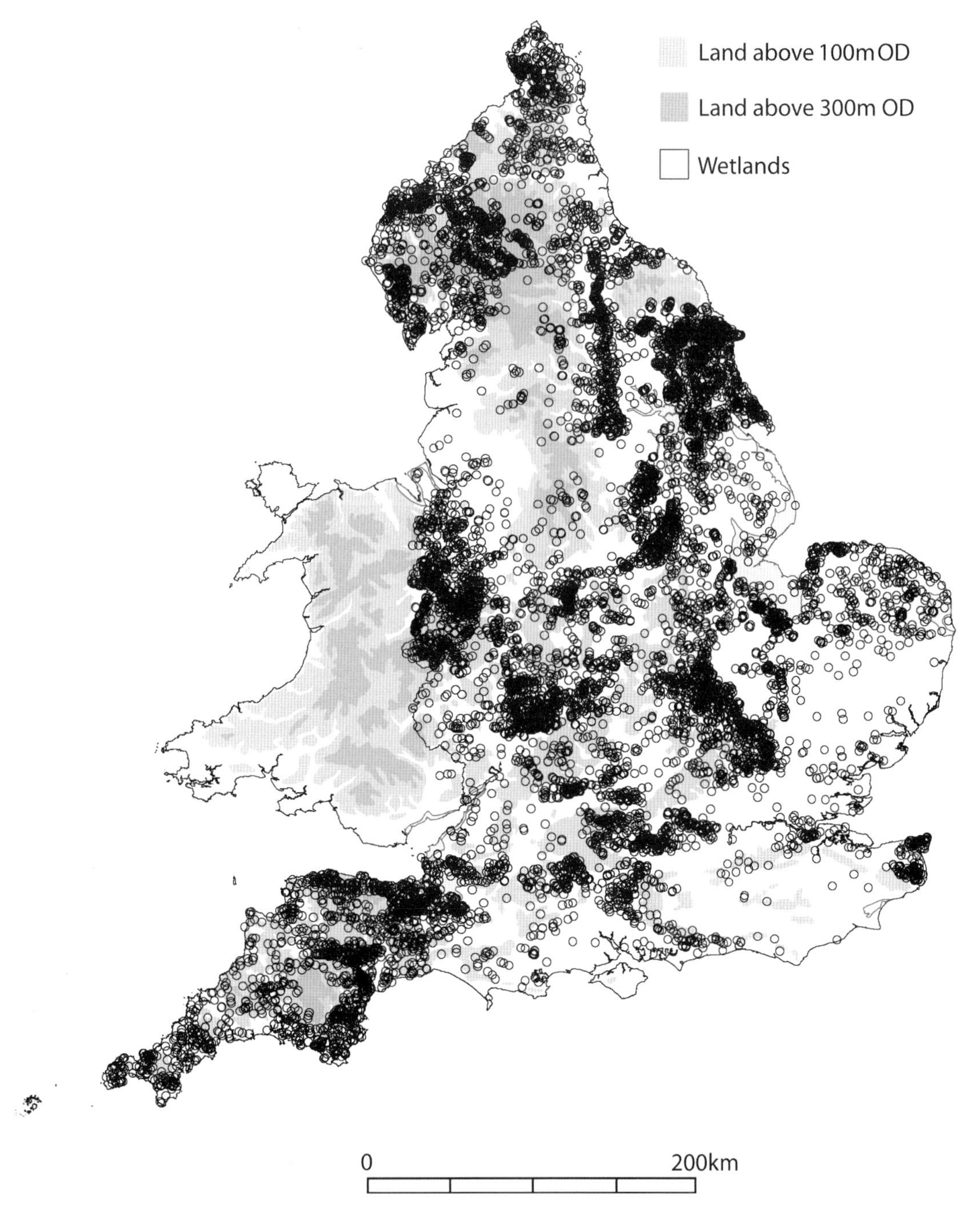

Figure 4.2 Distribution map of enclosed settlements

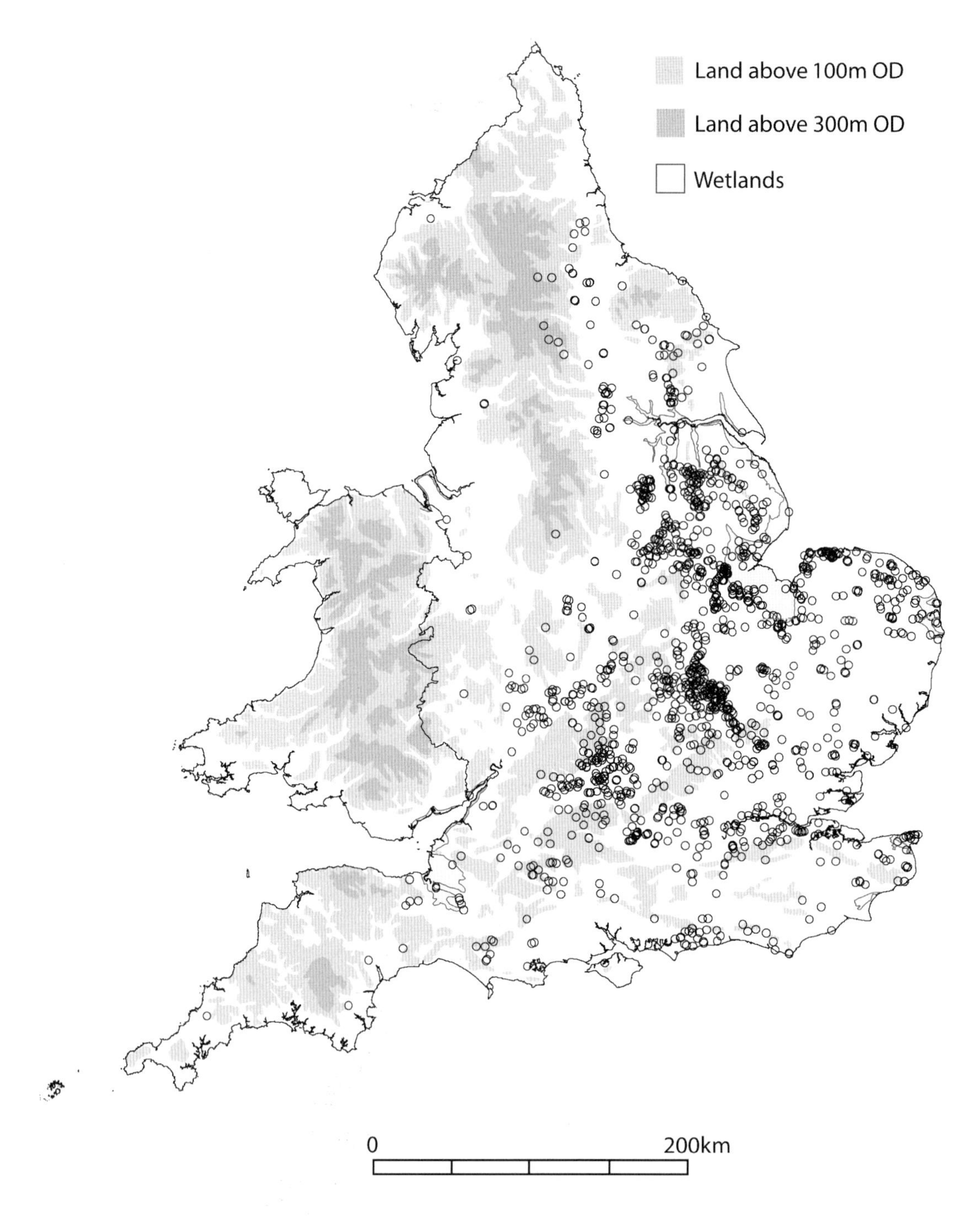

Figure 4.3 Distribution map of linear system settlements

(where recorded examples are frequently closely associated with military sites as *vici* or roadside industrial sites), they are a significant but minor element in settlement in much of the West Midlands. Strikingly absent from the South West, they are nevertheless very common across much of the rest of central and southern England. They are particularly abundant in a zone running from east Yorkshire to Wessex and across to Essex and Hertfordshire, and clearly constituted a significant if rarely dominant form of settlement in this area. The absence of quality cropmark evidence in some areas of Norfolk and particularly Suffolk at the time of the survey limits what can be said about their distribution in East Anglia, but they appear to be comparatively rare in this area. Likewise, the survey recorded very little information for the Mersey Basin and parts of the industrial North West, but the few records available suggest that the enclosure-dominated settlement pattern described for surrounding regions applies here too.

Open or unenclosed settlements (Fig 4.4) were relatively rare and unevenly distributed across the country. This almost certainly reflects the difficulty in recording open settlements where surviving earthworks are absent. As a result, they tend to be under-represented in the archives, an important consideration when comparing patterns of settlement nationally on the basis of the two more commonly recorded morphological types. Open settlements are common in some, but by no means all, areas with high levels of earthwork preservation, and have also been recorded in relatively large numbers in those areas in which much excavation has taken place in advance of modern development: thus significant numbers were recorded along several major English river valleys (ahead of mineral extraction along the Trent, Nene, and Thames, for example) and in and around some areas of major urban or infrastructure expansion (such as in northern Kent). It is noticeable that most well-dated excavated examples date to the Iron Age, suggesting that open settlements, as so far recorded at least, are a rare settlement form in the Roman period.

Settlement patterns by size – nucleated and dispersed settlements

Size of settlement was potentially a very valuable, if crude, indicator of the degree of nucleation of rural

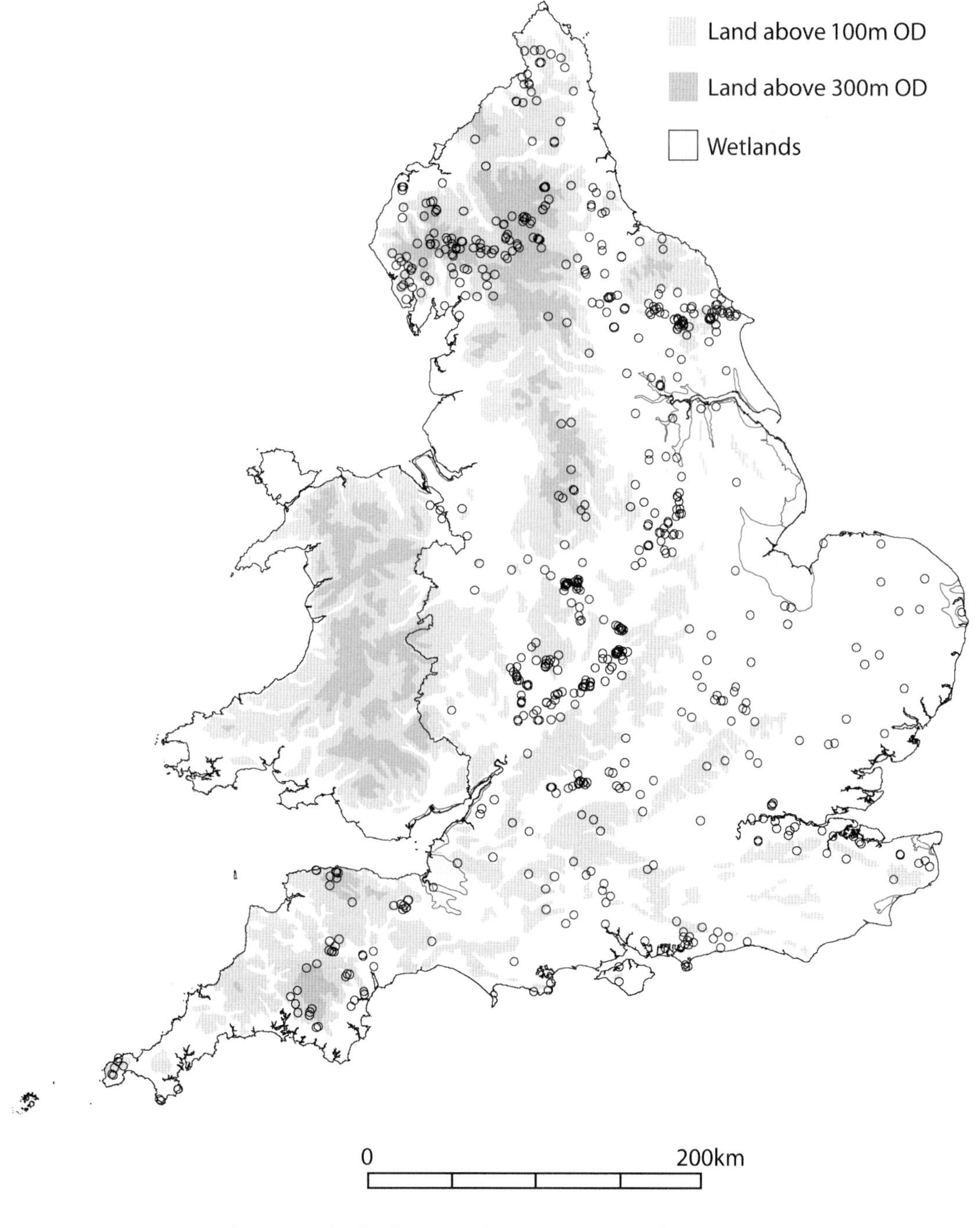

Figure 4.4 Distribution map of open or unenclosed settlements

Table 4.2 Numbers of enclosed settlements by size recorded for each sample area

	Cornwall	Marches survey	Devon	West Yorkshire	Hertfordshire	Total
0.1–0.5ha	75	334	35	74	103	621
0.5–1ha	55	40	7	26	47	175
1–2ha	19	19	7	3	11	59
2–4ha	3	14	1	1	4	23
4+ ha	2	6	0	1	4	13
Total	154	413	50	105	169	891

settlements in this period. As was noted above, however, the size of settlements was generally too rarely or inconsistently recorded by SMRs to be used in the national survey. That said, five areas with good levels of such evidence were used in order to provide a sample data set that would provide some guide as to the value of this approach and hint at broad patterns on a national scale.

Table 4.2 summarises the results from these test areas for enclosed settlements. Analysis of their size shows that enclosed settlements were overwhelmingly made up of small, dispersed sites (farmsteads or, for want of a better expression, farm clusters). For the test areas settlements less than 2ha in area (the dividing line chosen for the distinction between dispersed and nucleated categorisation) constituted 96% of all examples and never less than 94% in any one area. In fact, some 89% covered less than 1ha, a size suggesting that most are likely to have been akin to farm-sized settlements. Furthermore, the vast majority of large or nucleated settlement enclosures were recognised on closer inspection as Iron Age hillforts, most of which display little evidence for intensive settlement in the Roman period. This suggests that, within these small test groups at least, the overwhelming majority of enclosed settlements (though not all) recorded in the Roman period are likely to be dispersed (farmstead) sites.

Table 4.3 summarises the same results for linear system settlements. Here the analysis shows marked differences between regions, partly reflecting major variations in the presence or absence of linear systems as a settlement form. Thus the Devon and Cornwall samples recorded only a single example, reflecting the dominance of enclosed and, to a lesser degree, open settlement in this region. As a rule, the extent of linear system settlements are harder to define than enclosed ones, and therefore the figures in Table 4.3 summarise only those sites where cropmark or other evidence was complete or almost complete. While linear system settlements are generally bigger than enclosed ones (in part a function of the incorporation of non-domestic space into the core settlement area on these sites), the use of the 2ha division between dispersed and nucleated settlement still gives a good indication of the presence of larger nucleated settlements, which are comparatively common in the Hertfordshire sample but rare elsewhere. The figures for the Marches and West Yorkshire, being small, are harder to interpret, but they seem to suggest that the vast majority of examples were dispersed or at best small nucleated settlements. This seems to be a genuine difference, as on closer inspection of the individual records the Marches and West Yorkshire examples are all small, conjoined groups of two or

Table 4.3 Numbers of linear system settlements by size recorded for each sample area

	Cornwall	Marches survey	Devon	West Yorkshire	Hertfordshire	Total
0.1–0.5ha	0	4	0	1	2	7
0.5–1ha	1	6	0	3	3	13
1–2ha	0	1	0	2	2	5
2–4 ha	0	0	0	1	5	6
4+ha	0	0	0	0	5	5
Total	1	11	0	7	17	36

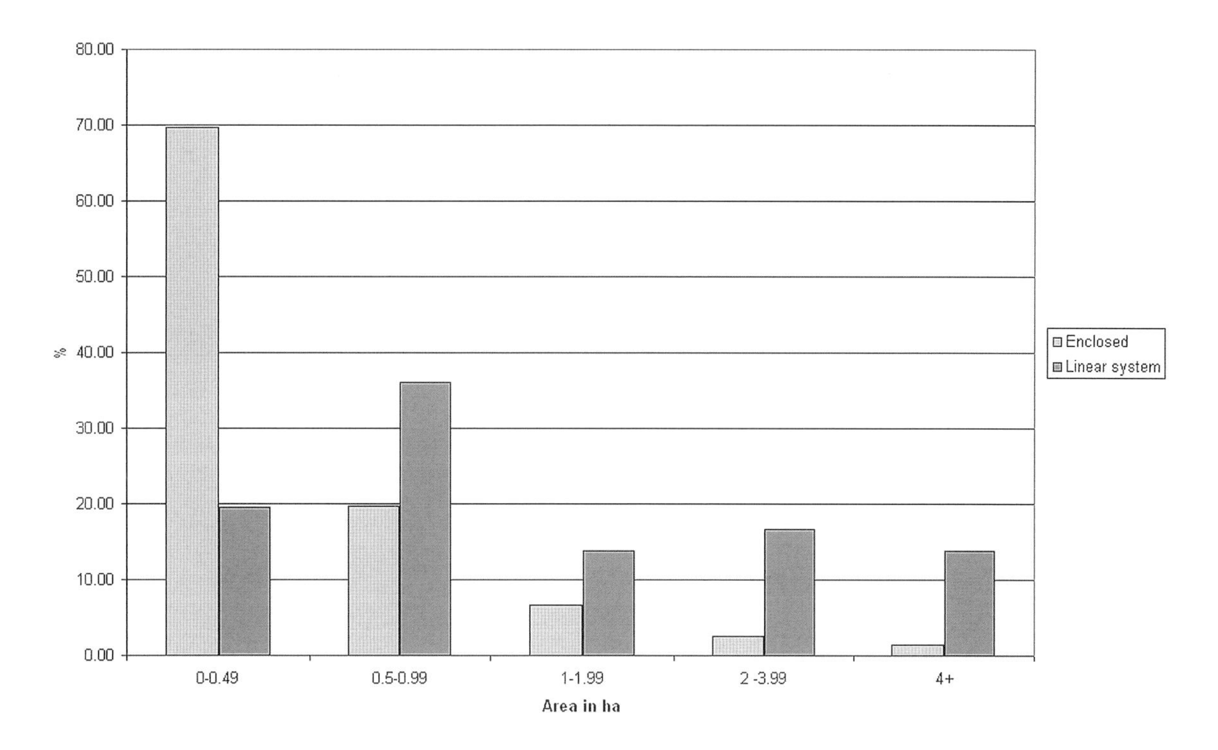

Figure 4.5 The percentage of enclosed (n=891) and linear system (n=36) settlements from sample surveys in each size range (in ha). Sites greater than 2ha were considered nucleated settlements for the purposes of the project

three or more enclosures, perhaps no more than one to three farms, while many of the examples from the Hertfordshire group represent large agglomerated or regular rectilinear complexes with several or even many separate areas seemingly occupied. Despite these regional differences, it is noticeable that nucleated linear system settlements constitute only some 4% of the total. Furthermore, there is a strong sense that, in the Hertfordshire example at least, there is a continuum of size ranges from small complexes that cannot represent more than a single farm, through medium-sized clusters to settlements as large as some small towns.

The problems of recording open settlements have been noted above and for the test survey areas they constituted too small a number to analyse quantitatively here. That said, however, ongoing work for the NMP in Northamptonshire (Deegan forthcoming) has focused on this issue with useful results. Here, a total of 76 open settlements have been recorded, of which 68 were less than 2ha in size (indeed, most were less than 1ha) – some 89% of the total. The vast majority of all the recognised examples, as is noted by the national survey, were either undated or dated to the Iron Age. This suggests that, while dispersed settlement was again dominant, in the Iron Age at least open settlement accounts for a small but significant proportion of nucleated sites in this area.

Settlement regionality by size and layout

By combining the morphological and size data it becomes possible to consider the regional and national character of rural settlement in the Roman period. At present it is only really possible to suggest the balance between different layouts and sizes of settlements in relation to enclosed and linear system types. The results of the national survey maps and the more detailed data from the survey case studies, however, do suggest certain clear trends in rural settlement. The suggestion from the individual morphological records is that, with the exception of Iron Age hillforts (the majority of which no longer appear to have acted as major settlement foci in the Roman period), most enclosed settlements recorded by the survey are of a size suggesting dispersed farmsteads or farm clusters (Fig 4.5).

Linear system settlements are largely absent from the far South West and the north (Fig 4.3). The few so far recorded in the Marches and West Yorkshire were also dispersed farms rather than larger nucleated settlements. In the East Midlands and Wessex, along with East Yorkshire, the East Anglian Fenland, and many parts of the South East, they are a common or even an abundant type that probably developed as both dispersed and nucleated forms. In most areas it is likely that dispersed forms were still predominant,

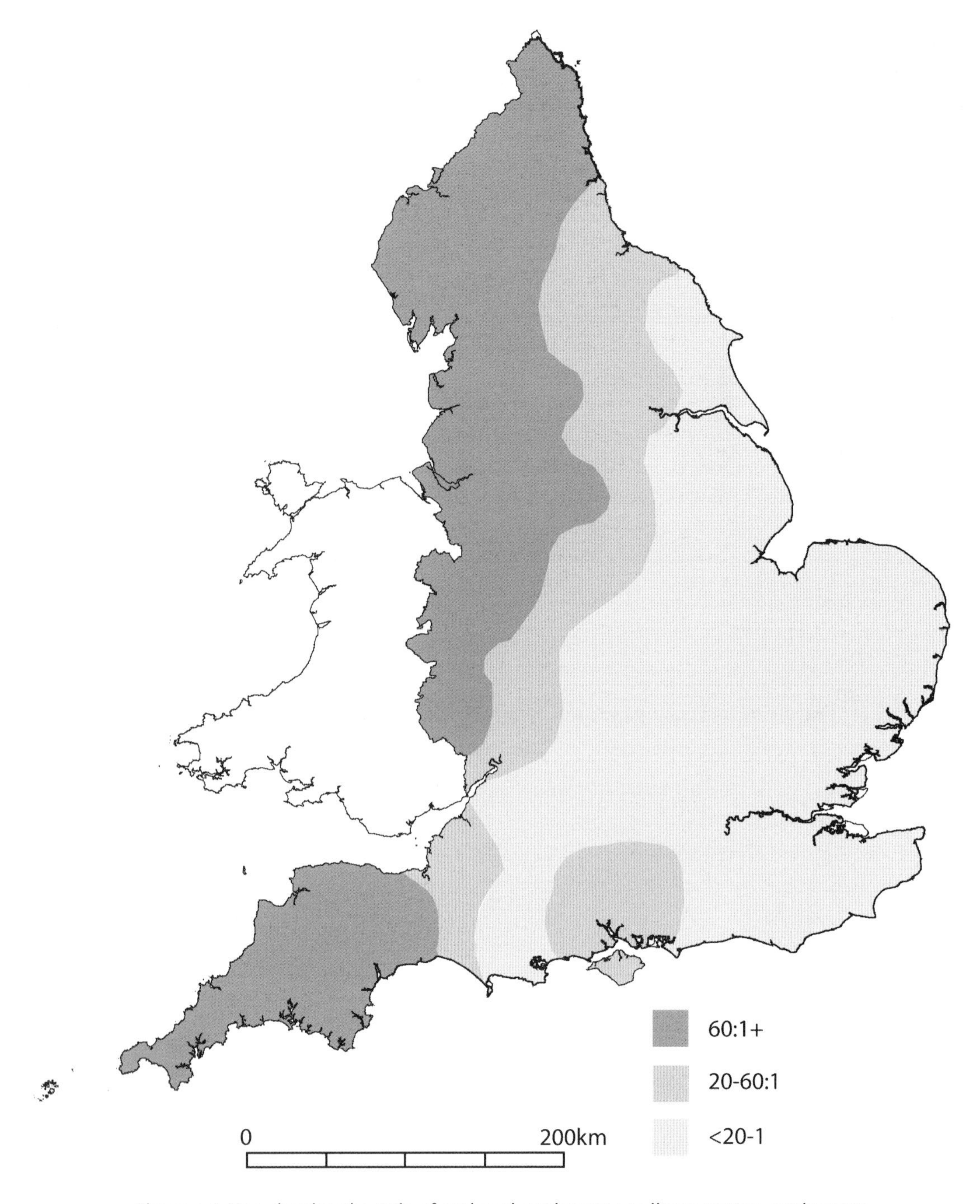

Figure 4.6 Map showing the ratio of enclosed settlements to linear system settlements

but nucleated examples could have represented as much as 10–30% of known enclosed and linear system rural settlements.

If we map the ratio of enclosed settlements (excluding hillforts) to linear system settlements nationally (Fig 4.6), it is possible to see a broad division between a rural settlement landscape dominated by enclosed (and possibly open) farmsteads in the South West, much of the English Marches, and the North West and North East, and a mixed landscape of enclosed and linear system settlements across the Midlands, the south, and the east. Furthermore, given that the vast majority of the mapped enclosed settlements were small, this northern and western enclosure-dominated landscape may also have been one of predominantly dispersed rural settlement. The mixed settlement landscape of the Midlands and south and east was, in contrast, possibly characterised by a far greater mix of settlement nucleation and dispersal. While still characterised by a marked degree of rural settlement dispersal in comparison with say, the champion lands of medieval England, these areas show a noticeable and, in some cases, such as Salisbury Plain (McOmish *et al* 2002) and the East Anglian Fenland (Hallam 1970), marked level of rural settlement nucleation in the Roman period.

Within this broad division it is possible, where survey data quality is good, to note further contrasts at a regional and even a local level. The Marches and West Yorkshire examples discussed above show that while, nationally, the presence of linear systems often acts as a good proxy guide to the presence of a rural settlement hierarchy it is not always the case locally. While the level of settlement nucleation in the Roman period indicated by the published evidence on Salisbury Plain is quite dramatic (McOmish *et al* 2002), nearby landscapes, such as those around Avebury, show a pattern of nucleated rural settlements developing in the Roman period within a landscape still dotted with significant numbers of smaller enclosed and open settlements (Fowler 2000).

Further inspection of Figure 4.6 in comparison to Figures 4.2 and 4.3 raises the possibility that Norfolk and northern Suffolk may represent a somewhat different rural settlement landscape characterised by locally mixed and often marked differences between areas dominated by dispersed settlement (such as parts of north Norfolk) and areas where linear system settlements were common, such as the fen-edge. While much of the north is characterised by a rural landscape of enclosed farms, parts of the Tees valley indicate the possible presence of a more mixed picture, with a small but significant number of probable nucleated sites associated with the road network and small-scale industry developing in the Roman period.

At present the national survey also suggests that within the broad zone in which rural landscapes are characterised by mixed settlement, there are areas such as southern Hampshire, around the New Forest, and parts of West Sussex that might be predominantly dispersed settlement landscapes. The absence of detailed published or archive surveys of this issue in the region, however, currently leave this suggestion open to question.

Additional settlement characteristics

Settlement architecture

Figures 4.7–4.9 map the distribution of basic patterns in vernacular architecture in rural settlements recorded by the survey. Clearly many records within the national survey did not note the forms of buildings from settlements, but the thinner distribution that remains still demonstrates clear regional patterns in architectural tradition. In northern England and the South West, various types of roundhouse architecture (Fig 4.7) form the overwhelming majority of examples in the Roman period and reflect the long-noted traditions in these regions of continuity of essentially Iron Age architectural forms. The few examples of rectilinear buildings recorded tend to come from military sites or *vici*, although in the North West and the northern Marches examples are found on rural sites that date to the mid–late Roman period.

Further south the evidence is more mixed. While roundhouses remain an abundant form in most regions they are comparatively scarce in south-eastern England, especially in parts of Essex, Hertfordshire, Surrey, and Kent. This pattern becomes clearer still when we search examples that can properly dated to the period (Table 4.4), demonstrating that most of the recorded roundhouses in this area are of late Iron Age date. Elsewhere in south and central England the pattern is more variable, but generally indicates the continuation of Iron Age traditions of architecture at least into the early Roman period. In those regions dominated by roundhouse architecture it is clear that the tradition is strong both in the Iron Age and Roman periods, although the continuity of roundhouses at the same location is noticeably greater in the South West than the north.

Buildings usually of types grouped under the heading of villas (Fig 4.9) only appear in any numbers south of the Tees and east of a line from the Pennines to the Severn estuary, being almost completely absent in Cornwall, Devon, and western Somerset. This confirms the distribution long known from published sources, although in places this survey has altered and extended somewhat their previously recognised distribution. In particular, they are found in moderate but greater numbers than previously thought in Norfolk and Suffolk, the middle and upper parts of the Trent valley, and in the West Midlands, clustered around the major Roman towns of Wroxeter and Chester.

Many other building traditions clearly existed in Roman Britain but the lack of agreement over a consistent vocabulary has led to a tendency to record them simply as building in an undifferentiated form. This frequently makes them difficult to assess from the national survey data alone but, as a group, many can be categorised under the simple heading of 'other rectilinear buildings' (Fig 4.8). It is apparent from this figure that this diverse group constitutes an important part of the settlement record, which needs to be incorporated within assessments of rural settlement importance in the future, especially as the total number of recorded examples outweighs that of villas. While clearly a simplistic classification hiding much diversity,

Table 4.4 Numbers of roundhouses recorded by the national survey by date

	Unknown	IA	Rom	IA/Rom	Total
North West	94	21	23	1	139
Yorkshire	147	52	33	46	278
East Midlands	81	23	25	40	169
West Midlands	109	6	9	6	130
East	80	19	60	25	184
South East	89	64	15	18	186
South West	89	32	32	60	213

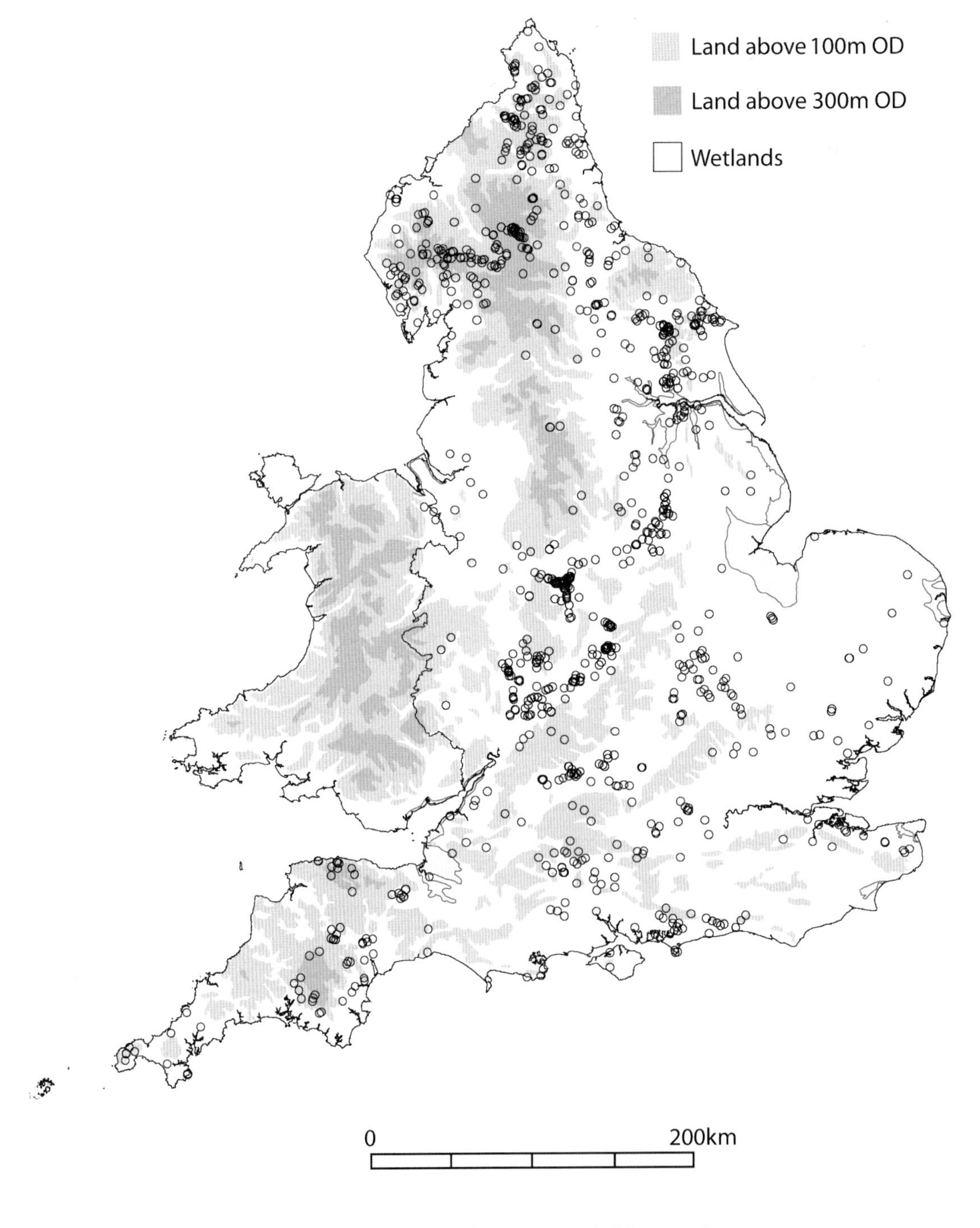

Figure 4.7 Distribution map of roundhouses recorded from settlements

Figure 4.8 Distribution map of rectilinear buildings (excluding villas) recorded from settlements

the pattern of rectilinear buildings is interesting because it largely coincides with and reinforces the distribution of villas. Taken together, the two provide an indication of the degree to which largely new traditions of rural architecture spread through southern, central, and eastern England in the Roman period. While there are notable gaps within this area in the distribution of villas (eg the East Anglian Fenland), these are largely filled by other rectilinear building forms. Thus though specific forms that are generally associated with high-status Roman settlements may be absent, the wider impact of new rectilinear architectural styles is not.

Although other forms of architecture were not systematically mapped as part of the survey due to frequent inconsistencies and omissions in the way they were recorded locally, it is worth noting two other potentially interesting regional developments in the Roman period. The first of these is the widespread development of so-called aisled buildings, which were clearly a very common, if not dominant, rural form in the later Roman period in central southern England and much of the East Midlands outside the Fenland (*cf* Taylor 2001). Their presence in part helps to explain the dense concentrations of rectilinear buildings seen in parts of Wessex, Northamptonshire, and

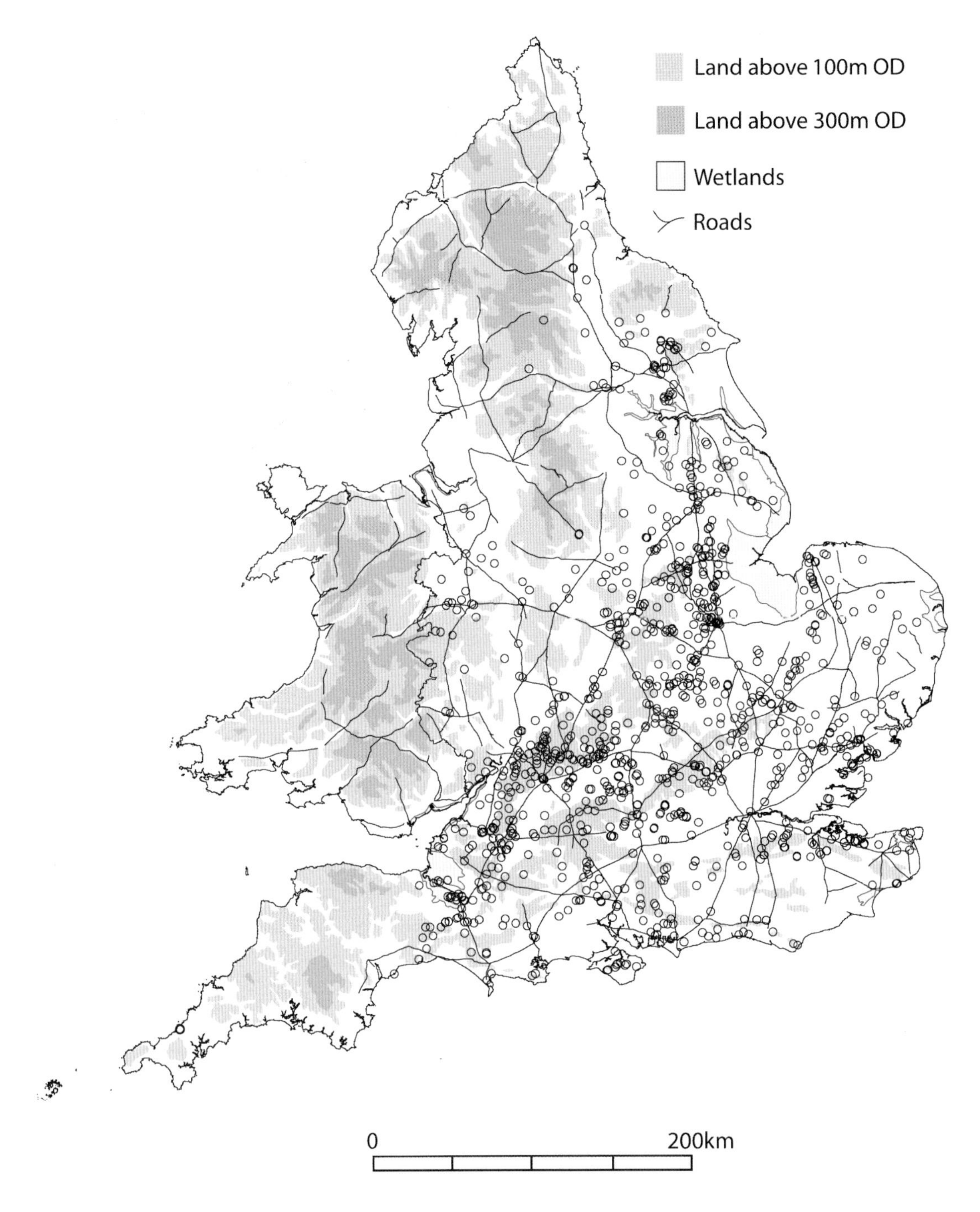

Figure 4.9 Distribution map of villa-type architecture recorded in relation to Roman roads

Lincolnshire. The second is the development of specialised forms of building in the South West. While it is true to say that rectilinear forms of building did not develop in rural contexts in the west of this region it is not true to suggest that roundhouses necessarily continued as the dominant form through the Roman period; rather, the region sees the development of locally specific traditions of building, in the form of courtyard houses in western Cornwall and ovoid or so-called boat-shaped buildings in Cornwall and Devon. In this respect the rural settlements of this region develop distinctive local architectural traditions in the Roman period that differentiate them from areas elsewhere in western and northern England.

Burial and ceremonial activity

While a detailed appraisal of the role and nature of religious practice lay outside the scope of this project it is worth noting broad patterns in practice in rural settlements in the Roman period in order that we may better characterise the various historic landscapes of the country. Figure 4.10 shows the recorded distribution of Roman shrines and temples from rural sites (the majority of urban examples are excluded from this map, although some on the margins of such sites have been incorporated where listed separately in the original SMR entries). This distribution reflects the degree to which rural landscapes saw the development of architecturally defined places of religious practice (excluding votive deposits or hoards alone, which were not recorded), and strikingly mirrors that of both regions with mixed settlement patterns and regions where villa and other rectilinear architectural traditions were adopted in Roman Britain. The few exceptions, in north-eastern and north-western England, are closely associated with military and urban contexts (lying within *vici* or in the immediate hinterland of sites).

The distribution of burial groups (more than five individuals found) and formal cemeteries (Fig 4.11) partly reflects the varying intensity of archaeological intervention through excavation and salvage recording, and partly also patterns in soil conditions which affect the preservation of human remains. That said, it is clear that traditions of both cremation and inhumation in rural contexts were characteristic of rural life in southern and eastern England in the Roman period. To the north and north-west, such groups survive far more rarely but, interestingly, where they do, they show a strong association with urban settlements and military installations. This may reflect the disproportionate extent of excavation

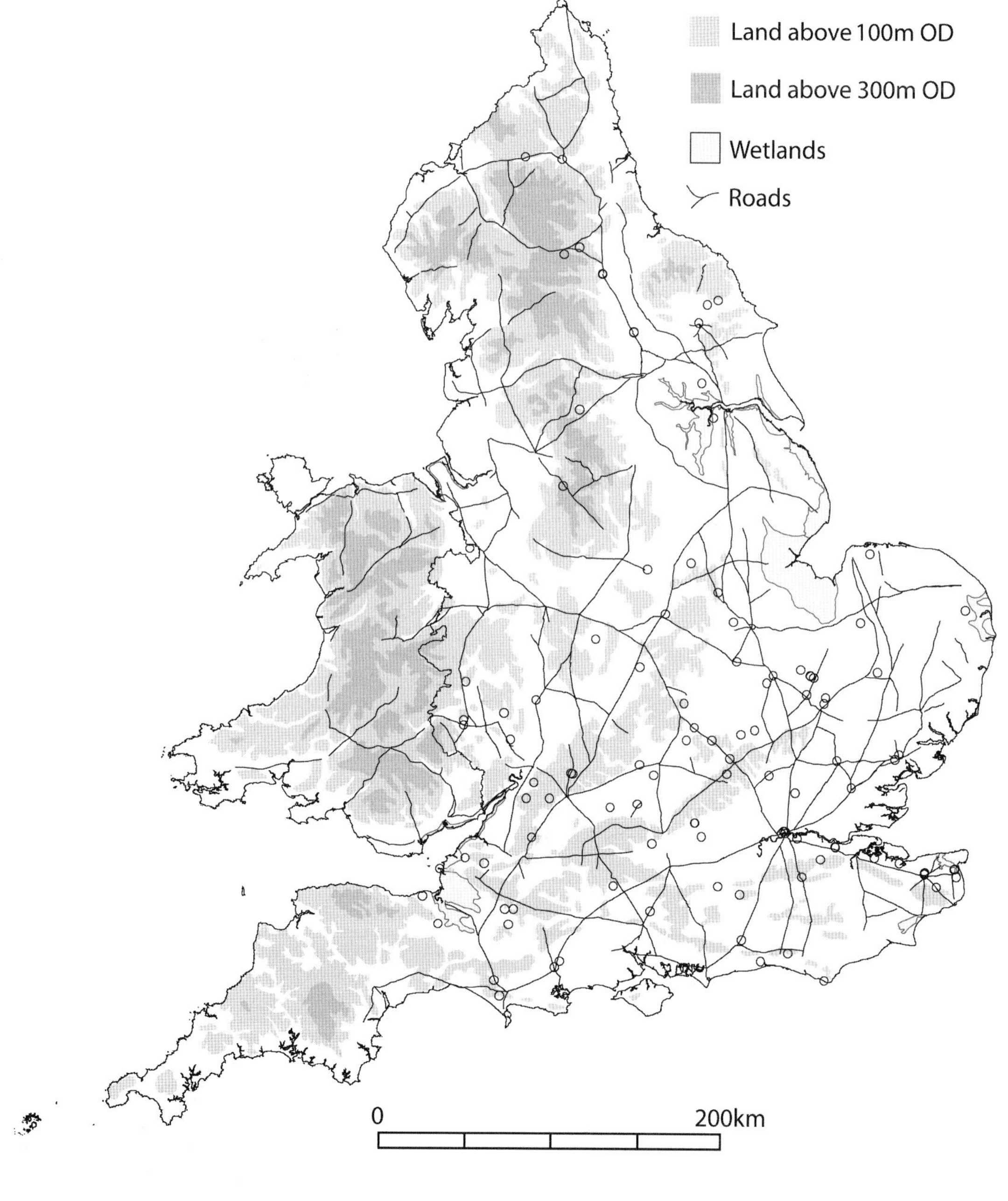

Figure 4.10 Distribution map of Roman rural shrines and temples in relation to Roman roads

carried out on these sites in these regions, but it still seems likely that we may be seeing a genuine difference in the degree to which human *burial* (as opposed to, say, excarnation) was a common rite in rural society across England. It is noticeable that those areas with marked traditions of burial in the late Iron Age also see many burials in the Roman period, although rites often changed. Outside these areas, especially in the North West and North East, the practice is rarely seen in rural contexts and may suggest that a different disposal rite was characteristic of rural beliefs here.

Rural crafts and industries

Figures 4.12–4.14 show the evidence for craft or industrial production of iron, pottery, and tile and salt associated with rural settlements across England. These readily recognisable and robust materials are reasonably consistently recorded in SMRs and could thus be used in the survey to identify the extent to which some craft practices were a significant part of regional rural economies. Figure 4.12 clearly delineates the three major iron-producing landscapes of Roman Britain: the Weald, the Forest of Dean, and

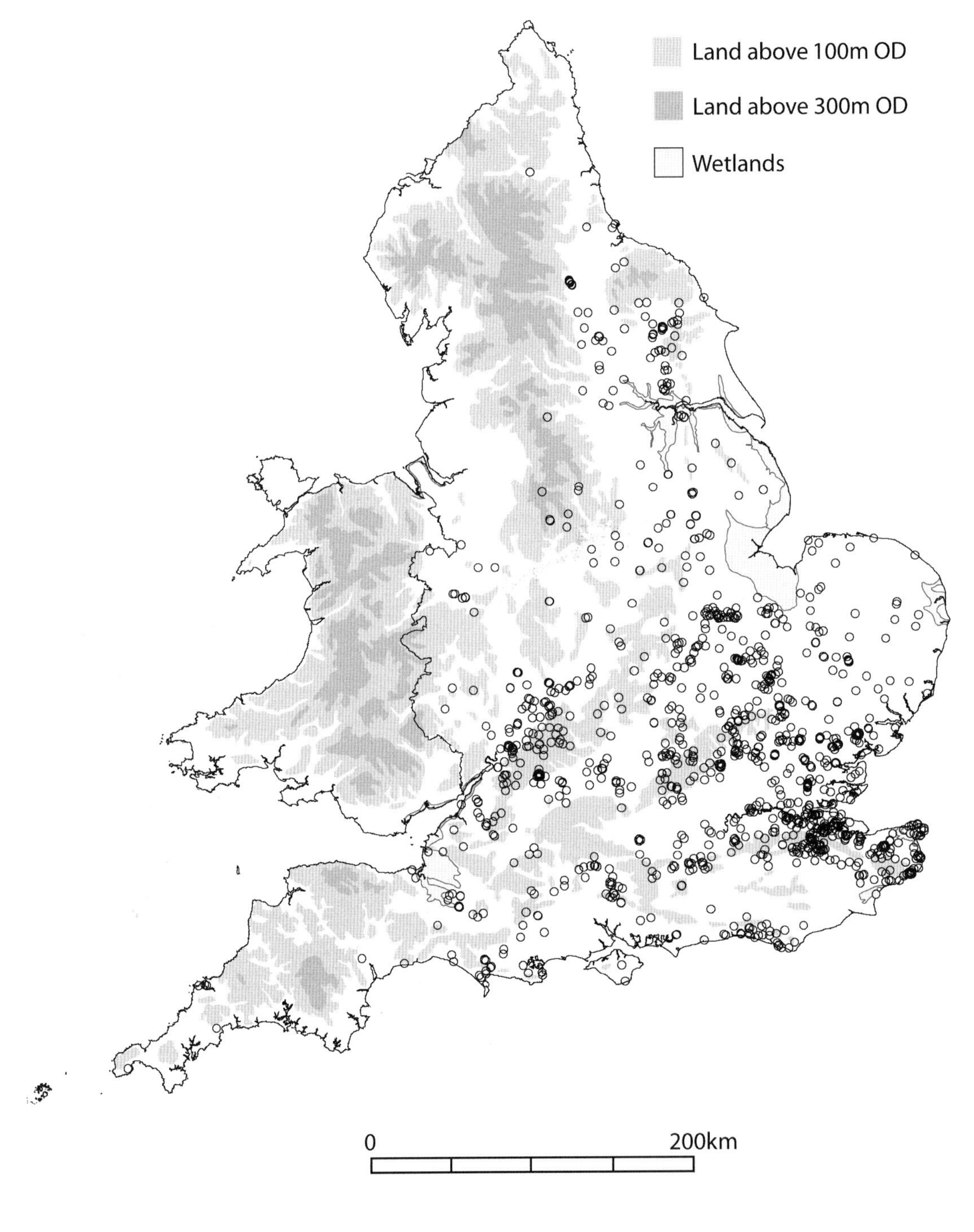

Figure 4.11 Distribution map of recorded Roman cemeteries and burial groups

the Jurassic ridge in Northamptonshire, Rutland, and south Lincolnshire. In these areas iron production is found on or in the immediate vicinity of a high proportion of rural settlements of all sizes. It was clearly a significant facet of the rural economy, which was orchestrated through the towns and road and riverine networks of the region. These industries are well known within the discipline, but less obvious until the current survey was the extent to which iron production (rather than smithing) was a widespread rural practice across many parts of the province. While this industry appears at its most extensive in the south and east, there is ample evidence for dispersed small-scale production in the North East and the Marches. Even in the South West, where evidence until recently was scarce, there are now suggestions of significant iron production in Exmoor and parts of Somerset.

Likewise, the map of pottery and tile production (Fig 4.13) accords with the long-recognised distribution of these industries in Roman Britain, but again shows the extent to which, at least in the earlier Roman period, dispersed patterns of production were common in the countryside across large parts of East

Figure 4.12 Distribution map of recorded Roman iron production sites

Anglia, the South East, and the East Midlands. Concentrating as it does on mapping production in non-military rural contexts, Figure 4.13 also emphasises the degree to which pottery and tile production in the countryside of Roman Britain was limited to the country's eastern and southern parts.

Perhaps the most interesting map of rural industry is that showing salt production in the Roman period (Fig 4.14). The location of salt production is inevitably heavily constrained by the presence or absence of the necessary environmental conditions and so the heavy bias seen towards coastal marginal wetlands is hardly surprising. More surprising, however, is that, to date, the survey has only recorded extensive evidence for such production in those parts of the province where we also see other industries, complex rural settlement hierarchies, and urban settlements concentrated. Wetlands in the North East and North West that on the grounds of available resources might have the potential for salt production do not seem to have seen the same degree of exploitation in the Roman period. The potential implications of this and other issues raised here are discussed in Chapter 7.

The results shown in the maps reproduced here do

Figure 4.13 Distribution map of recorded Roman pottery and tile kilns

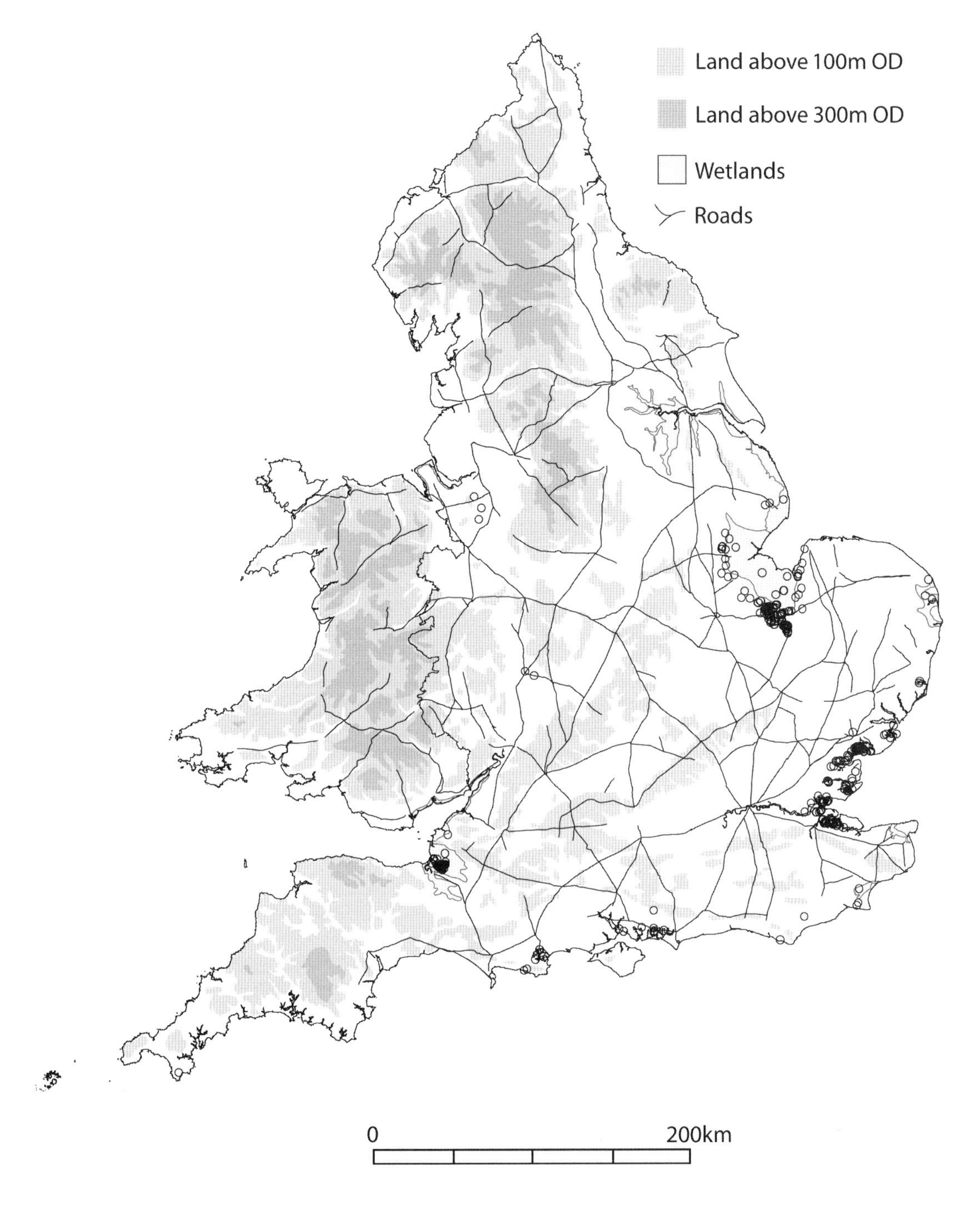

Figure 4.14 Distribution map of recorded Roman salt production sites

demonstrate how even the simple recording methods used by the survey enable us to build up a better overview of settlement diversity and regionality across the country. Although inevitably biased by local methods of recording and sometimes incomplete, they nevertheless provide a useful guide to the rural settlement evidence that takes into account important differences in the archaeological record nationally.

Regional characteristics

Having summarised some of the main national trends the remainder of this chapter deals with the evidence on a region by region basis (Fig 4.15). The regions are based for simplicity on those used by English Heritage, and provide the opportunity to discuss further particular local characteristics of Roman rural settlement, as well as strengths and weaknesses in the evidence from each part of the country.

The North East

Evidence for settlements recorded as earthworks shows that potentially the best-preserved settlements in the region are overwhelmingly found in the upland areas of Northumberland and Durham. Though perhaps unsurprising, Figure 3.2 clearly demonstrates the sheer scale and weighting of this bias in the surviving archaeological record, with few similar sites found outside these areas. Review of the summary statistics from elsewhere in the country indicates that this pattern generally holds true, something which has a number of important consequences for the evaluation of settlements (discussed below). The proportion of earthwork sites in the North East is very high in relation to the national figures and

Figure 4.15 Map showing the eight main regional divisions chosen for the current study

demonstrates the greater level of preservation seen in parts of the region that have long been rough ground or under pasture.

The earthwork sites provide primarily morphological evidence for settlement and are complemented nationally and in the region by aerial photographs of cropmarks and soilmarks. In Figure 3.3 it can be seen that cropmarks and soilmarks are located primarily in coastal Northumberland, the east Durham plateau, and the Tees valley. Their density varies considerably and the pattern seen in east Durham is typical of the levels found in lowland districts with suitable soils elsewhere in the country. Together, earthwork and aerial photographic evidence provide easily the single biggest resource for the study of settlement in the region (some 81% of the total).

The next most numerous source of evidence is finds scatters or groups, which occur in approximately 40% of recorded sites nationally. Figure 3.4, however, shows how long-noted national variability in the past use of portable material culture in the period is reflected in the form of recorded evidence for the North East. Finds groups are a very minor part of the archaeological resource north and west of the Tees valley, even though the cropmark distribution shows that there are extensive areas of modern arable cultivation within the

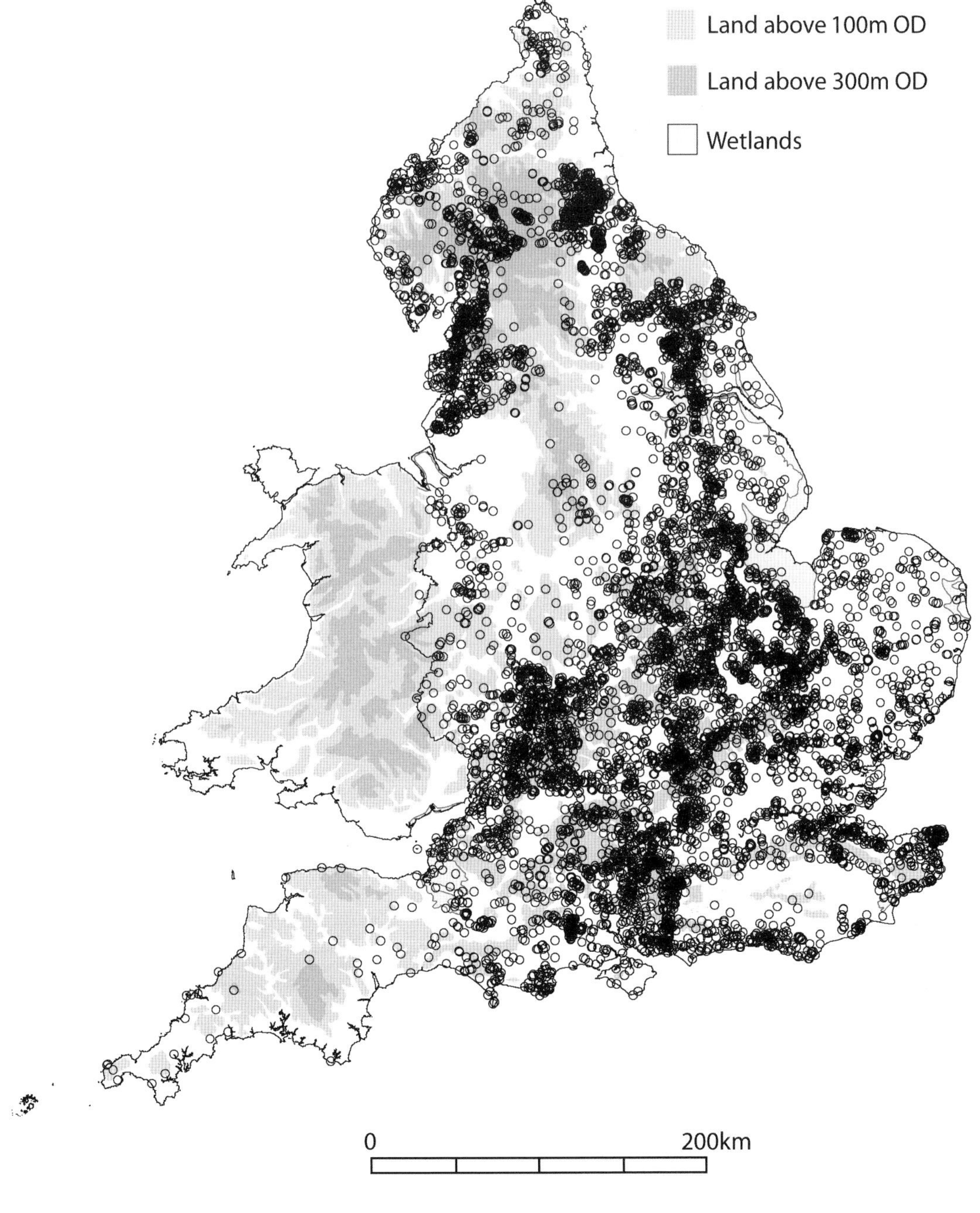

Figure 4.16 Distribution map showing settlements that remain unclassified

region. In Teesside artefact scatters begin to represent a significant potential resource (43 out of 150 recorded sites), one that becomes more apparent further south in Yorkshire. Other sources of evidence, such as documentary evidence and geophysical surveys, are, as has been noted, too infrequently and inconsistently recorded to be of real help but the distribution of sites with excavated evidence is generally very instructive of patterns of past archaeological interest; this is discussed further below.

Settlement evidence by type and period

Enclosed settlements (Fig 4.2) formed the overwhelming majority in many parts of Northumberland (some 372 in all), especially in the lowland areas dominated by cropmark and soilmark evidence. Open or unenclosed settlements were also relatively common in the upland areas but their distribution tended to be sparse in the region as a whole. This almost certainly reflects the difficulty in recording open settlements in the absence of surviving earthworks, as discussed above. Complex linear systems of settlement are very rare north of the Tees valley and the vast majority of recorded examples comes from probable or certain military *vici*. Importantly, this regional picture is very different from that further south, where, east of the Pennines, larger and more complex rural settlements start to become more common. The absence of such settlements is a defining characteristic of this region, and is in large part one shared by Merseyside and the North West. In both these areas rural settlement is dominated by predominantly small enclosed or open settlements interspersed with a few larger nucleated settlements with clear military associations.

The problems caused by insufficient evidence when attempting to characterise sites have been discussed above, and are illustrated in Figure 4.16, where it can be seen that unclassified settlement plans form the majority of recorded examples in parts of east Durham. In Durham, this was a consequence of the decision to place morphological information in supporting notes, rather than in the SMR's computerised records, but as many sites are evidenced by cropmarks their forms should be retrievable with further work.

Regional patterning in size and morphology

Figure 3.5 shows the distribution of the excavated sites for the North East. It is immediately apparent from the map that the distribution of recorded sites is relatively even across the region, although at its most dense in upland areas of Northumberland and Teesside. By and large this seems to reflect gross differences in the history of archaeological work in the region, with development threats not necessarily leading to major hotspots of activity. Although there has been a steady run of settlement excavations in the last twenty years, the impact of the work of George Jobey is still noticeable in Northumberland. An additional higher-density area of excavated settlements in Teesside is due in large part to work by local units in response to housing and industrial development around urban areas.

More significantly, however, the survey shows the marked regionality in settlement classes noted in the national survey. Northumberland and Durham are clearly dominated by enclosed settlements (predominantly small, with a few larger examples) and smaller open settlements. Interestingly, the distribution of open settlements partly counterbalances the impression from the national survey that settlement of this kind was essentially an upland phenomenon. This impression almost certainly stems from the difficulty of recognising open settlements until they are exposed through excavation ahead of development. Their presence in greater numbers in the North East may stem from a more systematic approach to the investigation of stripped areas, even when pre-excavation surveys have proved negative. These sites, however, still represent a relatively small proportion of the whole.

At first glance the distribution of the excavated sites, according to a simple twofold division by size (dispersed and nucleated), seems to be generally similar to the national picture, with small sites generally, but by no means exclusively, predominant. Linking this information with other characterisation criteria, however, shows that the nucleated Northumbrian and Durham settlements are clearly divided between *vici* and a small number of larger hillforts. With the exception of the vici, the vast majority of the settlements recorded in the survey are small sites of less than 1ha, demonstrating an overwhelmingly dispersed settlement pattern for the North East. Again, this distinctive characteristic of the region is shared by the North West and Merseyside but contrasts strongly with patterns further south.

The North West

Mapping the baseline survey evidence by form clearly demonstrated significant real patterns in the nature of the evidence (Fig 3.1). There are very many locally significant variations in the evidence mapped from the North West, but here there is only space to summarise the major trends that are already apparent.

The evidence for settlements recorded as earthworks indicates that the best-preserved settlements in the region are found in the upland areas of Cumbria; few similar sites are found outside these areas, with the exception of parts of Lancashire (Fig 3.2).

Figure 3.3 shows the distribution of cropmarks and soilmarks, which in this region are located primarily in the low-lying river valleys, on the coastal plains of Cumbria and Lancashire, and on small sandstone outcrops in otherwise poor areas of visibility in Merseyside and Cheshire. Their density varies considerably and largely reflects the tendency for cropmarks to form on particular soil types and the history of intensive survey carried out in the Solway Plain (eg Bewley 1994) and the river valleys of Lancashire. Together the earthwork and cropmark evidence provide 77% of the recorded evidence for the region.

Figure 3.4, however, shows that the North West has the lowest representation of sites through finds groups of any of the regions. Finds groups were a very minor part of the archaeological resource here, even though the cropmark distribution shows that there are some fairly extensive areas of modern arable cultivation within low-lying parts of the region. This would seem to be a genuine reflection of the scarcity of artefactual evidence recorded from rural settlements in the region, and mirrors the situation seen in the northern part of the North East.

Settlement evidence by type and period

Enclosed settlements (Fig 4.2) formed the overwhelming majority throughout the region. Open or unenclosed settlements were relatively common in the upland areas of Cumbria, but were rarely found elsewhere in the region (Fig 4.4). This, again, reflects the difficulty of recording open settlements in the absence of surviving earthworks. Complex linear systems of settlement were very rare throughout this region and the vast majority of recorded examples come from probable or certain military *vici*, a situation which contrasts with the picture elsewhere; for example, east of the Pennines and south of the Tees larger, more complex rural settlements start to become more common. This characteristic absence of such settlements in this region is similar to the picture in the North East. In both these areas rural settlement was dominated by small enclosed or open settlements interspersed with a few larger nucleated settlements with military associations (either next to forts or industrial sites associated with military supply), situated primarily on the major Roman roads.

In Figure 4.16 it can be seen that unclassified settlement plans form the majority of recorded examples in Lancashire. In large part this was because the majority of aerial photographic sites recorded in the SMR at the time of the survey did not specify what was recorded in any detail. Rectifying this problem would require a systematic search through the existing photographs.

Regional patterning in size and morphology

It is apparent from Figure 3.5 that the distribution of excavated sites was uneven across the region, being most dense in Cumbria. As with the North East, and for similar reasons, this seems to reflect differences in the history of archaeological work in the region. Although there has been a steady stream of settlement excavations in the last ten years, the impact of this work is only now being felt around the margins of the major urban areas in the region. The spread of excavated settlements in Cheshire and Merseyside is due in large part to this type of work, carried out by local units in response to the development of housing and industry in these areas.

There are striking regional biases in the settlement classes noted in the wider survey. The North West is dominated by small enclosed settlements, with small open settlements surviving in the uplands of Cumbria. The absence of large numbers of developer-funded excavations in the region means that the distribution of open settlements is still largely restricted to the uplands, but this picture may change in the next few years.

The data derived from excavations in the North West overwhelmingly support the impression of a region with a dispersed settlement pattern dominated by small, enclosed settlements, the vast majority of which are less than 2ha in size. As in the North East, the few nucleated sites recorded are divided between *vici* and a small number of larger hillforts. Unlike the North East, however, forts do not directly accompany some of these sites; rather, they seem to have acted as local industrial complexes along the major Roman roads.

Yorkshire

There are clearly very many locally significant variations in the nature of the evidence mapped from Yorkshire, which are affected not least by the varied history of recording by the various SMRs, but here only the major trends will be summarised. Evidence for settlements recorded as earthworks is generally rare in the region (Fig 3.1) and Figure 3.2 shows that the vast majority of well-preserved settlements is found in the upland areas of the Yorkshire Dales, the North Yorkshire Moors, and, to some degree, the Wolds, with few similar sites found outside these areas. The proportion of earthwork sites in Yorkshire is not particularly high in relation to the national figures, although this probably represents the under-recording in the current survey of such sites in the region. The high level of preservation seen in parts of the region long under pasture or rough vegetation is evident from the significant number of earthwork sites recorded from the Dales, Moors, and parts of the Wolds.

Cropmarks and soilmarks are distributed extensively across the region but are particularly dense across the limestone of west Yorkshire, and the Yorkshire Wolds and its fringes (Fig 3.3). The opposite is true of the Vale of York and the lower reaches of the main rivers running into the Humber. This reflects the geomorphology of this area, with much of the area of former wetlands immediately around the Humber west of the Wolds now better understood thanks to the work of the Humber Wetlands Survey (eg Van der Noort and Ellis 1997; 1998). The gaps in aerial photographic evidence are accounted for by the masking effects of clays and alluvial deposits of later date in the areas surrounding these rivers. The density of cropmark sites elsewhere in Yorkshire, however, is comparable with the levels found in lowland districts with suitable soils elsewhere in the country. Together, earthwork and aerial photographic evidence provide comfortably the single biggest resource for the study of settlement in the region (some 76% of the total).

The next most numerous source of evidence is finds scatters or groups, which constituted 22% of the records in the region. As with the North East, national variations in the past use of portable material culture are reflected in the recorded evidence for Yorkshire (Fig 3.4). Records of finds are particularly focused on the Wolds and the area immediately to the west and north, where a long tradition of fieldwork and extensive arable cultivation have led to the recovery of much evidence of occupation. There is also a concentration on the limestones of west Yorkshire, though here the records are primarily clustered in the main river valleys at lower elevations. Finds groups are a significant part of the archaeological resource of this region at lower elevations and are particularly important on arable ground on the margins of the former wetlands and in the Vale of York, where aerial reconnaissance is less effective. Overall, this picture is in marked contrast to that seen further north in the North East and North West regions, where fieldwalked information is scarce. Documentary evidence and geophysical surveys are, as has been noted, too poorly recorded to be helpful, but the distribution of excavated sites is, again, instructive of patterns of past archaeological interest.

Settlement evidence by type and period

Figure 4.2 shows that enclosed settlements formed the overwhelming majority recorded throughout the region, especially in those areas dominated by cropmark and soilmark evidence. Open or unenclosed settlements (Fig 4.4) were far more scarce but were nevertheless widespread throughout Yorkshire. There is some suggestion, however, that they were more common in lower-lying parts of the region, just off the Wolds and the Dales on the fringes of the Vale of York and the rivers draining into the Humber. This may reflect a genuine pattern in the settlement record or be a result of the greater dependence on excavation or observation ahead of development rather than aerial photographic information in these areas. Linear systems of settlement are relatively common in the region, especially in east and west Yorkshire (Fig 4.3). This differs from the regional picture further north and west, where such large and complex rural settlements are very rare, especially when not associated with military sites.

In Figure 4.16 it can be seen that unclassified settlements form a significant proportion of the records for north Yorkshire, parts of south Yorkshire, and some upland areas of west Yorkshire. They are also common though less numerous in parts of east Yorkshire. In the first two cases this is partly due to the use in the SMR of non-specific terms such as 'settlement' or 'farmstead' to describe sites, whereas in west and east Yorkshire it was partly due to the difficulty in distinguishing between complexes that could have represented field systems or been part of linear system settlements. In both instances much of this information could be retrieved by further evaluation of the archive records associated with these sites.

Regional patterning in size and morphology

Figure 3.5 shows a reasonable scatter of recorded excavations across most of the region, although there are significant gaps north-west of York and in Holderness. The rest of east Yorkshire and the Vale of Pickering, in contrast, have one of the densest patterns of excavated evidence in the north of England, a characteristic they have in common with the Midlands. In large part this reflects previous interest in Roman settlement across the region; in east Yorkshire, for example, a 'familiar' Roman pattern of materially rich villa and non-villa settlements associated with towns has seen much archaeological work. The rich but less recognisably Roman patterns of rural settlement in the rest of the region, in contrast, have seen little excavation especially by comparison with that shown to military sites. Consequently, while we have an enormous amount of recorded survey information on basic settlement forms and their distribution in these areas we know little in detail about the sites and their development through time. Since the 1960s the disparity in numbers of excavations between the upland and lowland parts of the region may also have been exacerbated by the greater numbers of, and emphasis given to, developer-funded excavations in the south and east of the region, in comparison to the situation further north and west. This imbalance is to a degree now being addressed via major infrastructure and other development projects in west and north Yorkshire and the signs for our future understanding of rural settlement in this important region are encouraging.

The marked regionality in settlement classes noted in the overall survey remains biased towards villas in this region. Over most of Yorkshire they were an uncommon form of settlement, yet they represent a majority of the available excavated data. This is particularly apparent in east Yorkshire, where excavations of Roman rural settlements without villa buildings are still rare despite the huge numbers indicated by the survey data.

Much of the north and west of the region was dominated by smaller enclosed settlements in the Iron Age architectural tradition. The distribution of open settlements recorded by excavation again partly counterbalances the impression from the national survey that settlement of this kind was essentially an upland phenomenon.

The distribution of the excavated sites indicates that small sites are generally predominant. A closer examination, however, indicates that the nucleated settlements in Yorkshire tend to be divided between *vici* and a small number of larger hillforts in the north and west of the region and larger rural linear system settlements that we might, for want of a better word, describe as 'villages' to the east and south. In the upland areas of north and west Yorkshire the vast majority of the excavated settlements recorded in the survey are small sites of less than 2ha (excluding the small number of *vici*), demonstrating an overwhelmingly dispersed settlement pattern. This distinctive characteristic of this part of the region is shared with most of the rest of northern England but contrasts significantly with the pattern in the limestone belt of west Yorkshire and neighbouring east Yorkshire.

The East Midlands

The extremely variable distribution of sites across this region largely reflects the history of archaeological interventions and the effects of local terrain and land use on the visibility of the evidence. Earthworks (Fig 3.2) are generally quite rare in the region's overwhelmingly arable and industrial landscapes but a major concentration of potentially well-preserved sites survives in the upland areas of the Derbyshire Peak District. Here upland grazing, abandonment, and more recent leisure use have aided the survival of settlements and field systems in a way seen nowhere else in the region. This pattern extends that seen in the Pennines, further north, and thereby contributes to a major area of preservation in the upland areas of the central spine of England. Elsewhere, small numbers of earthwork sites, primarily in the form of hillforts and larger enclosures, survive in upland areas of Leicestershire, Nottinghamshire, and Northamptonshire; hardly any survive in Lincolnshire.

The majority of information on settlement morphology in the East Midlands, however, as in most regions, is provided by cropmarks and soilmarks. In Figure 3.3 it can be seen that cropmarks and soilmarks display very clear patterning that is associated with the modern land use and underlying geology of the region. Dense concentrations of cropmarks are recorded on the Bunter sandstones of north-west Nottinghamshire and along the gravel terraces of the rivers Trent, Soar, Welland, and Nene. A major concentration is apparent on the sands and gravels of the fen-edge and on the silts of the Fenland itself, with less marked but nevertheless noticeable clusters along the Wolds and Lincoln Edge. Gaps in cropmark information are most apparent on the Coal Measures of central Derbyshire and west Nottinghamshire, and the claylands of central Leicestershire and north-west Northamptonshire. The remaining gap, around the Wash in Lincolnshire, represents the line of the former coast and its now-buried wetland margins.

The single most numerous source of evidence in the region is finds scatters or groups primarily recorded through fieldwalking (Fig 3.4). Within the region fieldwalked scatters are recorded pretty much throughout, the only exceptions being in the upland areas of the Peak District and the formerly submerged coastal areas of Lincolnshire. This is a consequence of a long tradition of amateur and professional field survey in the East Midlands; intensive and extensive surveys have been carried out by a variety of groups in the Fenland and fen-edge, the Nene valley, much of the clayland of both Leicestershire and Northamptonshire, the Trent valley, and the Coal Measures in Derbyshire (eg papers in Parker Pearson and Schadla-Hall 1994). Consequently, many of the gaps in the aerial photographic record have been filled in, demonstrating amongst other things that the clayland and Coal Measures were already extensively settled by the late Iron Age. The abundance and robustness of Roman ceramics in the region makes fieldwalking an ideal tool for survey and reflects the broader national pattern: the East Midlands lies within that southern and eastern part of the Roman province in which portable material culture was common across all sites. The only exception is the comparative scarcity of ceramics recorded from fieldwalking on sites in north Nottinghamshire and west Derbyshire, where levels are more akin to those found in neighbouring Yorkshire and Staffordshire, reflecting the picture more broadly seen in northern Britain.

Overall, the pattern of excavation (Fig 3.5) is good compared with many regions in England, with examples recorded from most of the varied landscapes found. Pressures of modern development, especially mineral extraction and urban expansion, have created significant clusters of archaeological interventions in the Trent, Soar, and Nene valleys as well as the iron-ore-rich landscapes of north-east Northamptonshire, Rutland, and south Lincolnshire. These clusters are complemented to some degree by local research and development-led excavation in other areas.

Settlement evidence by type and period

Figures 4.2–4.4 illustrate the results of the simple characterisation of rural settlement morphology for this region. Enclosed settlements were the most common form recorded and were dominant in Derbyshire, north-west Nottinghamshire, and Leicestershire. Open settlements were also found in upland areas of the Peak but in comparatively small numbers and no more commonly than in much of the Trent valley, for example. While open settlement is always under-represented in survey-based evidence such as this project, the good preservation of sites in the Peak District in particular mitigates somewhat against their simply not having being found in this region and suggests that the pattern of enclosed settlement is a genuine reflection of the rural landscape of the period. Within this pattern a further distinction can be drawn between the nature of wider land use in the Peak District and on the Bunter sandstones, on the one hand, and on the clayland of Leicestershire on the other. In the former case, enclosed settlements were directly associated with notable field systems, sometimes agglomerated and polyfocal, as in the Peak District, or regular and rectilinear, as across much of north Nottinghamshire. In Leicestershire enclosed settlements were far more rarely associated with field systems, a fact that may relate to archaeological survival or, perhaps more likely, to different traditions of land allotment.

Linear systems of settlement show a different pattern. Rare in Derbyshire, north-west Nottinghamshire, and much of Leicestershire, they were common in the Trent valley, Lincolnshire, Rutland, and Northamptonshire. While enclosed settlements were still common here, the rural landscapes of the east and south of the region have a characteristic settlement pattern consisting of a complex mix of smaller farmsteads alongside agglomerated rural settlements. This clear shift in the nature of rural settlement from one end of the region to the other is further emphasised when compared with the distribution of villas and small towns. Both of the latter parallel the distribution of complex linear systems of settlement well and were rare or absent from those parts of the region characterised by smaller enclosed settlements. The only real exception is in central Leicestershire, where villas were relatively common in a landscape of largely enclosed farmsteads.

Unclassified settlements formed a large minority in those areas that have seen much field survey (Fig 4.16) but have fewer surviving earthworks and have been less susceptible to aerial photography. They present a problem in areas of Leicestershire and Northamptonshire away from the main river valleys, the clay vale in Lincolnshire, and the Coal Measures in Derbyshire. As a consequence, while we can confidently map probable settlements in these areas we still have little evidence about their form.

Regional patterning in size and morphology

Figure 3.5 shows the distribution of the excavated sites for the East Midlands. A closer look at the subject of these excavations shows a wide variety of different rural sites being investigated. Although there is still a noticeable bias towards the excavation of villas and Roman urban sites in this region, intervention on a large and systematic scale ahead of mineral extraction has seen a wider range of rural settlements and industries being recorded in recent years. Away from the main areas of development, however, in parts of rural Lincolnshire, Leicestershire, and Derbyshire, for example, there is still a marked shortage of information from excavation about smaller rural settlements, which handicaps our understanding of the broader Roman rural landscape.

A study of the distribution of the excavated sites shows that small dispersed settlements tend to predominate. In Derbyshire and north Nottinghamshire almost all the rural sites where size could be recorded were small (essentially individual farmsteads). In Lincolnshire and Northamptonshire, however, a significant minority of rural settlements were somewhat larger, suggesting that nucleation was becoming more common in this area. Linking this information with other characterisation criteria shows that in the north-west of the region nucleated sites are divided between a small number of hillforts on the one hand, and military installations and their *vici* on the other. The vast majority of remaining settlements are small sites rarely covering more than 1ha, demonstrating the dispersed nature of rural settlement here. Further south and east, we see a continuum of settlement sizes ranging from less than 0.5ha for some of the enclosed settlements up to 8–12ha for some of the major linear system complexes, a figure that merges into the lower size range of some urban roadside settlements in the region. This, together with the presence of villas and other simpler settlement architecture, indicates a far more hierarchical structure to rural settlement in the east and south of the region.

The excavated sites suggest that in the north-west of the region the rural landscape was dominated by small enclosed or open settlements frequently associated with their own aggregate or rectilinear field systems. Other forms of settlement are very rare and urban development is limited to settlements founded alongside military installations. Architectural forms are conservative and show comparatively little classicising influence. Industrial activity is either located close to the few major urban foci (as with the Derbyshire pottery and lead industries) or is on a small scale and dispersed across the rural landscape (as with iron production in north Nottinghamshire).

The contrast between this area and the south and east is stark. In much of Lincolnshire, Rutland, and Northamptonshire (though not Leicestershire) enclosed and linear system rural settlements are interspersed across a landscape with many local civilian centres. Rural industry is common, often on a significant scale and seemingly well integrated with local roadside settlements/small towns by the later Roman period. Only in the Fenland and parts of the landscape distant from the road network is this pattern less marked, though here larger linear system settlements (hamlets or villages, for want of better terms) are also common.

The West Midlands

Earthwork sites were recorded throughout the region in small numbers but are only really common in the far west of the region (Fig 3.2). This corresponds well with the known survival of earthworks in the upland parts of the Marches, where a long history of pastoral farming has aided their survival. This pattern continues the trend seen elsewhere in England for the presence of high numbers of potentially well-preserved sites in the upland margins of modern agricultural practice in the north, the south-west, and England's central spine.

Cropmarks and soilmarks were also concentrated across the Marches, although they are noticeably predominant in or along the margins of the main river valleys (Fig 3.3). This mainly riverine distribution pattern is further extended to the east and north, where earthworks are far rarer, and is especially clear along the river Severn and the Warwickshire Avon, where free-draining sand and gravel soils have produced very extensive cropmark evidence. The centre of the region, in contrast, shows less of this type of evidence, in part because of the massive growth of Birmingham and its satellite communities, and the consequent masking of sites. Together, earthwork and aerial photographic evidence provide the single biggest resource for the study of settlement in the region (some 73% of the total).

The next most numerous source of evidence is finds scatters or groups (Fig 3.4). The distribution of finds groups complements that of the earthwork evidence as a result of the differing modern pastoral and arable balance between the west and east of the region. In the west, lower levels of arable land have limited the extent of fieldwalking and consequently the number of discoveries of finds scatters associated with settlement. It also, however, probably demonstrates a genuine difference in the past use of portable material culture in Roman Britain (Fig 3.4). Finds from excavated sites in the region are notably rarer in the north and west and especially so from rural settlements away from the immediate hinterland of towns or major military sites (*cf* White 1998). In the east and south of the region, in contrast, significant quantities of robust portable material culture are found on all sites, a fact probably due in part to their proximity to the pottery kilns recorded by the current survey.

In the north and west, excavation has been comparatively rare and shows a marked trend towards military sites, towns, and other roadside settlements at the expense of rural settlements. In the east the pattern is more widespread and denser; however, here the effect of developer-funded excavation ahead of aggregates quarrying can be seen in the disproportionate amount of work which has been carried out in the major river valleys.

Settlement evidence by type and period

Enclosed settlements were the majority form across the region as a whole, overwhelmingly so in the upland areas of the western Marches. While this partly reflects the nature of the surviving evidence it is fair to say that this pattern of enclosed settlements is a genuine indication of the rural landscape of the period. Open or unenclosed settlements were generally rare, and the small numbers recorded were unevenly distributed across the region. Their distribution largely reflects the fact that confirmed examples are mainly recorded from excavation, currently indicating more about the pattern of modern archaeological intervention than any significant pattern in the past. Linear system settlements showed a clear and distinct pattern. Almost totally absent from Herefordshire, Shropshire, and Staffordshire, they were comparatively common in and around the Severn, Avon, and upper Trent valleys in the east. This is an important pattern, indicating a shift in the nature of rural settlement from one end of the region to the other.

Unclassified settlement plans form a significant minority of examples over much of the region, and are a notably high proportion of listed sites in the south and east (Fig 4.16) as a result of a lack of aerial photography, geophysical survey or excavation to support fieldwalking results. Therefore, although many of these sites can be recognised as settlements, their form and frequently their extent remain unknown. The distribution of field systems parallels the overall pattern of earthwork and cropmark evidence, although distinct patterns within this distribution are apparent at a local scale (see Chapter 5).

Regional patterning in size and morphology

Figure 3.5 shows the distribution of the excavated sites for the West Midlands. While the distribution of recorded sites is reasonably even, there are some notable gaps and clusters. The largest concentrations of excavations are found in the Severn valley and its tributaries and also along the road networks across the rest of the region, where they are associated with urban settlements. A closer look at the remaining examples from the wider landscape reveals a noticeable bias towards the excavation of villas in the west, leaving us, again, with a shortage of information on broader rural settlement. To the east the balance between villas and other forms of rural settlement architecture is more even, though here the excavation of rural sites reflects the predominance of developer-funded work on the gravels and little is currently known about the nature of rural settlement on the interfluves and claylands surrounding the main valleys. In contrast, a traditional research-led interest in the military towns and villas has dominated in the north and west.

At first glance the distribution of the excavated sites by size seems to be generally similar to the broader picture from all the surveyed sites, with small sites, again, generally predominant. Further analysis using other characterisation criteria, however, shows that in the west nucleated sites are mainly divided between hillforts on the one hand and towns and *vici* on the other. The vast majority of remaining settlements are small sites covering no more than 1.5ha, demonstrating the dispersed nature of most rural settlement in much of the region.

Regional differences in the distribution of settlement classes is marked. In the west, the rural landscape is dominated by a dispersed pattern of small, enclosed farms interspersed with a few larger nucleated settlements with clear military associations. In the east, in contrast, there is far greater variety, with both small, enclosed settlements and enclosure complexes alongside some larger nucleated rural settlements and towns with few military associations.

The contrast between a landscape of dispersed

enclosed farmsteads in the Marches and uplands of the west, and the far more diverse pattern of dispersed and nucleated settlements to the east is further reflected in the nature and layout of field systems with which the settlements are associated. In the west, settlements appear alone or in association with nucleated or polyfocal field systems that reflect the fragmented and dispersed nature of land division. In the river valleys of the east, however, rural settlements are frequently well integrated with a system of trackways and extensive rectilinear field systems that commonly cover large uninterrupted tracts of the landscape. This pattern is far more in keeping with the East Midlands and is discussed further in Chapter 5.

East Anglia

Earthworks are rare in the region, with few recognisable clusters of sites surviving in good condition (Fig 3.2). A small group survives in the Fenland, probably as a result of the continuation of permanent pasture land use in former marginal wetland areas, and others exist along the Essex and north Norfolk coasts. The latter were mostly saltern mounds or 'redhills' that survived in marginal coastal grasslands and former wetlands.

The best information on settlement morphology in East Anglia was provided by the relatively abundant settlements that show as cropmarks or soilmarks. Figure 3.3 shows very clear patterning of this type of evidence across the region, reflecting not only underlying soil types (and thus cropmark visibility) but also the development of cropmark records within the relevant SMRs at the time of the survey. Dense patterns of cropmarks are discernible in the Fenland and the major river valleys, and on the permeable geologies of Cambridgeshire and Hertfordshire, providing a good overall record of settlement and past land allotment. Less dense but nevertheless significant patterns of cropmarks are also present across most of Norfolk and parts of Essex. Notable gaps in our evidence, however, exist through much of north-west Essex and Suffolk, where heavier clay soils are generally not conducive to cropmark formation. The remaining gap, in the northern Fenland around the Wash, represents the line of the former Roman coastline.

The single most numerous source of evidence for settlement in the region is finds scatters or groups primarily recorded through fieldwalking (Fig 3.4). Scatters are recorded throughout the region, with particularly dense clusters in areas such as the Fenland and the Norfolk and Suffolk fen-edge, and the former Soke of Peterborough in Cambridgeshire, where major campaigns of fieldwalking have taken place. The only real gaps occur on the Oxford clays of central Cambridgeshire and the clayland margins of Hertfordshire. A major benefit of the fieldwalked data, however, is the way in which they demonstrate the patterns of settlement in those parts of Suffolk and Essex with poor cropmark information (Fig 3.4). In this way it is possible to see that this part of the region was also quite densely settled, with a seeming preference for the major river valleys and coastal plains of the two counties.

The region is generally well served by excavation and there are notable concentrations of evidence around the historic towns of the region, in the river valleys of Cambridgeshire and Hertfordshire, on the fen-edge, and in eastern Essex. Less well known through excavation are the upland and clayland parts of Hertfordshire and Cambridgeshire, western parts of Essex, and central and north Norfolk. All these areas generally lie away from the pressures of mineral extraction and urban development, and have also suffered from the relative scarcity of local research-orientated excavation.

Settlement evidence by type and period

A major limitation, for the purposes of the present survey, was the comparative scarcity of cropmark, earthwork, and extensively excavated sites in Suffolk, leading to a shortage of detail for the characterisation of settlements. Consequently, it could be argued that settlements in Suffolk and to some degree parts of Essex were under-represented in the classified data sets recorded by this survey.

Enclosed settlements were the most common form recorded and could be seen everywhere across the region (Fig 4.2). In Hertfordshire and Cambridgeshire they represent a significant majority of the classifiable settlements, a pattern less clearly repeated in much of Essex. In the north-east of the region, however, particularly in Norfolk and northern Suffolk, the balance between enclosed settlements and linear system settlements was more even, suggesting a rather different pattern of settlement and land allotment in this area. Open settlements were rare across the region but the small number recorded came overwhelmingly from the east and south of the region, in Hertfordshire, Essex, Suffolk, and south Cambridgeshire. There are no particular reasons to believe that this is an artefact of survival and visibility and, though numbers are small, it may represent a genuine pattern of regional settlement.

Linear systems of settlement were commonly found throughout East Anglia (Fig 4.3). Especially common in the river valleys of the west of the region and in the Fenland, they were nevertheless seen in all other areas as well. As noted above, they formed a comparatively high proportion of settlements in Norfolk, north Suffolk, and the Fenland. Thus, while enclosed settlement were still common here, the rural landscape of this part of the region consisted of a more complex pattern of smaller and larger farmsteads and 'hamlets' or 'villages' linked to often extensive field systems. This clear division in the nature of rural settlement is further emphasised when compared with the distribution of villas, which largely parallel the distribution of linear systems of settlement across the region, with the possible exception of small clusters in areas of predominantly enclosed farmsteads in the far north-west and south-west of the region.

Unclassified settlements formed a significant minority of examples in Cambridgeshire and Hertfordshire and a majority in Suffolk. The latter reflects the dependence on fieldwalking and metal detecting in order to record settlements in the clayland areas of Suffolk. This represents a problem not just here but in other clayland parts of the region, where settlement activity is clearly present but where as yet it cannot be classified and further assessed.

Regional patterning in size and morphology

Figure 3.5 shows the distribution of excavated sites for East Anglia. A wide variety of different rural sites have been investigated and although there is still a noticeable bias towards excavation of villas, military foci, and Roman urban sites in East Anglia, interventions in a variety of different situations and a long tradition of amateur research and rescue excavation have seen a wider range of rural settlements and industries being recorded than in most regions.

Analysis of the excavated sites showed that dispersed settlements tended to predominate in the west of the region, although here, and also in the north-east of the region, the landscape was also dotted from the late Iron Age onward with larger nucleated linear system settlements ranging in size from small farm clusters (*c* 1–3ha in size), to village-size groups and major complexes of urban and proto-urban status (*c* 20ha+). This complex hierarchical pattern of rural settlement parallels the rise of a well-developed network of roads, villas, and towns in most parts of the region. The addition of other characterisation criteria regarding industrial activity to this analysis shows that much of Cambridgeshire, Hertfordshire, Essex, and probably Suffolk were well integrated within the Roman provincial economy. Exceptions seem to lie in the Fenland – its distinctive and well-known pattern of settlement lacked villas or industrial activity beyond salt production – and in parts of Norfolk and the claylands of Cambridgshire, where settlements do not appear to have been well integrated with wider networks of settlement and economic activity.

The contrast between these areas is more in quantity than absolute form but the survey has nevertheless been able to demonstrate distinctive differences within the region. Rural industry is common, often on a significant scale and seemingly well integrated with local roadside settlements/small towns by the later Roman period. Only in the Fenland and parts of the landscape distant from the road network is this pattern less marked, though even here larger linear system settlements ('hamlets' or 'villages') are present.

The South East

Major gaps and concentrations exist in the distribution of sites across the region, and require brief explanation here. Earthworks were found scattered in relatively significant numbers throughout the region as survivals in present and former woodland, such as the New Forest, and in pockets on the chalkland landscapes of Sussex, Kent, Berkshire, and Hampshire (Fig 3.2). Those on the chalks represent the fragmentary remains of far more extensive systems that were extant in the earlier part of the 20th century but which have been destroyed by ploughing over the last 50 years. Elsewhere, small numbers of earthwork sites, primarily in the form of field systems and saltern sites, survive on coastal fringes in areas of former or present marginal wetlands around the Thames estuary, the Isle of Thanet, and the Sussex coast.

While these earthwork sites provide very valuable and fragile information on settlement and field systems, the majority of information on settlement morphology in the South East is provided by cropmarks and soilmarks (Fig 3.3). Dense concentrations of cropmarks are recorded on the chalklands of Hampshire and Berkshire as well as on the North and South Downs and the sand, sandstone, and gravel soils of the Sussex coast, the Thames estuary, and especially the Thames valley in Berkshire. Cropmark density is lighter but still significant on the predominantly boulder clay and chalky till soils of Buckinghamshire and the margins of Greater London in Surrey. The most prominent gap in cropmark information, however, curves in a great arc through south-western Kent and northern parts of east and west Sussex. This large break in cropmark evidence corresponds to the clay Weald and Romney Marsh, regions known not to favour the formation of such evidence. This gap is one major reason why cropmark evidence constitutes less than 30% of recorded sites for this region in the survey, with consequent effects on our ability to classify settlement form.

The single most common source of evidence in the south-east comes from finds scatters or groups primarily recorded through fieldwalking (Fig 3.4). Within the region fieldwalked scatters are heavily recorded throughout much of Buckinghamshire, the Thames valley and estuary, and the Hampshire and Sussex chalklands. This distribution is partly a consequence of the predominantly arable regimes of these areas which over the last 30 years have brought much material to the surface, especially in areas with formerly well-preserved earthworks of Roman and medieval date. Much of the work involved in collecting this information has been carried out as a result of local amateur interest, but recently there has also been increasing amounts of development-led work (such as the Channel Tunnel Rail Link through Kent) and locally intensive research, such as the East Hampshire survey (Shennan 1985), the Danebury Environs Project (Cunliffe 2000), and the Maddle Farm (Gaffney and Tingle 1989) and East Berkshire surveys (Ford 1987). While this has inevitably biased the overall distribution of recorded sites towards the areas indicated, it probably also partly reflects a genuine imbalance in the density of settlement across the region as a whole. While many of the clayland areas of the Weald have not seen similarly rigorous arable cultivation or archaeological survey, the work which has been done (primarily ahead of development or as part of work on the Wealden iron industry) suggests that settlement here was very scarce in the Iron Age and Roman periods. Indeed, the majority of scatters and groups recorded from the Weald on Figure 3.3 relate to evidence for Roman ironworking sites. Consequently many of the gaps in the aerial photographic record may reflect real gaps in the evidence, rather than merely the probability that this area is not generally susceptible to cropmark formation.

On the whole, however, the abundance and robustness of Roman ceramics in the region makes fieldwalking an ideal tool for survey and reflects the broader national pattern, in that the South East lies within that southern and eastern part of the Roman province in which portable material culture was common across all sites.

Overall, the pattern of excavation is rather more evenly spread than some of the other sources of evidence already discussed, and therefore helps to fill in gaps in our knowledge for parts of the Weald, for the margins of greater London (especially to the south and east), and for the extensive urban conurbations now present along the Sussex coastal plain and the Solent. Pressures of modern urban development have clearly had an impact here, as have major infrastructure projects such as the Channel Tunnel Rail Link (excavations along the course of which help to explain the 'line' of sites recorded in Figure 4.1 through central Kent). Earlier research tended to focus on the study of the hillforts and villas of the region, alongside the survey of some of the impressive array of rapidly disappearing earthwork field systems on the chalk, and ironworking sites in the Weald. Today a far more diverse range of settlements are undergoing investigation, although frequently only on an evaluative level, before mitigation ahead of development. The latter, while widening our appreciation of the range of rural settlement in the region, has tended to produce often fragmentary evidence about individual sites, especially where settlement boundaries are not easily defined.

Settlement evidence by type and period

A particular problem, not confined to the South East, is the use of generic but vague terms such as 'settlement' and 'occupation' for a very wide range of settlement forms. This is especially apparent in those counties such as Buckinghamshire and Hampshire, where fieldwalked material is a major component of the overall record for settlement and where occupation and settlement are used as fairly standard terms for such evidence. This contrasts with the situation in Kent and Berkshire, for example, where aerial photographic evidence is relatively abundant, and the Isle of Wight, where a preponderance of excavated evidence has resulted from a focus on the county's well-known villas.

Enclosed settlements were commonly recorded wherever aerial photographic and excavated evidence was available (Fig 4.2). Small enclosed settlements were, however, comparatively scarce in the Chilterns and on the South Downs in Sussex and southern

Hampshire, and very common in eastern Kent, northern and western Hampshire, and the Thames valley. Open or unenclosed settlements were comparatively rare, but those recorded were relatively evenly distributed across the region. That said, the presence of a notable concentration of such sites recorded as former earthworks and through excavation on the South Downs and parts of the Hampshire chalklands suggests they may have been a relatively common form of settlement in these areas, where, as was noted above, enclosed settlement is relatively uncommon. The absence of open settlements from most areas of Buckinghamshire, in contrast, may suggest the relative insignificance of this form north of the Chilterns – a situation which contrasts with that seen to the south-east of the Chilterns in the East Anglian region.

Linear systems of settlement were common in the South East compared with most regions within the survey. They were found pretty much wherever earthwork and cropmark evidence was recorded but were an especially significant part of the settlement landscape of the South Downs and the Thames valley and its immediate tributaries. Common also in eastern Kent and Buckinghamshire, they were nonetheless rare in central and southern Hampshire and the Weald. While this partly reflects the balance of surviving evidence it is fair to say that this pattern may be a reasonable reflection of the rural landscape of the period.

Unclassified settlements formed a significant proportion of the total in those areas that have seen much field survey but which have few surviving earthworks and have been less susceptible to aerial photography (Fig 4.16). This is particularly apparent in eastern Hampshire, Buckinghamshire, and the Weald, as well as in the southern fringes of Greater London. Consequently, while we can map probable settlements in these areas we still have little evidence about their form. The distribution of field systems is obviously linked to that of cropmarks and earthworks, and showed some interesting patterns in relation to settlement forms, being especially common on the Berkshire Downs, in parts of the Thames valley, and on the South Downs, where they are associated with the relatively large number of linear system settlements.

Regional patterning in size and morphology

There is a generally high number of excavations across the region, and few areas have not seen some significant excavation (Fig 3.5). The most notable gaps are in the clayland parts of the Weald, where many years of observation and survey have failed to identify much evidence for widespread settlement on a significant scale in the Roman period. This appears to be a genuine phenomenon and, as such, represents one of the few places in England where rural settlement in the Roman period was genuinely sparse or absent. Other, smaller, gaps tend to be areas that today are relatively quiet rural districts devoid of major development threats or areas that underwent significant urban expansion and renewal before rescue excavation was well established. The biggest concentrations of excavated evidence occur in and around many of the region's historic towns (that also happen to have been Roman centres), around the fringes of modern urban expansion on the south coast and greater London, and in those areas, such as the Thames valley, that have long been threatened by mineral extraction.

Closer inspection of this evidence suggests that, while there is still a noticeable bias towards excavation of villas and Roman urban sites in the South East, intervention on a sometimes large and widespread scale has demonstrated that all forms of rural settlement were present in the rural landscape of the period. Away from the main areas of Roman urban growth, the roads, and the coastal ports, evidence for rural settlement change is often more conservative and to a degree less pronounced but, by the 3rd century if not before, all parts of the region had been profoundly affected by the Roman presence and were integrated within the wider Roman economy and society.

Study of the distribution of the excavated sites shows a landscape largely characterised by dispersed farmsteads (enclosed, unenclosed, and linear systems), interspersed to a greater or lesser degree with larger linear system settlements on the scale of farm clusters or even, on the chalkland, for example, larger 'village' sites. While enclosed settlements are the predominant form in places like the Hampshire chalklands and linear systems are very common on the South Downs, no one form is ever as dominant as is seen in some other regions within this survey. Consequently, wherever we look within the region (with the exception of the aforementioned Weald) we see a landscape dotted with a very diverse range of rural settlements linked through a network of roads and trackways that enabled the redistribution of the diverse range and large quantity of agricultural and industrial resources produced in the region.

Alongside this complex hierarchical pattern of rural settlement we see the widespread development of villas; this occurred very early on the south coast, and later elsewhere. Villas developed in most parts of the region alongside a dense and well-developed network of roads, towns, and coastal ports, and almost irrespective of the specific balance in the proportions of dispersed and nucleated rural settlements in any one area. Consequently, the rural landscape of the South East is best characterised as one where dispersed and nucleated enclosed and linear system rural settlements are interspersed across a landscape with many local civilian centres. Rural industry is common, often on a significant scale and seemingly well integrated with local roadside settlements/small towns by the later Roman period.

The South West

Major trends can be seen in the overall distribution of this evidence, with heavy concentrations of sites recorded in the upper Thames valley, Gloucestershire, eastern Somerset, east Devon, and the Penwith peninsula (Fig 4.1). Earthworks are abundant in the upland areas of the west of the region and in some coastal districts of northern Somerset (Fig 3.2). The latter are mostly salterns, which survive in the marginal coastal grasslands and former wetlands of the Somerset Levels. Smaller concentrations survive in the Mendips and the Salisbury Plain Training Area in Wiltshire. This overall pattern reflects the national picture, where the major concentrations of sites surviving as earthworks are found in coastal margins or former wetlands, and in upland areas where pastoral farming regimes or moorland have preserved upstanding earthworks.

Alongside earthwork evidence most information on settlement morphology in the South West is provided by the relatively abundant pattern of settlements showing as soilmarks or cropmarks. In Figure 3.3 it can be seen that particular concentrations of evidence were found in the Exe valley and to the east of Dartmoor in Devon, northern Somerset, the Mendip Hills, and the upper Thames valley. Less dense patterns were found across much of eastern Cornwall (complementing the largely earthwork-based evidence from the west), much of the rest of Devon and Dorset, the Cotswolds, and parts of Wiltshire. Notable gaps in our evidence are relatively few, but include north-west Devon, eastern Dorset, and the Swindon and Bristol conurbations. The remaining gap covers the upland core of Dartmoor, which current archaeological evidence suggests was largely devoid of permanent rural settlement in the Roman period (*cf* Fleming 1988; Pettit 1995).

Finds scatters or groups primarily recorded through fieldwalking were very rare on the acidic soils and pastoral landscapes of Devon and Cornwall (Fig 3.4). Further east, however, they constitute a significant and even a major part of the archaeological resource for the period. Scatters are recorded in large numbers in the Thames valley and Gloucestershire (apart from the Forest of Dean), and across Wiltshire, and Dorset. Particularly dense clusters are apparent in areas of systematic fieldwalking, such as the Somerset Levels. In the east of the region gaps are relatively rare and tend to be due to the presence of major urban conurbations such as Bournemouth, Swindon, and Bristol, or protected landscapes, such as the Salisbury Plain Training Area.

Figure 3.5 highlights the clear bias in excavation towards the east of the region, with less excavated evidence from Cornwall, Devon, and north-western Somerset, including Exmoor. This reflects the overwhelmingly rural land use of the region in the recent past, its comparatively sparse modern population and the relatively limited impact of mineral extraction. One exception within this area is the number of excavations recorded in western Cornwall, a reflection of a strong tradition of local research-led fieldwork. Excavated sites are far more common across the east of the region and reflect a similar degree of intervention to that seen elsewhere across much of southern England. For the period under study here particularly intensive areas of excavation can be seen in the Cotswolds, the Thames valley, the hinterlands of Ilchester and Dorchester, and southern Wiltshire. Less well-known through excavation are the areas immediately north of Salisbury Plain, western Dorset, and the Taunton area of Somerset. These patterns generally reflect the relative intensity of the pressures of mineral extraction and urban development but in some areas have also been affected by the scarcity of local research-orientated excavation.

Settlement evidence by type and period

Figure 4.2 shows that enclosed settlements were abundant across Cornwall, Devon, and Somerset, and common elsewhere across the region. Open settlements were relatively common here, compared with many other regions, and are particularly apparent on the upland margins of Exmoor, Dartmoor, and western Cornwall (evidenced by large numbers of surviving earthwork sites), as well as in the upper Thames valley, where they have been discovered during rescue excavations ahead of development (Fig 4.3). The pattern of examples elsewhere across the region, however, suggests that there are no particular reasons to believe that the presence of open settlements in reasonably large numbers is solely a result of survival and visibility and, therefore the surviving pattern may be a genuine reflection of settlement regionally.

Complex linear systems of settlement were almost entirely absent from the west of the region but become progressively more common as one moves further east. Especially common in the Thames valley, Wiltshire, and Dorset, they clearly represent a major, if not *the* major, form of settlement in the Roman period in these areas. Thus, while enclosed settlements were still common here, the rural landscape of this part of the region consisted of a more complex pattern of enclosed, open, and linear system settlements linked to often extensive field systems. This clear division in the nature of rural settlement between enclosure-dominated west and mixed east is further emphasised when compared with the distribution of villas, which largely parallel the distribution of linear system settlements across the region, with the possible exception of eastern Devon. Elsewhere in the South West, areas with fewer or no linear systems of larger rural settlements also tend to have few, if any, accompanying villas.

Unclassified settlements formed a significant proportion of the whole across most areas east of Somerset. In part this reflects the higher numbers of sites recorded as finds scatters or through partial observations, but it also shows the problems apparent in the classification of complex linear system settlements, as noted above. This represents a problem not just here but across much of southern England.

Regional patterning in size and morphology

Figure 3.5 shows the distribution of excavated sites for the South West. Closer inspection of the data suggests marked variability in the balance between the numbers of rural settlements, military foci, and Roman urban sites investigated. There is also a notable bias in the circumstances of excavation in different parts of the South West, with a low proportion of developer-funded excavations in Devon and Cornwall. This situation is gradually changing as the number of developer-funded interventions picks up in Devon and Cornwall and new research and rescue excavation have seen a wider range of rural settlements and industries being recorded. Particular biases regarding the types of site excavated are still apparent in the record, with an overwhelming focus on villa excavations in the Cotswolds and the predominance of military and urban contexts in Devon.

Dispersed settlements dominated the settlement pattern of the west of the region. With the exception of the hillforts (about which we still have little excavated evidence, although most appear Iron Age in date), the vast majority of the settlements recorded in the survey are small sites of less than 1ha. This overwhelmingly dispersed settlement pattern is shared by the North East and North West, and contrasts strongly with patterns further east.

In the eastern half of the region, particularly in Wiltshire and Dorset, the landscape was also dotted with larger nucleated linear system settlements ranging in size from small farm clusters (*c* 1–3ha in size), through village-size groups and up to major complexes of some 20ha, of probable urban and proto-urban status (eg Catsgore, Somerset – Leech 1982; Ellis 1984; Charlton Down, Salisbury Plain – McOmish *et al* 2002), that developed from the early Roman period. Locally common, these nucleated settlements were part of a complex hierarchical pattern of rural settlement that developed, especially from the 2nd century AD, alongside a well-developed network of roads, villas, and towns in the east of the region.

If we factor in characterisation criteria concerning industrial activity we can see that rural settlements from easternmost Devon and eastern Somerset to Dorset, Wiltshire, and Gloucestershire were well integrated within the Roman provincial economy. To the west of this region, and especially west of Exmoor and Exeter, we see a landscape dominated by dispersed rural settlement with little evidence for marked integration, with no urban or other nucleated settlements, a poorly developed road network and little evidence for the intensive industrial use of available resources.

The survey has demonstrated a contrast within the South West between east and west which is in many respects quite stark; although it hides further subtle internal distinctions, it shows that the modern region sits astride a major national divide in the Roman rural landscape.

Chapter 5
Settlement and landscape

The discussion in this chapter seeks to place the development of settlements within an understanding of some of the broader patterns apparent in the development and form of field systems across the landscape. Building upon the insights into settlement form and pattern outlined in the previous chapter, it sets out the evidence for broad patterns in field-system layout and scale across the country that can act as a guide to the possible evolution of different systems of land allotment and enclosure. This is then followed by a consideration of the inter-relationships between the broad patterns in settlement form seen in Chapter 4 and these field systems in order to begin to address the nature of rural land use regionally. A thorough discussion of debates surrounding land allotment in prehistory and the Roman period would be impossible within a short overview such as this; instead, it is my intention to show how the *variety* of field-system forms seems to relate to some of the settlement patterns already discussed and consider how this might impact upon our understanding of the regionality of rural society in Roman Britain.

Introduction

In looking at field systems we are looking at histories of land allotment and demarcation, an important means of defining land use and ownership in rural society. There has been much work on this in British prehistory and elsewhere in the Roman world but, perhaps surprisingly, little here (eg Bowen and Fowler 1978; Bradley *et al* 1994). The systematic recording and mapping of fields was clearly beyond the scope of the current project but here an attempt is made to give a brief overview of the diversity in field systems across the country (*cf* Fig 5.1), before discussing some potential trends from region to region using published and some unpublished case studies.

In particular, the summaries that follow emphasise three aspects of the evidence: first, field-system layout, which may be used as a potential guide to the development and organisation of field systems; second, the overall scale of individual systems, which may act as a guide to scale of enclosure, and a possible index of larger-scale intercommunal patterns of rural land use and communication; third, the nature of contemporaneous settlement forms, which may be compared with the field systems in order to investigate the relationships between the dispersed, mixed and nucleated settlement patterns noted in Chapter 4 and possible wider land-use patterns in the Roman countryside.

Regional overviews

Here, again, this evidence will be summarised region by region, using the same structure as in Chapter 4. It is worth emphasising once again that these regions are not chosen to represent any significant archaeological pattern, but serve as a convenient way of structuring the overview.

The North East

The North East is characterised by a great deal of regional variation in field systems that in part reflects gross differences in the nature and level of their preservation. In lowland areas limited archaeological survival and aerial photographic mapping means that we still have comparatively little detailed knowledge in places like Durham and coastal Northumberland (eg Harding 1979). Fortunately, large-scale excavation and geophysics are increasingly showing the presence of such systems and are serving to highlight a possibly important distinction between the south-east of the region and the remainder. In the Tees lowlands, we see settlements associated with extensive networks of

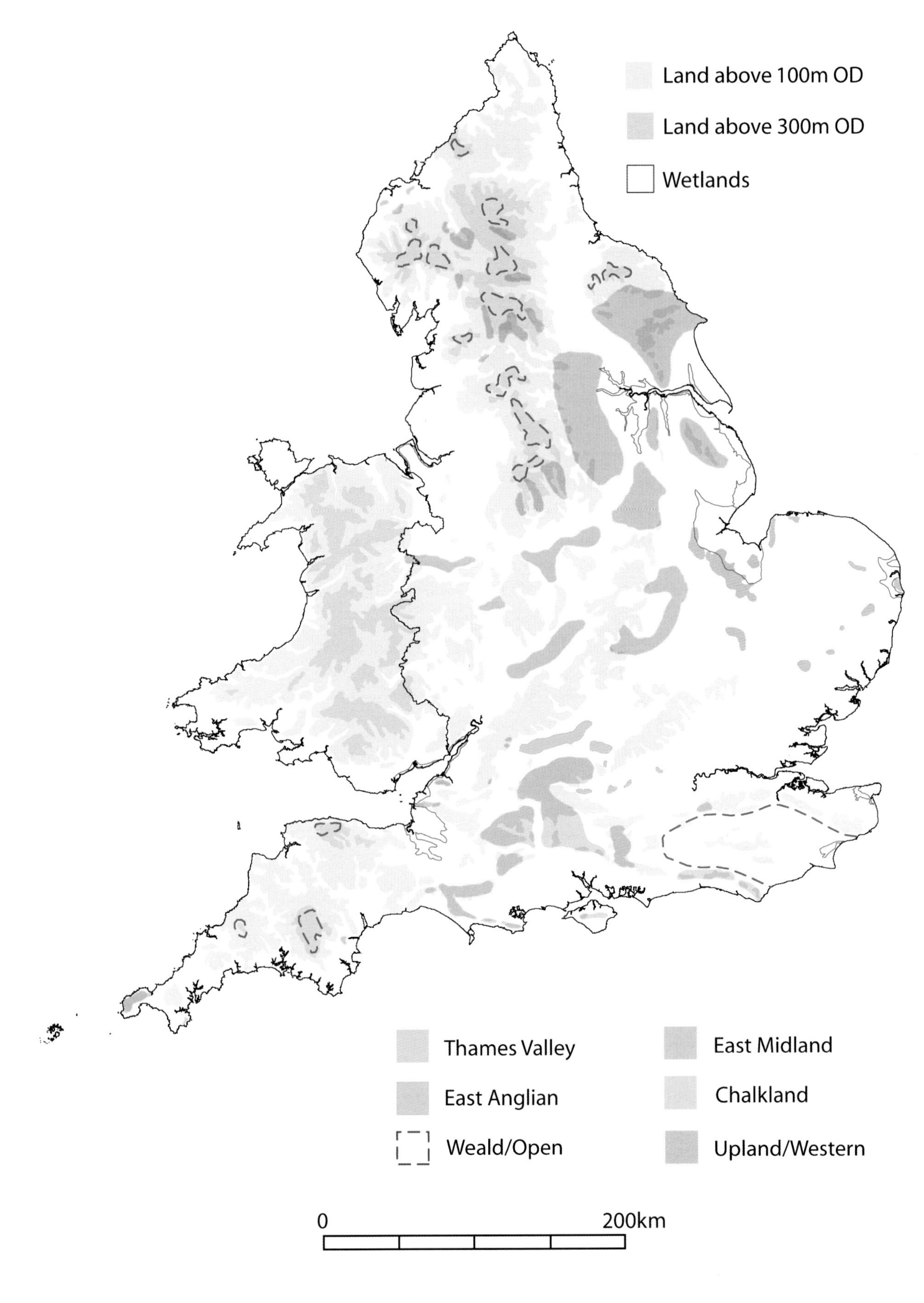

Figure 5.1 Stylised map of different forms of field systems across England

fields and trackways (Still and Vyner 1986; Inman 1988; Still *et al* 1989; Annis 1996) at sites such as Ingleby Barwick (ASUD 2000), and it is possible that this may also be the case in the lower Tyne and Wansbeck valleys to the north, as evidenced from recent excavations at Pegswood and Great Park (Proctor 2002).

In the uplands, in contrast (and especially in Northumberland), aerial photography and ground survey have been extensive (eg Gates 2000; 2004a; Oswald 2004). Areas of cord rig known to be present throughout the first millennium BC probably continued into the Roman period alongside cross-ridge dykes, such as that at Wether Hill (Topping 2004), which were constructed in the Iron Age but continued to function through the Roman period. In the majority of cases the extent of the arable plots defined by cord rig is small; Gates' (2004a; 2004b) survey of the Hadrian's Wall corridor shows that, there, they range from 0.5 to 3ha in size, but rarely exceed 1 ha. While this may be as a result of their variable preservation, Gates' evidence suggests land cultivation on a comparatively small scale associated with the overwhelmingly dispersed patterns of rural settlement known here. This does not, however, suggest that broader land use was not extensive, as the presence of cross-ridge dykes and localised networks of fields associated with small hollow-ways and tracks may indicate more extensive use of the wider landscape for both enclosed and open stock management (Fig 5.2 (1)). Further south, in Weardale and Teesdale, the picture is a little less well developed but work by Coggins (1986a; 1986b) and Young and Webster (forthcoming) seems to point to a pattern of dispersed settlement associated with small enclosures in an otherwise open landscape predominantly associated with stock management.

Together, the surveys mentioned above suggest that upland areas of the region were largely characterised by dispersed patterns of settlement associated with localised cultivation; these areas, in turn, were located within wider networks of dykes and occasional enclosures probably associated with extensive stock management, in a largely open landscape. In lowland areas our evidence is poorer, but there is some suggestion from the Tees lowlands that at least in the south-east of the region there were some complex and extensive field systems associated with a small number of larger settlements, alongside localised networks of fields around neighbouring small settlements.

The North West

Aerial and ground-based survey in the Eden valley in Cumbria (Higham 1979; Higham and Jones 1975) has shown that dispersed enclosed settlements were often associated with the fragmentary remains of small field systems, but only where preservation is good, as at Yanwath Woodhouse, has a better appreciation of their form and scale been possible (Higham and Jones 1985). Here, broadly rectilinear fields which were focused on the settlement covered an area of approximately 10ha, with further sinuous linear boundaries extending over a total of 3km. Higham and Jones took this to suggest a landscape of often densely spread but dispersed enclosed settlement, the occupants of which practised enclosed arable farming as well as more widespread but only partially enclosed stock rearing in the intervening areas (Fig 5.2 (2); Higham and Jones 1985, 82).

As an upland zone much of the Cumbrian Massif was simply too high and inhospitable for established settlement in the Roman period and here most evidence for occupation is limited to the few sheltered valleys and lakes. The best-known example, at Aughertree Fell, suggests another local cluster of dispersed settlements sharing a relatively extensive field system covering *c* 1.4 square km of the valley side. The irregular shape and large size of individual fields were taken by Higham and Jones (1985, 94) to suggest areas of enclosed pasture on these poorly drained and acid soils. To the east and north, on the edge of the Cumbrian Massif, we see settlements seemingly without attendant field systems; rather, they possessed occasional irregular enclosures, possibly for stock management, set within an otherwise open landscape.

Away from the Massif on the limestone uplands and boulder clays of the Eden–Lune watershed, the pattern is again subtly different. Here, distinct groups or clusters of dispersed settlements are associated with localised field systems and, further afield, long dykes separate these areas from unenclosed land. In contrast, intervening upland areas between these settlement groups seem to consist of largely unenclosed and unoccupied land at this time. The shortage of modern excavation in these areas again raises problems of the absolute chronology of these systems but Higham and Jones (1985, 85) saw the dykes as significant boundaries designed to separate areas of open pasture from the cultivated lands of these localised groups of settlements.

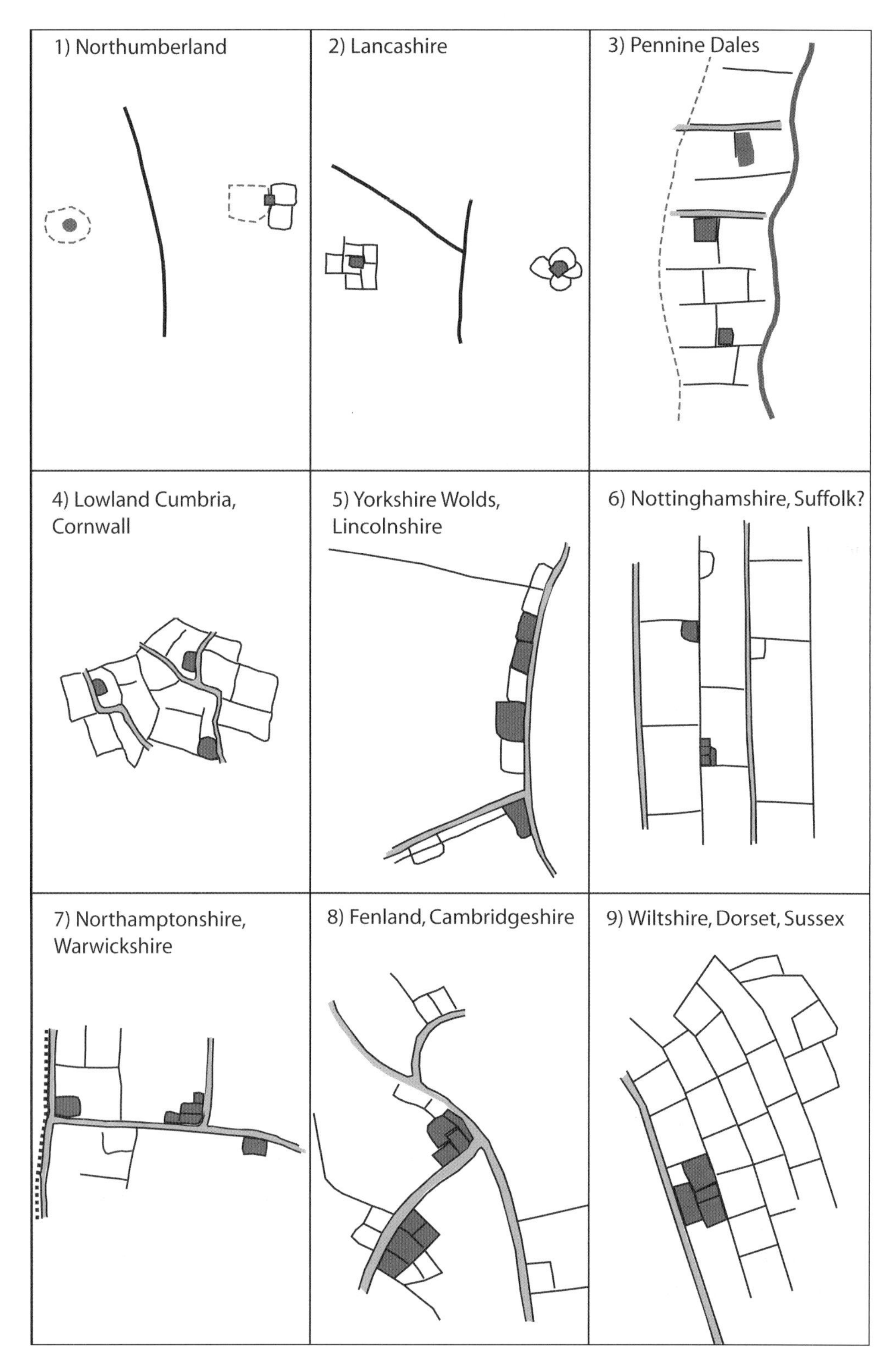

Figure 5.2 Schematic plans of different field system forms identified by the national survey. Black lines indicate boundaries; dark shaded areas are settlements; dashed lines indicate boundary of enclosed cultivated land

In lowland areas of the North West, in contrast, evidence for the survival of field systems is less common and the few that have been proposed are by and large poorly dated (Petch 1987; Higham 1993). Philpott has noted field boundaries in association with cropmark settlements in Cheshire and the Mersey Basin (Cowell and Philpott 2000, 190) that indicate relatively small complexes of broadly rectilinear fields closely associated with individual dispersed enclosed settlements. Here, he suggests these fields may not represent the full extent of land use surrounding settlements but rather mark the extent of arable land around them, thus creating small-scale systems of land allotment attached to individual farms rather than a pattern of more extensive systems that partition large areas of the wider landscape.

This picture of settlement-focused, localised field systems seems to be mirrored in the Solway Plain, where a long tradition of aerial survey and synthesis provides a fuller picture of later prehistoric and Roman settlement and land use (Higham and Jones 1975; 1985; Bewley 1994). Here dispersed settlement groups tend to cluster on the drier soils in association with localised blocks of rectilinear enclosed fields covering *c* 6–10ha in area (Higham and Jones 1985; R Philpott pers comm). In places, the dense clustering of settlement creates continuous patterns of fields over larger areas, though there is little evidence to suggest that they represent large-scale extensive or 'planned' systems (Fig 5.2 (4)).

While varying in detail, the evidence from different parts of the North West suggests patterns of settlement and field layout that are similar to those noted in many areas of the North East. Again, networks or clusters of dispersed settlements tend to lie within locally enclosed groups of fields or even in seemingly unenclosed land showing little evidence for the construction and maintenance of clearly defined longer-distance droves or trackways. Fields, when present, appear as small- to medium-sized blocks focused in an aggregate pattern around individual farms or neighbouring groups of farms within a wider landscape with far less evidence of overt boundary demarcation than in the south of the country.

Yorkshire

In some respects the area of Yorkshire about which we know least is the North Yorkshire Moors. Earlier work, by Don Spratt (1989) in particular, has done much to demonstrate the significance of the visible and sometimes major later prehistoric and medieval boundary divisions on and immediately around the moors. Unfortunately, there appears to be far less evidence for the nature of this landscape during the Roman period (Hartley 1993). On the high moors there is little settlement or field boundary evidence that can be dated to the period but on the edges and vales there is some suggestion that small fragmentary coaxial systems, probably of prehistoric origin, were used during the Roman period.

The Yorkshire Dales, as with so many of England's upland areas, have the frustrating combination of often good preservation but correspondingly little archaeological excavation (*cf* RCHME 1995). While they are poorly dated, there is mounting evidence for the use of sometimes quite extensive coaxial systems that were developed from the mid–late Iron Age onwards. These are overwhelmingly concentrated on dale sides and occasionally extend onto the moorland fringe, although they are rarely found above 400m AOD. Access is provided through these systems by droveways down into the valley bottom (Fig 5.2 (3); Horne and MacLeod 2004). Further up into the Pennines, particularly on the high peat moorland to the west, we see a largely unenclosed landscape with little settlement. Fleming (1998) suggests that the Daleside systems recorded in Swaledale date from the middle Iron Age on, but to the west, in Littondale, the excavated evidence suggests that the system here was of mid–late Roman date (Maude 1999). All were certainly in use in the Roman period and the available evidence suggests that livestock management was a primary concern within such systems, with droves running from moor to dale bottom, probably allowing optimal seasonal grazing alongside localised cultivation. Settlement was sometimes quite densely distributed along the dale sides but, again, was primarily dispersed in character.

To the east of the Pennines, in the Vale of York and along the Magnesian Limestone belt at its western edge, recent systematic survey (Jones in prep) alongside PPG16-related excavation and smaller-scale research projects have markedly improved our understanding of the landscape in the Iron Age and the Roman period (eg Jones in prep; Halkon and Millett 1999; Millett 2006; Roberts *et al* 2001). In the Magnesian Limestone belt south of Tadcaster are landscapes with a mixed pattern of 'brickwork' (cohesive) and nuclear (aggregate) strip field systems that developed in the latter part of the Iron Age and into the Roman period. This pattern extends south of the rivers Aire and Don to the west of the Humber wetlands as far as Rossington in south Yorkshire (Deegan 2001; Riley 1980). A similarly mixed landscape is seen extending into the areas between the Ouse and Derwent, south of York, but not seemingly beyond (Jones in prep).

By contrast, we see a markedly different landscape in the eastern Vale in the area to the east of the River Derwent and extending over the Wolds and Vale of Pickering. Extensive aerial survey and fieldwork here provide us with a clearer picture of developments on the Yorkshire Wolds, where the rural landscape was in large part structured around long-distance linear earthworks dating back to the late Bronze Age. By the late Iron Age these formed major territorial divisions across the Wolds that determined the direction of long-distance trackways providing access into and out of the Wolds from Holderness (eg Stoertz 1997; Fenton-Thomas 2003). During the late Iron Age and the Roman period some of the large territories demarcated by these boundaries were subdivided with infill land division and both nucleated (ladder) and dispersed enclosed settlements along the main trackways (Fig 5.2 (5)). Some of these bounded zones, especially those enclosing Wold tops, were left to remain as large open tracts respected by settlements. These were thought by Stoertz and Fenton-Thomas to represent extensive pastures for the keeping of large flocks of sheep, notable in the faunal records of excavated sites such as Garton, Rillington and the Rudston villa. In this landscape, the late Bronze Age ditches and dykes can be seen to act as both boundaries between different zones of land use and settlement, and trackways enabling movement over longer distances across the Wolds. Intensive and long-term survey and excavation through the Heslerton project (Powlesland 2003) shows this pattern extends into and across the Vale of Pickering to the north.

At the southern end of the Vale of York and along the lower reaches of the rivers Foulness, Aire and Wharfe lie the wetlands of the Humber. Here the work of the Holme-on-Spalding Moor survey (Halkon and Millett 1999) and the Humber Wetlands Survey (Van de Noort 2004) suggest localised nuclear (aggregate) patterns of enclosure associated with settlements lying on slightly drier 'islands' or river banks (Fig 5.3). These small field systems are closely associated with ditched droveways that run from them out into lower-lying unenclosed land in their vicinity. These marginal areas of both fresh and saltwater marsh were probably used as feeding grounds for sheep and cattle. The vast majority of the settlements associated with these nuclear field systems were dispersed, but a small

Figure 5.3 Aerial photograph of localised aggregate field system around settlement in the Holme on Spalding Moor area, East Yorkshire (NMR 12097/77, 23 August 1990 © Crown copyright. NMR)

number of large nucleated settlements akin to ladder settlements or possibly even small urban ribbon developments have been recorded at key loci along the major watercourses of the region (eg Sutton-upon-Derwent, Chapman *et al* 1999; Hull, Didsbury 1990; Addingfleet, Fenwick *et al* 1998).

While undoubtedly a gross oversimplification of an extremely complex and nuanced situation, it is possible to suggest that in this region we see major contrasts in land use that reflect a broader change in the nature of the rural landscape nationally. On the North York Moors and the northern end of the Vale of York, as well as the Yorkshire Dales, the patterns and extent of field systems are not dissimilar to those seen in other parts of the North East and North West, with localised fields or dyke systems demarcating areas around individual settlements or clusters of settlements with seemingly open landscapes beyond. Some of the daleside systems in Yorkshire are admittedly on a significantly larger scale than those encountered further north, but the presence of droves running from settlement and fields to open land (rather than linking settlements over long distances) is still a characteristic of many. In the Magnesian Limestone and sandstone areas of west and south Yorkshire, on the Yorkshire Wolds, and in the Vale of Pickering, however, are much more extensively demarcated rural landscapes characterised by a mixture of small fields and larger fields or enclosed blocks of land linked by droves.

The West Midlands

In the upper Severn valley and the Shropshire Plain aerial photographic evidence for settlement and field systems is extensive but patchy. Thanks to a long history of aerial survey (synthesised by Whimster 1989 and Baker 1992) a picture is emerging of separate but nonetheless extensive areas of bounded landscape within the Severn valley, especially around Wroxeter and modern Bridgenorth (Baker 1992; Webster 1991). In places the construction of pit alignments perhaps dating to the late Bronze Age or early Iron Age probably formed the founding framework for some of these field systems, but much of the rest appear to have been of late Iron Age and Roman date (Wigley 2007). Work on this aerial photographic evidence in conjunction with rescue excavation (eg Ellis *et al* 1994; Gaffney *et al* forthcoming) around Wroxeter suggests that where detailed evidence is available, field layouts were on a similar orientation to those of the modern landscape. Ellis *et al* (1994, 103), supporting Bassett (1990), suggest that this may be taken to indicate that here, at least, some elements of the modern field pattern can be seen to originate in the pre-Roman period.

To the north-east of the upper Severn valley, in eastern Shropshire and western Staffordshire, as well as the fringes of the West Midlands conurbation, there has been little detailed study in the past and subsequently we are not able to say very much about field systems in these areas, although ongoing aerial photographic work by Gill Barratt may help to remedy this situation in the future.

South-west of the Severn valley, in the Marches, work on possible field systems rather than settlements of this period has until recently been comparatively rare. Now, however, analysis of the evidence from modern mapped field systems for the Herefordshire Historic Landscape Characterisation (HLC) project (Ray and White 2004), and the results from subsequent smaller-scale field projects, are rapidly changing our understanding of this area's field systems. Recent survey in the Arrow valley in particular (White 2003) has led to the suggestion that the orientation, if not the exact form, of the modern field pattern is derived from the layout of field systems dating to the later Iron Age and the Roman period. This pattern of relative conservatism in post-Roman field layout is increasingly being noted elsewhere within the area. In the middle Wye valley around Kentchester, Ray (2001) has also noted that while the boundaries of modern fields have migrated over time, the field pattern has maintained its scale and general orientation potentially since the Iron Age, though this remains to be tested on the ground.

Certainly some of the multivallate dispersed enclosed settlements seen in the region, such as that at Coleswood, lay within contemporary field systems. The morphology of these systems is varied; frequently they have sinuous but broadly rectilinear boundaries arranged into complex aggregate blocks, but some appear to be coaxially arranged (Ray 2001, 83). Elsewhere, however, surveys on Bircher Common and Yarsop have identified smaller aggregate systems attached to settlement enclosures. Few of these systems have been closely dated but most tend to show a pattern of contiguity in form and development that might suggest the relative long-term stability of land-use patterns in this area, as implied by the HLC work. One possible exception to this comes from the Wye valley, where Ray and White (2004) have argued that a coaxial system of probable later prehistoric origin was reorientated to lie perpendicular to the Roman roads constructed in the area of Kentchester. Further south, in the lower Wye and Severn valleys and the Forest of Dean, the picture is still very patchy, although in the latter case recent work by Robin Jackson may shed more light on the situation.

In contrast to this picture, the landscapes of the Vale of Evesham and the Warwickshire Avon are similar to those in many of the major river valleys of the East Midlands (below) and, indeed, seem to share a common heritage with the landscapes of the Nene, Welland and parts of the Soar and Trent. Here, settlements of both dispersed enclosed and complex kinds sat within a landscape that from the late Bronze Age onwards underwent a substantive phase of land division using pit alignments and linear ditches. On the gravels of the valleys themselves, at least, many of these early boundaries become primary components, by the late Iron Age and into the Roman period, in the development of extensive field systems associated with droveways that linked settlements together in well-integrated agricultural landscapes. Extensive excavations at Wasperton (Crawford 1982; 1983; 1984) and elsewhere have shown how small enclosed settlements of the middle to late Iron Age sat alongside long-lived pit alignments or ditched boundaries. During the later Iron Age and the Roman period these boundaries continued to provide a primary axis for the construction of extensive field systems and droveways linking settlements of both simple enclosed and linear system forms (Fig 5.2 (7)). This pattern has recently been demonstrated to extend onto the light sandy soils of Dunsmore (Palmer 2002), but as yet there is insufficient evidence on the heavier clay soils of the Feldon area to develop an understanding of the wider landscape here (Hingley 1996).

The East Midlands

In north-east Staffordshire and the Peak District we encounter a very different range of field systems and patterns of enclosure. The latter area has a very productive tradition of survey and in upland areas often good levels of earthwork survival, but has suffered from a scarcity of excavation and the consequent difficulty in dating sites. That said, sustained work has helped to demonstrate that on the eastern and high moors of the Peak District there is evidence for contraction of settlement away from the high moorland at the end of the Iron Age or early in the Roman period (Barnatt and Smith 1997; Bevan 2003). Along the Manifold, Derwent and Dove valleys, on the other hand, there are dense patterns of settlement and fields along the dale sides that probably extended to lower elevations, though here modern agriculture has largely removed traces of field systems (Cleverdon 1995; Bevan 2003). Makepeace (1998) suggests that in the limestone plateau areas settlement and fields are largely restricted to daleside shelves, though again this may in part be a result of the effects of later historic land use.

For many years the comparatively meagre dating evidence available was used to suggest that much of this region was colonised in the 2nd century AD (Hodges 1991; Branigan 1991), but recent work by Makepeace (1998) and Bevan (2005) has questioned this. Instead it is now thought that the Dales see a significant degree of continuity from the late prehistoric period, associated with a decline in woodland that begins in the Iron Age and continues throughout the Roman period. Within this context the morphology and scale of field systems tend to reflect the dissected nature of the landscape, with high and low altitudes separated by steep-sided valleys and only limited areas suitable for fields (Bevan 2005, 53). The fields themselves vary greatly in detail and size, from very small examples to specimens as large as those found on the sandstones of Nottinghamshire, but they are mainly ordered into fairly small rectilinear systems around a mixture of mostly dispersed enclosed and unenclosed settlements with access to extensive open grazing on neighbouring moorland (Bevan 2003).

To the east of the Peak District on the Coal Measures and to the south on the clays few cropmarks or earthworks are recorded and as a result it is not yet possible to characterise the nature of land use. Immediately to the south, however, in the upper Trent and Tame valleys, cropmark and excavated evidence is more abundant (eg Smith 1977; 1979; Coates 2002). Here, the pattern of land division is characteristic of many of the river valleys of the East Midlands, where a primary phase of land division, employing pit alignments and ditched terminal boundaries that are thought to date to the early Iron Age, exists (Coates 2002). These then formed part of the framework for the subsequent partition of the landscape, from the mid–late Iron Age onwards, into large rectilinear ditched fields with associated settlement and stock enclosures. By the late Iron Age and early Roman period a system of ditched droves linked neighbouring settlements across the field network, creating a well-integrated agricultural landscape by the late 1st century AD.

Further down the Trent valley, to the north of

Newark, we see far more extensive examples of such rectilinear, sometimes coaxial field systems. These too are often related to an early phase of blocks of pit alignments and ditched boundaries at intervals along the valley, which then acted as a focus for subsequent extension of land allotment patterns in the later Iron Age and the Roman period. The origins of this pattern are not as well understood here as they are further to the south, but they are seemingly a relatively late development, with some components dating to the late Bronze Age/early Iron Age transition but most to the late Iron Age and early Roman period (Garton 2002; Knight and Howard 2004a). The extent of this system of enclosure is such that in its fully developed form (probably during the first two centuries AD) it constituted a dense network of settlement set within a closely allotted and managed landscape of fields with interconnecting droveways running over sizeable parts of the valley.

In places the scale of individual field plots, their orientation and association with droves, and the often coaxial nature of the Trent valley systems, prompt comparison with another extensive tradition of land allotment immediately to the west and north, along the sandstones of north Nottinghamshire and south Yorkshire. These so-called 'brickwork plan' (cohesive) field systems (Riley 1980, 11) are characterised by long parallel ditches or trackways between which perpendicular boundaries run, breaking the landscape into fields of between 0.5 and 2.8ha (Fig 5.2 (6)). The origins of these system seem to lie in the late Iron Age, although the majority of them would appear to be of Roman date (Garton 1987; Chadwick 1999; Knight *et al* 2004). The apparent homogeneity and coaxial appearance of this landscape can create the impression that it was created in a single deliberate phase and this has led to speculation that it constituted a single 'official' intervention. Excavation and detailed analysis of parts of this system, however, have shown it to be created in a more piecemeal fashion; the ordered coaxial layout is a function of its final form (Robbins 1998; Chadwick 1999) and the ease with which it was possible to lay out systems over the gentle terrain of the sandstones with long trackways running perpendicular to the course of local rivers. While cohesive systems were predominant over much of the sandstones of this region, other forms of field-system development were present. In particular, nuclear plan field systems, in which an enclosed settlement formed the core around which similar large strip fields were laid out, become increasingly common further north in modern south Yorkshire, around Rossington and on into the Aire valley.

To the east and south of the Trent valley the completion of recent major aerial survey projects has helped clarify our understanding of a further characteristic landscape feature of much of the East Midlands (Bewley 1998; Deegan 1999; forthcoming). Here, patterns of land allotment seem to have been structured around large single, double and triple dyke/ditch systems, often in association with pit alignments. Originally noted by Pickering (1978; 1979), these boundaries can be seen to extend in a band across the east and south of the Midlands from the Humber to the Nene. While dating the origin of these dykes is still difficult and it is clear that the final form visible on aerial photographs is a consequence of often long sequences throughout the Iron Age of recutting and multivallation of an original component, their origin would seem to lie in the late Bronze Age or early Iron Age (Willis 2006).

While the subsequent development trajectories of these initial phases of land boundaries were complex, a common pattern of development saw the broader open spaces demarcated by these boundaries being progressively broken up into smaller blocks through the construction of single ditched boundaries (sometimes recutting and redefining pit alignments) during the middle to late Iron Age. This process created the so-called 'washing line' pattern of settlements and other enclosures associated with sinuous linear boundaries apparent in much of the cropmark evidence (Figs 5.2 (5) and 5.4). During the course of the later Iron Age and into the Roman period this pattern underwent further gradual change, in which the lines of long boundaries remained the foci for settlements but were converted to ditched tracks that formed probably very extensive but still patchily understood networks (eg Meadows 1995; Taylor 1996; Deegan forthcoming).

Away from the main river valleys and the more freely draining soils, a complementary pattern of enclosure emerges. In the clayland landscapes of the uplands and interfluves of Leicestershire and Northamptonshire a mixture of somewhat patchy aerial photographic evidence and increasing numbers of PPG16-related excavations indicates the presence of late Bronze Age/early Iron Age boundary-defined systems similar to those already mentioned, albeit more sinuous and fragmentary in nature. These smaller systems sit alongside as yet undefined and possibly partly unenclosed landscapes, or ones with patterns of more irregular aggregate enclosure (a pattern seemingly common on the clays in Bedfordshire). This indication of a more piecemeal pattern of field enclosure seemingly dates to the mid–late Iron Age and appears, again, to continue, with alteration and extension in places, through the earlier part of the Roman period (Pickering and Hartley 1985; Kidd 2004; Deegan forthcoming; P Clay pers comm).

The absence of multiple ditch or dyke systems in eastern Lincolnshire seems to be a genuine reflection of the character of land allotment, as the soils of the Wolds, in particular, are conducive to cropmark formation but show no signs of such monumental features in the landscape (Boutwood 1998). In this area Jones (1988; 1998) has mapped a rather different landscape, with recorded settlement generally scarcer and both multiple dykes and pit alignments absent. Instead, we see a pattern of more localised dispersed blocks of fields, in which the accretion of enclosures along a network of trackways between both dispersed and nucleated settlements is characteristically seen. In areas where coverage and cropmark response have been good, such as the Lymn valley, a pattern of small broadly rectilinear blocks of fields clustered around the roads and interspersed with larger open areas is apparent. In this respect the field systems here (especially when associated with ladder-like nucleated settlements, as at Welton-le-Wold) bear some similarity to the Roman-period pattern seen on the Yorkshire Wolds. The most important difference is that the

Figure 5.4 Aerial photograph of so-called 'washing line' enclosures and boundary systems with neighbouring Roman road, near Ruskington, Lincolnshire (NMR 3118/342, 24 July 1986 © Crown copyright. NMR)

Lincolnshire examples appear to have developed around primary trackways, whereas in Yorkshire the trackways were themselves structured by an extant system of dykes dating back to the late Bronze Age.

East Anglia

Further south in Lincolnshire, and extending to the east across much of northern Cambridgeshire and west Norfolk, lies the largest single area of former wetlands in England, the Fenland. This region has perhaps had a longer and more substantial tradition of study of its Roman-period landscape than any other part of the country (eg Phillips 1970; Hall and Coles 1994; Crowson *et al* 2000). The combination of ground-based survey and aerial photography (very effective on the light soils of the Fenland) by Hallam (1970), Hall (1987; 1992; 1996) and others gives a clearer picture of land allotment patterns than is usually possible.

Much of this early work recognised that this landscape was predominantly colonised in the Roman period, events linked by Salway (1970) and later Potter (1981; 1989) to a historical narrative of imperially inspired colonisation in the Hadrianic period. The picture now emerging, however, is more complex, with clear evidence for Iron Age settlement and wetland exploitation on the 'islands' and fringes of the Fenland (Hall and Coles 1994; Taylor 2000b; Fincham 2002). On the islands there is some evidence of fairly small aggregate (nuclear) field systems associated with localised clusters of settlements dating to the Iron Age (Evans 2003, 263–9). During the Roman period, thanks partly to natural marine regression, and partly to attempts to construct local drainage networks, much former wetland became available for settlement and agricultural exploitation. This drying-out of the region was not a uniform process (Waller 1994), but it enabled a pattern of steady encroachment into the Fenland from the drier fringes and islands throughout the 1st and 2nd centuries AD.

The overall impression of Roman exploitation in these areas is of a landscape dominated by long sinuous trackways laid out along the course of roddons upon which settlements were established (Fig 5.2 (8)). Fields defined by ditched boundaries were then laid out perpendicular to the tracks, producing localised axial field systems running from high roddons down into the former wetlands (Palmer 1996). In places this network formed a straggling but continuous system in which whole swathes of the landscape were encompassed within a pattern of trackway-linked settlements with attendant fields by the middle of the Roman period.

Away from the Fenland, across the rest of East Anglia, however, we encounter a rather different situation. Here, a combination of the apparent post-Roman land-use patterns and a strong regional tradition of the analysis of land allotment within landscape history have created a situation where there is much recognised potential for the delineation of early field systems but as yet little detailed archaeological evidence for their chronology. The observation of apparent relationships between field patterns and the courses of known Roman roads on the one hand, and the identification of the remains of earlier regular field systems 'fossilised' within more modern field patterns on the other, has led several authors to suggest that relict, largely coaxial systems survive in many areas across East Anglia. Hesse (1992; 1998), working in north Norfolk, and Harrison (2002) and Oosthuizen (1998; 2003), in Cambridgeshire, have all suggested that, within areas of later open-field agriculture, the long axial furlong boundaries and tracks of the medieval and later landscape were founded upon a pre-existing coaxial framework of probable later prehistoric or Roman date.

This pattern, however, is not confined to the areas of medieval open fields of Rackham's 'planned countryside' of central England. Elsewhere, in what Rackham (1986) referred to as the 'ancient countryside' (a landscape characterised by the limited extent of open fields and the early inception of piecemeal enclosure) a number of authors have suggested that extensive coaxial systems form the underlying structure for later cohesive patterns of enclosed fields. Williamson (1987a; 1993; 1998) has identified several such systems, around Yaxley in north Suffolk, in the Scole-Dickleborough area of south Norfolk, and in the Stonham Aspal area of Suffolk (Fig 5.2 (6)). Warner (1996) has noted that the key characteristic of these systems was not the fields themselves but the long parallel axial boundaries, often surviving as lanes, that usually ran perpendicular to the major local watercourses. Warner also noted that these coaxial lanes were widespread across much of north-east Suffolk and south Norfolk.

In Essex similarly extensive systems of early boundaries have been claimed for the Dengie peninsula, Thurrock and the Little Waltham area (Drury 1976; Rodwell 1978). The main problem with much of this work, however, is the lack of supporting evidence from excavation or other detailed archaeological survey for these field systems' suggested early origins. This has led some, such as Martin (1999), to question many of the assertions made through such topographical studies and to point out that a Saxon date for their origins would better fit the known settlement evidence on the claylands of Suffolk. In the few cases where excavation has taken place, it is becoming clear that some of these seemingly ordered, planned coaxial systems have complex histories of development and alteration that stretch across much of the first millennium AD. In the Rochford region of Essex, for example, Rippon (1991) has demonstrated that elements of a highly ordered rectilinear field system can be dated to the Roman period but that the surviving form is predominantly of later Saxon date. Wilkinson (1988), publishing the results of work on the Grays bypass in southern Essex, showed that while some landscape survival had occurred from the Roman period within later systems most of the rectilinear field pattern seen was of later date, while in south Cambridgeshire and north-eastern Northamptonshire, Upex (2002) used excavation to suggest that some but by no means all furlong boundaries perpetuated Roman field patterns at a local scale.

More recently, excavations at Burnham Sutton, north Norfolk, close to Hesse's survey, have identified a pattern of small coaxial fields 'originally laid out in the late Iron Age or, perhaps, in the early Roman period' (Percival and Williamson 2005, 11). Though these early fields were narrower than their medieval counterparts, Percival and Williamson used the available excavated and cartographic evidence to suggest that prehistoric or Roman coaxial field patterns were gradually made more regular and their constituent fields larger in the post-Roman period. In this way, the later open-field furlong pattern 'ghosted' the original system of land division (Percival and Williamson 2005, 15). Smaller rectilinear field patterns of this kind, dating to the Iron Age, have also been found on the sandy soils of the Sutton Hoo area (Martin 1999).

The ongoing plotting of aerial photographic evidence around Snettisham and Heacham in north Norfolk for the NMP has recognised an extensive network of late Iron Age and Roman settlements and small rectilinear fields linked to the coastal plain by droveways. In many respects these mirror the results of earlier work in the east of the county around Cantley and Lothingland (Edwards 1978), where similar extensive systems of small rectilinear fields (of up to 0.7ha) associated with ditched trackways were recorded. Their layout and form would seem to represent farmsteads surrounded by their own fields and interlinked by complex networks of tracks and droves.

Work by Morris and Wainwright (1995) on the dipslope of the Chilterns in Hertfordshire suggests a similar, if more mixed, pattern. To the north, small settlements were associated with localised irregularly shaped fields interspersed with meandering droveways. Further south, long droveways ran parallel and perpendicular to the scarp edge and defined large blocks of rectilinear fields separated from each other by seemingly unenclosed tracts of land that were possibly used for grazing.

The South East

The Thames valley has long been a focus of intensive archaeological survey and excavation (eg Benson and Miles 1974; Gates 1975), and the aerial photographic evidence, in particular, has been subject to further recent reanalysis (Fenner 1994; Baker 2002). As a result we have a good understanding of the development of patterns of land allotment, which indicates subtle variations in the nature of the landscapes of the middle and upper Thames valley. Within the valley there appears to have been a characteristic late Iron Age and early Roman landscape of dispersed enclosed and linear system settlements linked by an extensive network of trackways. The latter were often established upon an earlier first-millennium BC framework of settlement and land use but, by the late Iron Age, boundary-defined field systems seem to have been limited to clusters of enclosures in and around settlements and along the trackways. Intervening areas of the landscape were seemingly unenclosed (or at least demarcated in a way that no longer survives).

At the confluence of the Thames and Thame the landscape of the late Iron Age and early Roman period was focused around trackways linking rectilinear enclosed settlements with attendant clusters of fields or paddocks, with seemingly unenclosed land beyond (Baker 2002; a pattern akin to that seen in Figure 5.2 (8)). While late Iron Age and Roman settlement here partly relates to pre-existing foci of the middle Iron Age, the trackways and field enclosures appear to create a new framework for the wider landscape. In contrast to this, to the north, around Stanton Harcourt in the Windrush valley, the broad structure of land use appears to be established by the middle Iron Age, with local clusters of settlements arranged around a core area of possibly communal pasture with areas of arable cultivation located outside this zone. This pattern continues into the earlier Roman period, even though it is accompanied by localised settlement reorganisation and, as at the confluence of the Thame and Thames, the establishment of trackways linking settlements into a single network (Lambrick and Allen 2004). A similar pattern of trackway-associated clusters of enclosures is apparent at Farmoor (Lambrick and Robinson 1979), but at Yarnton areas of arable cultivation on the gravel terraces do not appear to have been bounded by ditched enclosures (Hey 1996; Henig 2000). Evidence from the neighbouring Kennett valley, in Berkshire, would suggest that the river gravels here were also densely covered with rectilinear field systems associated with extensive trackways by the end of the 1st century BC (Lobb and Rose 1996). Much of this pattern continued into the Roman period, albeit with some evidence for expansion into the more marginal areas and localised reorganisation of settlement at this time.

Further down the Thames the widespread encroachment of Greater London restricts understanding of the wider landscape in the Roman period, though Bird (1996; 2000) has noted that rural settlement was strongly biased towards the lighter soils of the gravels and sands. Rectilinear field systems are known from a number of sites but how extensive these were and how they articulated with the wider landscape is not clear.

On the chalk uplands of the Lambourn Downs in Berkshire some 30 years of fieldwork has demonstrated that while many of the field systems present may have been established during the later Bronze Age, the major phase of use now visible dates to the Roman period (eg Richards 1978; Fowler 1981; Gaffney and Tingle 1989; Bowden *et al* 1993; Miles *et al* 2003). While the detailed patterns vary, coaxial, narrow, predominantly strip-shaped fields dominate (Figs 5.2 (9) and 5.5; Small 2002). While extensive, these systems did not cover the entire landscape, and areas of the most exposed clay-capped soils seemingly remained unenclosed. Small also noted a second distinctive form of field system, found on the highest ground along the northern edge of the chalk escarpment and consisting of large ditched fields enclosing areas of between 1.2 and 4ha. These systems appear to have complemented the coaxial systems and, though poorly dated, they may have been constructed in the late Bronze Age, and then later recut to be incorporated into the later Iron Age and Roman landscape (Lock and Gosden 2001; Small 2002, 20–4).

Traces of similarly extensive strip-field systems and settlements have been found over much of the South Downs in west Sussex (Drewett *et al* 1988). Excavation and survey at a number of sites indicates that many of these systems, which were established in the late Bronze Age or early Iron Age, were reused and in places expanded in the Roman period (eg Rudling 1982; 2003; Barber *et al* 2002). These strip fields were often laid out perpendicular to long-established trackways and some pre-existing fields were subdivided in the Roman period as part of localised reorganisation. Evidence for the development of a substantial network of late Iron Age settlements and rectilinear field systems is also beginning to emerge on the Sussex coastal plain (Bedwin and Pitts 1978; Bedwin 1983; Bedwin and Place 1995; Davenport 2003). Here the fields are defined by ditches designed to help improve drainage on this somewhat marginal land and there seems to be greater evidence for partial discontinuity or reorganisation of occupation in the late 1st century BC and 1st century AD.

Similar evidence would seem to be in comparatively short supply for the North Downs in Kent and Surrey, in part because of the effects of subsequent arable cultivation here (though aerial photography does indicate many as yet undated 'Celtic' fields on the chalklands of east Kent: Champion 2007). Field systems have been recorded on Mickleham Downs and at several other places on the chalk in Surrey but not elsewhere (Hanworth 1987; Bird 2004), and recent overviews of the evidence in London and Surrey (Poulton 2004; Bird 1996; 2000; 2004) have suggested only limited settlement expansion in the Roman period onto the heathlands and London clays from existing areas of settlement on the lighter soils of the valleys of the Thames, Wey and Blackwater; as yet, however, the nature of attendant land use in these formerly open or wooded landscapes is little understood.

To the south of the Downs the heavy clays of the Weald are still dominated by evidence for the Roman period related to iron production and little else (Gardiner 1990). While there are some indications of settlement and agriculture in the area between Farnham and Guildford, in Surrey (Bird 2004), most of the region still sees little or no surviving evidence for land division or cultivation. In the continuing absence of evidence to the contrary, the idea of the Weald landscape as still heavily wooded in the Roman period remains prevalent, although this may not have been true of the heathland soils at the heart of the Weald in the Ashdown Forest area of east Sussex.

Here, dispersed enclosed settlements dated to the late Iron Age were associated with as yet undated field boundaries (Gardiner 1990, 43).

On the south coast in Romney Marsh (Eddison 2000) much of the Roman land surface is today covered by later deposits, but the available evidence suggests that while salt production was possibly important up to the 2nd century AD, this area was probably used on a seasonal basis; there is no associated evidence of land allotment. By *c* AD 200 rising water levels appear to have made the area largely uninhabitable.

To the west of the region, on the Hampshire chalk, there is widespread evidence for land allotment and cultivation in the form of further 'Celtic' (in this case small strip) fields. Work by Cunliffe (1973; 1977) around Chalton indicated that during the Roman period field systems reached their greatest extent, blanketing large parts of the landscape. In places, these were built upon the reuse and expansion of earlier systems but elsewhere the presence of more regular strip fields, usually coaxial in appearance but constructed perpendicular to the many trackways running across the landscape, suggests the enclosure and cultivation of new areas. While extensive, these systems did not cover the whole landscape. Unenclosed land, thought likely to be pasture by Cunliffe, survived on the highest parts of the Downs in a pattern similar to that suggested for the Lambourn Downs. A comparable picture emerges from the many years of aerial and ground-based fieldwork in the environs of Danebury hillfort (eg Palmer 1984; Cunliffe 2000; 2003a), where large areas of field systems were laid out in the second millennium BC, subsequently undergoing many subtle shifts and changes in use and form but seeing significant reuse in the Roman period. While most of the earlier work focused on the prehistory of this landscape the results of the more recent Danebury Environs Roman project (Cunliffe 2003a; 2003b; 2004), at Flint Farm and Rowbury Farm in particular, indicate the reoccupation and reuse of field systems from the late Iron Age into the Roman period. Similar, though rather less detailed, evidence for extensive lynchetted fields exists for the central chalk belt of the Isle of Wight, but few of these systems appear to have been dated through ground-based fieldwork (Basford 1980).

Figure 5.5 Photograph of ploughed-out strip fields ('Celtic' fields) on the Lambourn Downs (NMR 15207/02, 3 January 1995 © Crown copyright. NMR)

The South West

The evidence for field systems on the chalklands of Dorset and Wiltshire is equally impressive. Here, an archaeological focus on the later prehistory of these landscapes has provided an excellent understanding of the development of field systems and patterns of land use, particularly in the Bronze Age (eg Bowen and Fowler 1978; Bradley 1984; Barrett *et al* 1991; Gingell 1992; Bradley *et al* 1994). The study of the subsequent development of these systems, however, has been far less systematic or intensive and consequently our picture of the landscape in the Roman period is perhaps less clear than we might have hoped. On Salisbury Plain at least some of the coaxial systems established in the middle Bronze Age appear to have seen extensive reuse and cultivation in the 1st and 2nd centuries AD (Bradley *et al* 1994; McOmish *et al* 2002), which was accompanied by the extension of field systems onto the High Plain in the Roman period (Fulford *et al* 2006, 202). The presence of less regular rectilinear aggregate fields in the areas between these systems may be further evidence of extension in the late Iron Age or Roman period, though as yet there is relatively little published excavated data available for them (Entwhistle *et al* 1994; 2006; Crutchley 2000; McOmish *et al* 2002; Fulford *et al* 2006). Fowler (2000), working on the Fyfield and Overton Downs, has demonstrated a similarly extensive reorganisation of the agricultural landscape in the first centuries BC and AD that involved the laying-out of new, and the reuse of old, field systems that were now integrated with a network of trackways running across both the Downs and valleys. Settlement here had been dispersed (and was, indeed, apparently rare) in the Iron Age, but in the Roman period the development of nucleated settlements such as Overton Down South led to a mixed settlement landscape through most of the Roman period (Fowler 2000). Immediately to the north, on the Marlborough Downs Gingell (1992, 157) noted similarly extensive re-establishment of arable cultivation on the chalk as well as the development of a new field system on Totterdown in the earlier Roman period.

The development of such systems in the late Iron Age and the Roman period is less clearly understood to the south, across the chalk downs of Dorset, although extensive systems are apparent across much of this landscape (RCHME 1970; 1972; Barrett *et al* 1991). Excavation and survey in the area around Maiden Castle and along the south Dorset Ridgeway suggests that we are again seeing the establishment of structured field systems from the second millennium BC (Woodward 1991), followed by a comparative lull in their cultivation and development during much of the Iron Age and renewed intensification in tillage during the Roman period (Smith *et al* 1997). Here the re-emergence of settlement outside the hillforts in the late Iron Age provided a precursor to the pattern of early Roman settlement around Dorchester. While evidence from some sites is still limited, it is clear that here, too, an early pattern of predominantly dispersed rural settlement is superseded by a more mixed pattern of dispersed and nucleated settlement as some sites expanded to cover as much as 20ha by the 4th century AD.

In the upper Thames valley in Gloucestershire, large-scale excavation and survey at Lechlade (Allen *et al* 1993) and Claydon Pike (Miles *et al* 2006) provide good comparative material with that from further downstream in Oxfordshire. The late Iron Age and 1st century AD saw significant settlement shift in the former region but again within a wider network of droveways and field systems. The fields and droves were most clearly defined by the 2nd century AD but undoubtedly existed before this date. The rectilinear field systems were again clustered close to settlement and along droves with seemingly larger open areas beyond in a similar pattern to that seen in Oxfordshire. The dipslope of the Cotswolds is surprisingly short of information considering the long tradition of villa excavation in the region. In places there is good localised information on villa-associated field systems, as at Barnsley Park, but far less is known about the situation further afield. Some groups of small rectilinear 'Celtic' fields are known in several areas above tributary streams running off the dipslope (RCHME 1976; Aston and Iles 1987), but these have seen little systematic research. Work currently mapping the aerial photographic evidence as part of the Gloucestershire NMP, however, alongside the publication of Moore's research (forthcoming) may well change this perception.

Rather more is known about the developing landscapes around the Severn estuary, especially in the wetlands, thanks to a range of surveys and excavations in recent years. It appears that at the end of the Iron Age much of the alluvial wetlands around the estuary were saltmarsh and mudflats. During the Roman period a large proportion of the land north of the now defunct river Siger was reclaimed and a number of relict field systems of Roman date have been recorded in the northern levels (Rippon 2000). Here artefactual and environmental data, in conjunction with morphological analysis of surviving boundaries, have led Rippon to suggest that farms displayed a threefold zonation consisting of settlement, surrounded by clusters of paddocks or small heavily manured cultivated plots, with larger rectilinear fields beyond (1997). The overall pattern, while locally coaxial, appears to relate to localised piecemeal drainage of the wetlands in a similar manner to that noted above for the East Anglian Fenland. This contrasts starkly with the evidence from the Wentlooge Levels, across the estuary in south Wales, where a landscape of long narrow rectilinear fields over large areas of former wetlands appears to have been designed as a single project, possibly associated with the supply of the legionary base at Caerleon.

Less is known about the dryland fringes and uplands around the Somerset Levels but several areas of largely undated small rectilinear 'Celtic' field systems associated with dispersed enclosed or linear system settlements survive on the Bleadon Hills, Brean Down and the Polden Hills (Fowler 1978; Bell 1990; Rippon 1997; Gerrard forthcoming). Elsewhere in Somerset, Leech (1982) and others working on the period have said little about field systems, and even less appears to be known about the situation on the Blackdown Hills. To the west of the Levels the archaeology of the Quantocks is comparatively poorly known but the publication of recent NMP photographic mapping alongside excavation and geophysical survey by King Alfred's, Winchester, will transform our knowledge of rural settlement in the area during this period.

In lowland areas of Devon even less is known, and the extent to which the sometimes dense pattern of dispersed settlement and complex local field systems seen in the medieval period may have earlier origins is still unclear (S Turner pers comm). One of the few indications of the possible nature of field systems at this time comes from the limestone uplands around Newton Abbott, where local field survey has identified fragmentary remains of a number of field systems of probable Iron Age and Roman date surviving as earthworks (Gallant *et al* 1985). In most cases these systems appear to have survived as irregular or rectilinear accreted fields, but the overall extent of such systems is not known. That said, recent paleoenvironmental studies in mid-Devon indicate the broad continuity of predominantly pastoral land use within a largely open landscape from the middle Iron Age through the Roman period, accompanied by only gradual clearance of some of the remaining areas of woodland (Fyfe *et al* 2004). In this region of dispersed settlement arable cultivation is indicated only in the immediate vicinity of the few excavated sites, with grassland dominant beyond (Fitzpatrick *et al* 1999).

On the moorlands of the south-west the later first millennium BC is generally seen as a period of retreat from the high moors, with settlement and agriculture focused on its fringes (Griffith 1994). On Dartmoor there is little evidence for any permanent presence on the uplands from the late Iron Age and only a handful of sites are known (Quinnell 1994; Gerrard 1997). Paleoenvironmental evidence suggests that during this period the upland was used only for seasonal grazing. On Exmoor well-dated excavated evidence is still in very short supply, but environmental evidence from the blanket bogs on the high moor suggests a similar pattern to that on Dartmoor (Francis and Slater 1990; 1992). Nearer to the fringes of the moor there is some suggestion of the occasional reuse or conversion of relict Bronze Age field systems but little evidence for other systems of possible Iron Age or Roman date, the one possible exception being the undated system on Withycombe Hill (Riley and Wilson-North 2001). The presence of probable Iron Age and Roman enclosed settlements on the wider moor suggests that some of these areas at least were still suitable for settlement, possibly associated with stock rearing on largely open land, rather than arable farming.

In Cornwall a similar picture emerges, though here survey, excavation and HLC work have all helped to refine the view. Aerial photography, earthwork survey and excavation have long demonstrated the dense pattern of dispersed enclosed settlements across the better farming lands of the county (eg Thomas 1966; Quinnell 1986; Rose and Johnson 1982). In recent years, systematic mapping through the ongoing Cornwall NMP, and the increasing use of geophysical survey, are beginning to demonstrate the extent of the field systems associated with these settlements (eg Shiel 1995; Rose and Preston-Jones 1995; Jones 2001). The combination of this work with the pioneering work carried out as part of the HLC project (Herring 1998), is beginning to reveal the possible extent and complexity of fields in the Cornish landscape of the time.

The HLC suggested that 57% of the Cornish landscape is covered with so-called 'Anciently Enclosed land of medieval or earlier origin' (Herring 1998, 40). An unknown proportion of these extensive irregular field patterns is based upon later prehistoric or Roman origins, but in some areas, such as the fringes of Bodmin Moor (Johnson 1994), parts of the Lizard peninsula (Johns and Herring 1996) and Penwith, the evidence is becoming clearer. Best-known and preserved of these systems are the extensive, irregular but broadly rectilinear lynchetted fields associated with the rounds and courtyard house settlements on the granite uplands of west Penwith (Fig 5.2 (4); Rose and Johnson 1982; Quinnell 1986). Several of these systems extend over hundreds of hectares between neighbouring settlements and in many places form the basis of the modern field pattern.

Elsewhere in the county Rose and Preston-Jones (1995) have suggested a more mixed and piecemeal survival, with later prehistoric and Roman-period field systems surviving within the modern pattern in some areas, alongside zones where the earlier field pattern was lost and later replaced by new fields of a different form in the medieval period. In the latter case they have suggested that this may indicate a phase of retraction or abandonment of land, especially in more upland margins in the post-Roman period, before later re-enclosure within medieval strip fields (Rose and Preston-Jones 1995). In between these extensive enclosed landscapes lay areas of upland, such as Bodmin Moor and the more exposed reaches of Penwith and the Lizard, that, as elsewhere in the South West, appear to have been fringed or avoided by settlement and agricultural enclosure, suggesting open seasonal grazing on moor, heath or downland.

Discussion

While it has not been possible in such a short sketch to encompass properly or assess the sheer variety and complexity of patterns of field layout and use across the country in this period, it is possible to suggest one or two characteristic differences that are worthy of comment. First, the field arrangements summarised in Figure 5.2 (1–3) all seem to reflect differing forms of infield–outfield farming. In Figure 5.2 (1) and (2) we can suggest patterns of individual infield and individual outfield holdings, while in Figure 5.2 (3) we see individual infield but communal outfield holdings. In all these cases the outfield areas are largely open, the main distinction being the use of dykes to delineate the individual extents of this open land between settlements in Figure 5.2 (1) and (2) but not in (3).

Figure 5.2 (4) can be seen as a more developed or intensive form of this pattern where, instead of individual, separate infields, we see complex infield patterns held individually or communally between small clusters of settlements with more distant communal outfields, usually demarcated from neighbouring clusters. Most of these landscapes are dominated by patterns of dispersed settlement with communities occupying individual farmsteads, although the daleside systems seen in Figure 5.2 (3) also include examples of smaller nucleated settlements.

In direct contrast, the other examples cited in Figure 5.2 (5–9) are all forms of landscape characterised to some degree by very extensive patterns of field enclosure, often to the extent that there are few areas of unenclosed land. They are also, noticeably, landscapes in which settlement and fields are linked often over very long distances by extensive networks of tracks and droves. Many of these had developed before the Roman conquest, although some were developed or extended in the Roman period to create, as Baker (2002, 27) notes, a 'joined-up' landscape of rural settlement and land use. In these landscapes we see both the development of mixed hierarchical patterns of rural settlement, incorporating both dispersed and nucleated examples (compare Fig 4.6 with Fig 5.1) and the appearance of the majority of villas (*cf* Fig 4.9).

The implications of this observation are many and some are discussed in more detail in Chapter 7, but here one point is worth noting. Figure 5.1 is a map of the wide variety of field systems discussed above, simplified geographically and linked to the predominant patterns in settlement form discussed earlier. In it the systems noted in Figure 5.2 are collated as Upland/Western forms (Fig 5.2 (1–4)), as East Midland forms (those in Fig 5.2 (5–7)), as East Anglian forms (Figure 5.2 (6) and (8)) and as Chalkland forms (Figure 5.2 (9)). Weald/Open landscapes are those where there is currently little evidence of field systems and permanent rural settlement of the period. In the case of Upland/Western forms we appear to be looking at a range of landscapes in which individual farms or clusters of farms lie at the core of their respective landscapes of enclosed fields. In many if not most of these cases, beyond the often comparatively limited extent of these fields we see areas of the landscape that do not appear to be so clearly demarcated, or that are open or possibly wooded. Notably, many of these types are found in regions with neighbouring extensive uplands that were often open landscapes at this time. In the remaining examples (except the Weald or open areas), we see landscapes in which settlements appear to be far more integrated within networks of long trackways or droves and extensive and often continuous or cohesive systems of fields. These landscapes incorporated both small farms and larger foci by the late Iron Age and the Roman period and show the clearest evidence for agricultural specialisation or expansion during this time. In short, these appear to be rural landscapes in which both agricultural integration between communities and the mobilisation of agricultural resources between and beyond these communities were achievable.

Chapter 6
Settlement characterisation case studies

Introduction

The majority of probable late Iron Age and Roman rural settlements recorded in the national survey were known primarily or solely through surface finds or aerial photographic evidence. While this served to generate an effective overview, much of this evidence was recorded in an inconsistent or simplistic manner, hindering attempts to characterise or research the sites identified more profitably. Consequently, much potentially useful information regarding, for example, the size, broad morphology, and chronological development of settlements was inaccessible. Despite these obvious limitations, clear distinctions in the predominant morphology of rural settlements were apparent across the country. In order to understand the significance of these patterns better, and to see, particularly, whether similar patterns might be observed in the size and chronological development of settlements, more detailed information was needed. Consequently, several case studies were carried out in order to look at the extent to which such information might be available through different forms of survey evidence (Fig 6.1).

Case studies 1: the aerial photographic surveys

Aerial photographic evidence provides one of the most abundant resources available for this type of study. Three areas were chosen in order to address specific trends and possible weaknesses identified in the national survey.

The Nottinghamshire/Lincolnshire survey

The NMP surveys for Nottinghamshire and Lincolnshire provided an ideal case study for several reasons. First, they constituted one of the largest contiguous areas of systematically mapped land within the country, and their results could be checked against the national survey data on a scale not possible elsewhere. Second, the national survey had also suggested several characteristics of rural settlement across this region that were of further interest. Settlement densities, for example, varied greatly across the region, being very high in the Trent valley and in north-west Nottinghamshire, relatively high on the Wolds and Lincoln Edge, and lower elsewhere. It was uncertain as to whether this related to a genuine absence of evidence or simply variability in the quality of records available.

The national picture also suggested that, while north-west Nottinghamshire was dominated by enclosed settlement, a more mixed pattern was apparent in parts of the Trent valley and Lincolnshire. It was thought that these differences might correspond to the degree of local settlement nucleation and settlement hierarchy in different areas. Additionally, there was uncertainty over whether some sites classified as linear system settlements in this area were in fact field systems. Finally, and most importantly, the combined survey areas also provided an important opportunity to assess a possible boundary identified in the national survey (*cf* Chapter 4) between primarily dispersed settlement landscapes and those with a far greater mix of both dispersed and nucleated settlement forms.

The Nottinghamshire and Lincolnshire NMP projects covered a large cross section of the East Midlands, taking in the eastern Pennine fringe, the Sherwood sandstones and mudstones, the Trent valley, the Lincoln Edge, clay vale and Wolds, and part of the western fen-edge (Fig 6.2). The Fenland, however, was explicitly excluded from the Lincolnshire NMP and is not considered here. The Lincolnshire survey, one of the first commissioned after the formal inception of the NMP, began in 1992. The results were selectively published as a series of papers on specific

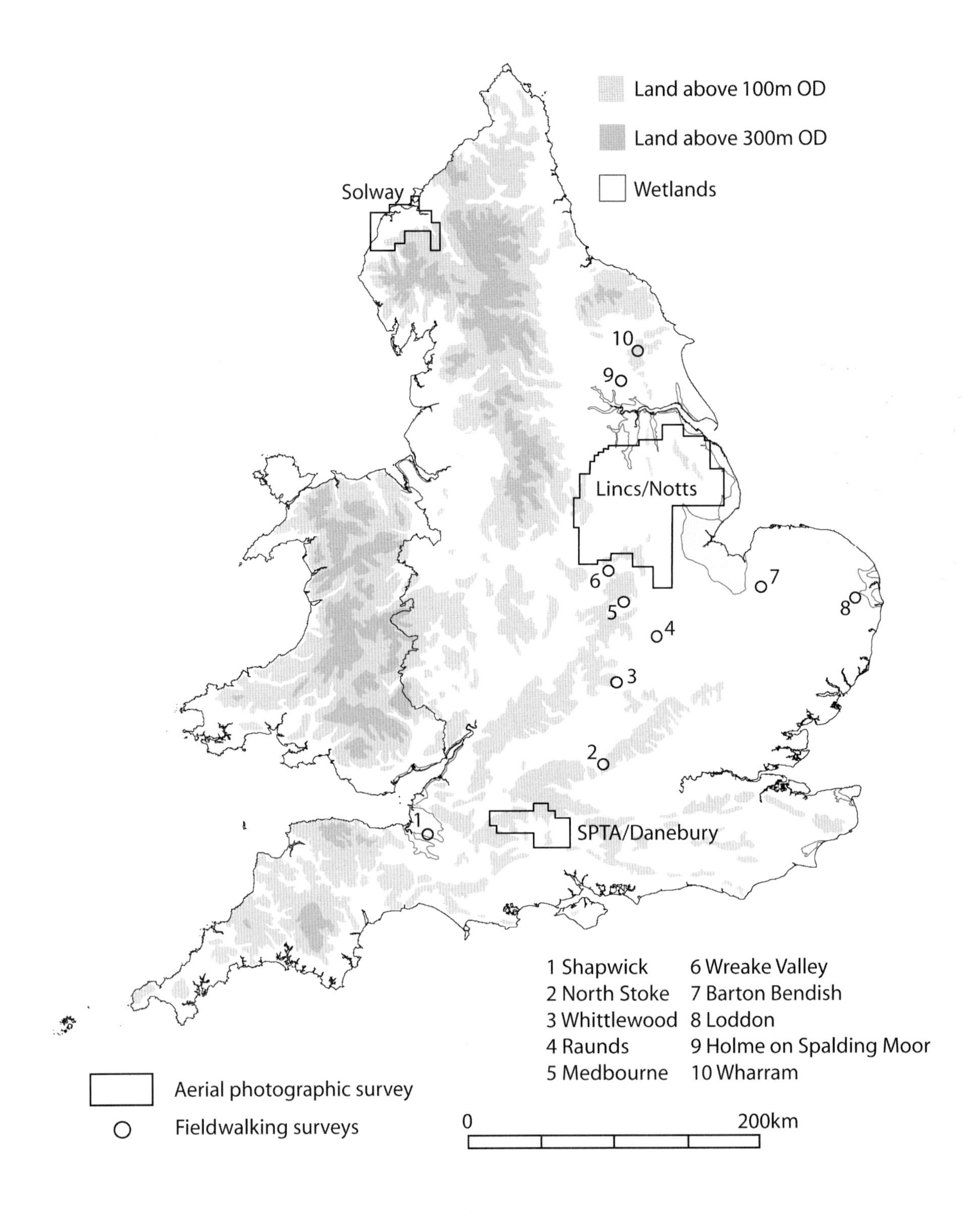

Figure 6.1 The location of the three aerial photographic and ten field survey case studies

themes in 1998 (Bewley 1998). The Nottinghamshire project started in 1991, initially as a county-specific survey supported by a grant from the RCHME; it was incorporated within the NMP in 1993. Its results were drawn together in an internal report for the RCHME in 1999 (Deegan 1999).

The current survey acquired both map overlays and digital data sets from the MORPH2 [see Abbreviations] database (in the form of Access records) held by the NMP. These were then reclassified using the Roman rural settlement project's methodology so that they could be compared with the original national Roman rural settlement data set based on SMR data. Both data sets were compared in order to study the

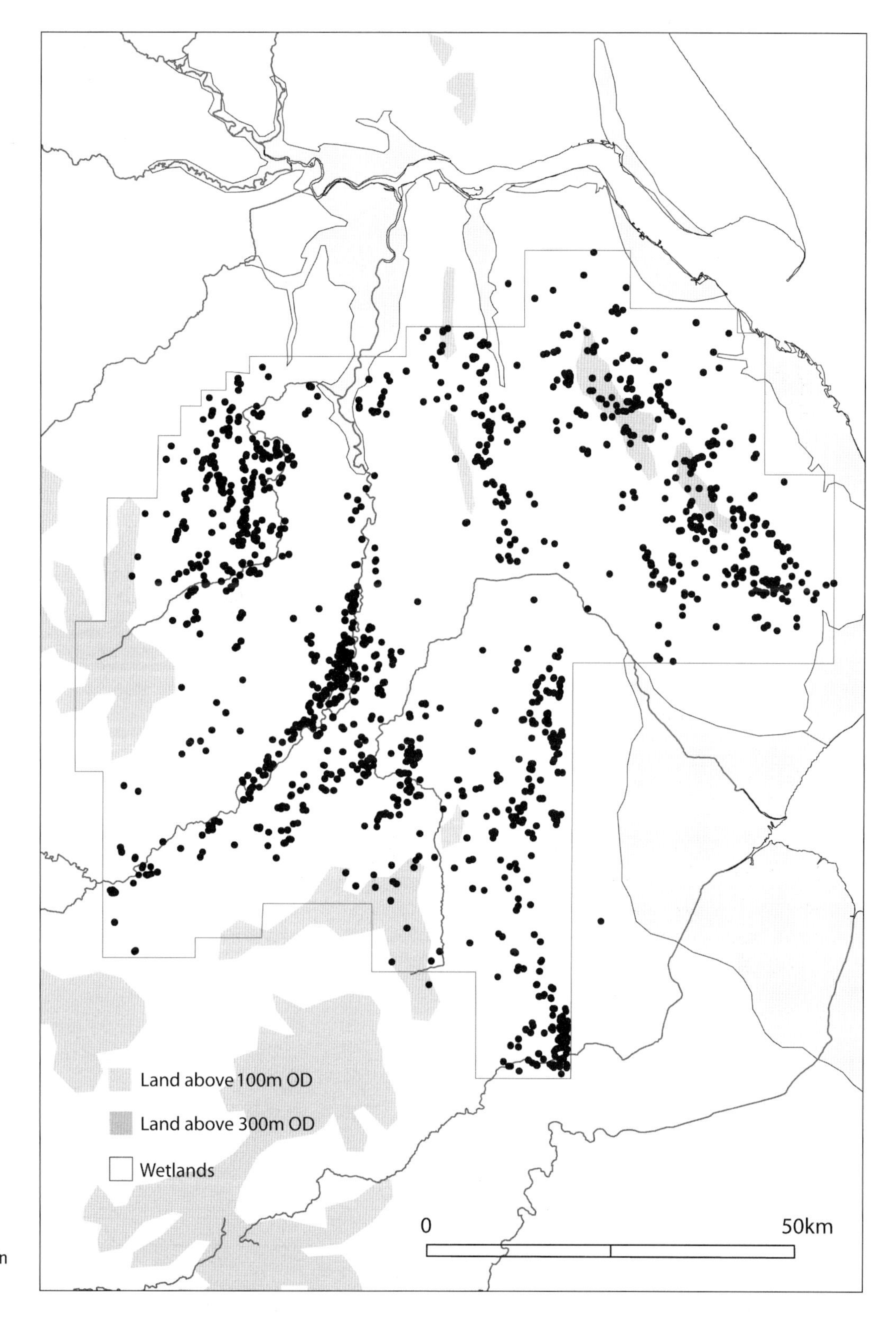

Figure 6.2 The Nottinghamshire/ Lincolnshire survey area, showing all probable Roman settlements recorded in the case study

settlement patterns derived from the two sources and to examine the issues raised above.

Figure 6.2 shows the distribution of all probable settlements recorded by applying the rural settlement project's national survey criteria to the NMP data. A total of 1639 sites were recorded by the case study; as is apparent, their distribution is biased markedly towards specific areas within the region. Much of this pattern is a reflection of the suitability or otherwise of certain soils and underlying geology for the formation of cropmarks (Deegan 1999; Boutwood 1998; Carter 1998). The higher numbers of recorded sites in Nottinghamshire, however, also reflect the longer and more intense history of aerial photographic survey here. In particular, work by Riley and Pickering on the Sherwood sandstones of north Nottinghamshire

(Riley 1980), and in the Trent valley by the Cambridge University Committee for Aerial Photography (Whimster 1989) provides some of the most comprehensive coverage anywhere in the country. The overall pattern is thinner in Lincolnshire, partly as a consequence of less intensive aerial survey coverage in the county but also as a result of the poor susceptibility to cropmark formation of soils in the clay vale, the marshland, and parts of the eastern fringe of the Trent valley and the Kesteven uplands (Carter 1998). Despite this, the case study does provide large numbers of sites for consideration along the Lincoln Edge, the Lincolnshire Wolds, the western fen-edge, and parts of Lincoln Heath. In this regard the distribution of settlement mapped by the case study largely parallels that noted from a wider range of sources recorded in the national survey. Given these localised biases in cropmark recovery, it is also important to remember that the settlement maps generated below are qualitative rather than quantitative guides. In other words, it is better to analyse the balance between different forms and sizes of settlement in any area rather than differences in their overall density in order to gain an insight into the different settlement landscapes across the region of the case study.

Figures 6.3 and 6.4 map the distribution, respectively, of enclosed and linear system settlements, using the NMP data. Unenclosed settlements were not mapped in this way because, as was often the case nationally with cropmark sites, they were recorded only comparatively rarely and only where cropmark formation was particularly good. Small numbers of unenclosed settlements were noted in the Trent valley and rarely elsewhere but, as was noted in the national survey (Chapter 4), this pattern is likely to be unrepresentative of the wider distribution of these sites.

A comparison of Figures 6.3 and 6.4 shows that small enclosed settlements are the most common settlement form across the whole region. Collating these different patterns produces a distinctive map of the balance of rural settlement form across the region that highlights varying patterns of dispersed or mixed dispersed and nucleated settlement (Fig 6.5). Within this pattern there are some important variations. As a proportion of the total mapped in any one part of the region, small enclosed settlements constitute the dominant settlement form along the north-western and western fringes of Nottinghamshire and possibly in south-western Nottinghamshire (Fig 6.5 (A): this pattern is also thought to extend, outside the case study area, into south Yorkshire and Derbyshire). Elsewhere, while still common in most places, they are generally accompanied by a wider variety of settlement forms.

On the Sherwood sandstones of north Nottinghamshire the small enclosed settlements are accompanied by dispersed linear system settlements in significant numbers (Fig 6.5 (B)), with a small number of nucleated linear system settlements located on the very easternmost fringe of this area. The latter component of this pattern parallels that seen in the Trent valley, where small enclosed settlements are especially common, alongside significant numbers of both small and nucleated linear system settlements. A closer examination of the size of the large linear systems in the Trent valley, however, shows that most lie within the range 2–6ha, only just over the 2ha division between dispersed and nucleated settlement suggested above, indicating settlements akin to 'hamlets' or small 'villages' rather than larger villages or even potential 'small towns'.

In Lincolnshire small enclosed settlements form a significant proportion of the total settlements along the Lincoln Edge and the Wolds (Fig 6.5 (C)). Here, however, both small and large linear system settlements are quite common. Analysis of the large linear system sites shows that they cover a much wider range of sizes than the Trent valley examples (from 2.5 to 10+ha). Recent analyses of the excavated and field survey evidence for these sites suggest a picture of a widespread group of aggregate nucleated settlements present here from the late Iron Age (Todd 1991; May 1996; Willis 2001; Thomas 2005). The difference between these sites and other aggregated complexes to the south (in Northamptonshire) and west (in and beyond the Trent valley) lies not only in their size and morphology, but also in differing aspects of their material culture, namely their patterns of material consumption and access to 'prestige items'.

Though many aspects of these large linear systems settlements remain to be studied, it appears that many of these sites were substantial multifunctional settlements and that several, such as Sleaford (Elsdon 1997), Owmby, Kirmington, Ludford, Ulceby, and Dragonby (May 1984; 1996), were high-status foci involved in the production, use, and consumption of coinage, personal metalwork, and imported ceramics on a significant scale in the late Iron Age. Several sites in this group, such as Dragonby, Kirmington, and Nettleton (Willis and Dungworth 1999), also show evidence for votive deposition; the presence of significant numbers of Iron Age coins and brooches might

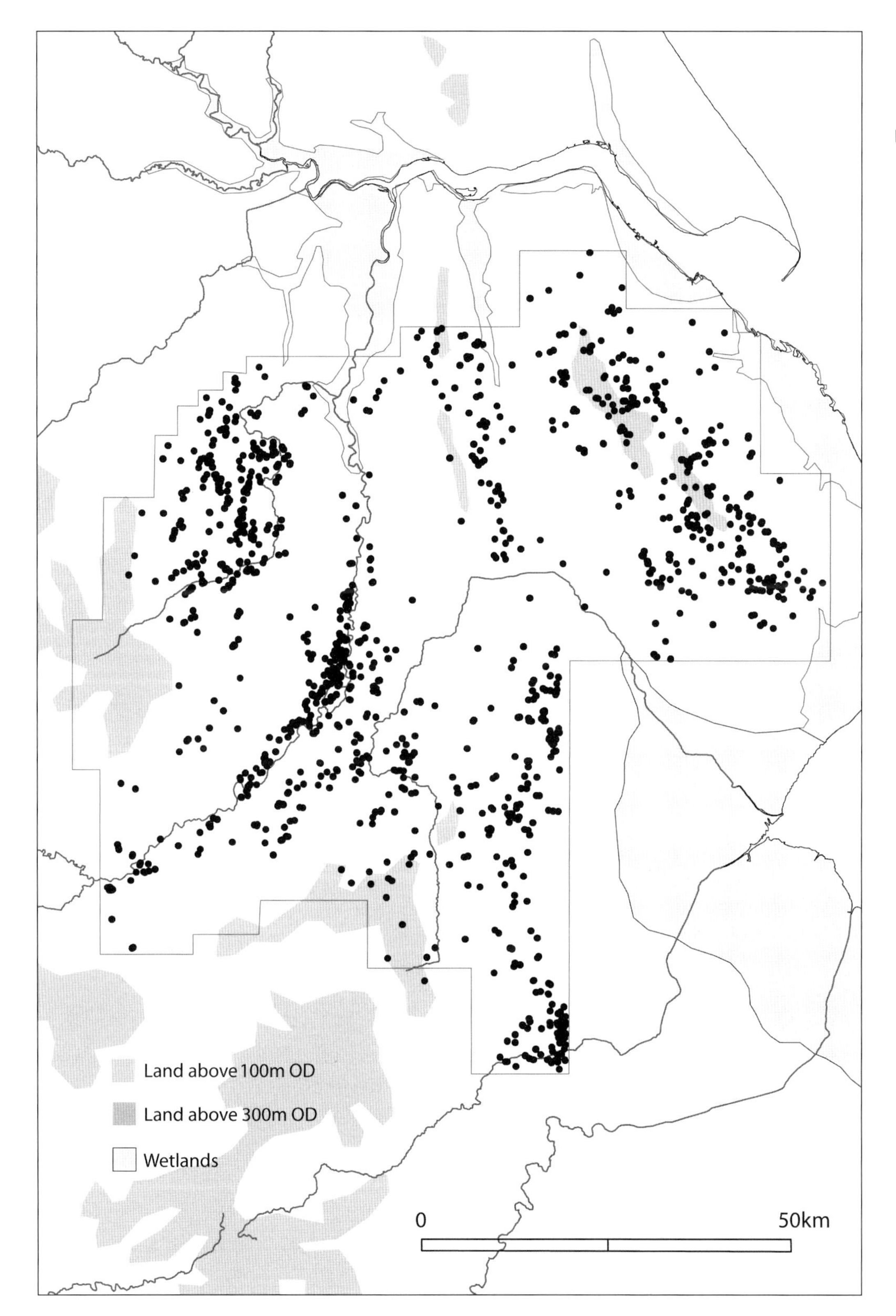

Figure 6.3 Distribution map of all enclosed settlements in the Nottinghamshire/Lincolnshire case study

have more to do with religious activity and ritual deposition than simple indices of 'high status'. When the coin evidence is removed from the broader picture, the Roman-period evidence for these 'major centres' seems far more ordinary (Willis 2001).

The NMP survey data studied here indicates that these 'centres' represent the largest and wealthiest sites within a mixed pattern of rural settlement comprising both dispersed and further nucleated rural foci. While detailed dating evidence for many sites is absent it is clear that this region had a very well-developed and complex settlement hierarchy in the late Iron Age and the Roman period, in which some of the larger settlements also acted as religious/political foci in a distinctive social landscape that extended as far south as the Ancaster Gap (Fig 6.5 (D)). This pattern seems to

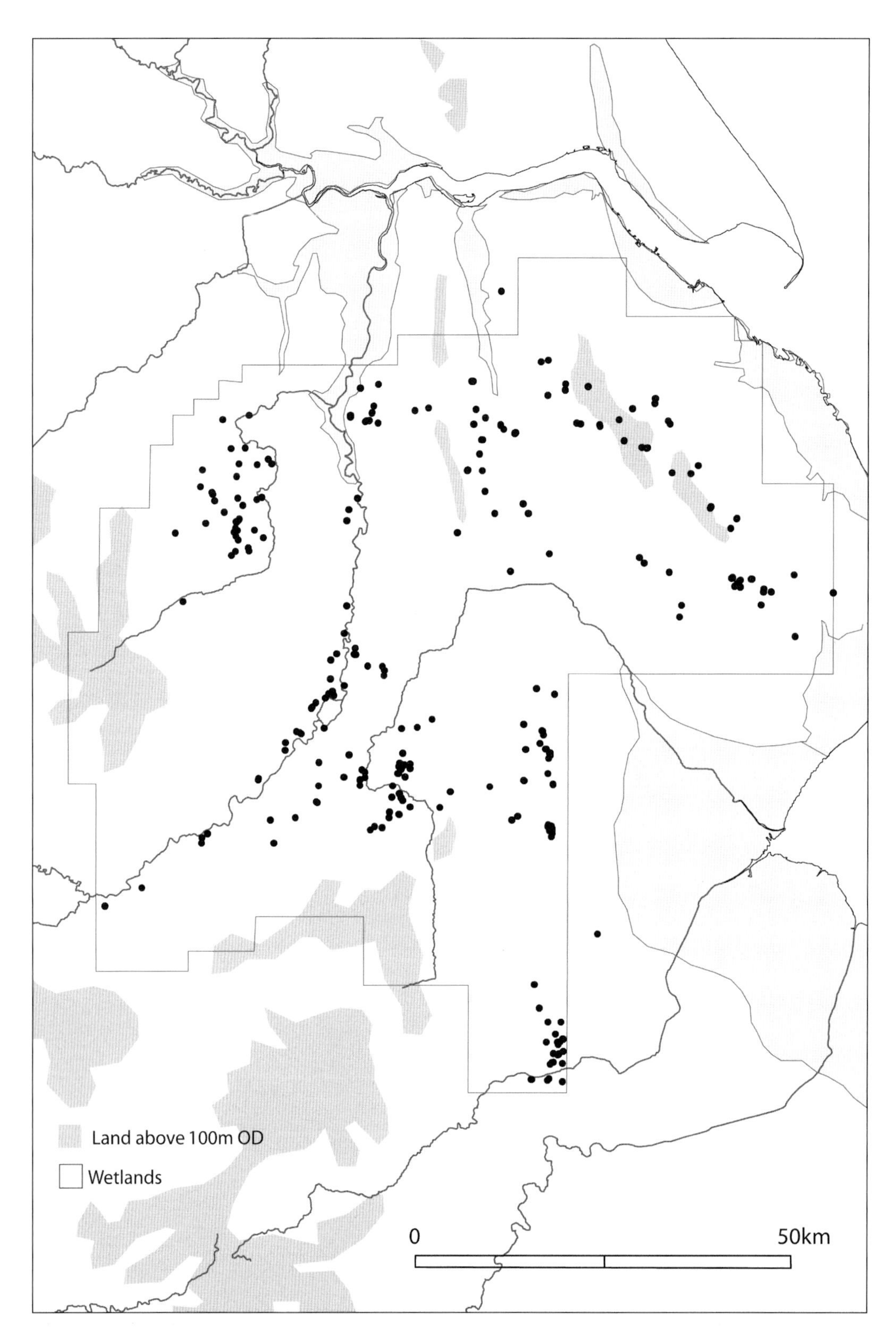

Figure 6.4 Distribution map of all linear system settlements recorded in the Nottinghamshire/Lincolnshire survey

extend as far west as the Trent valley in Nottinghamshire, where Knight and Howard (2004a, 100) have noted major aggregated settlements at Lockington, Ferry Lane Farm, Collingham, Rampton, and Brough-on-Fosse – although, as noted above, they are rarely on the same scale as those of the main group in Lincolnshire, and do not possess late Iron Age material culture of comparable richness.

South of the Ancaster Gap and away from the fen-edge, dispersed enclosed and linear system settlements dominate the landscape, with larger foci scarce. The national survey suggests that this dispersed settlement pattern extends into Leicestershire, and it also seems to extend to the west of the Ancaster Gap into the Vale of Belvoir and the eastern fringes of the Trent valley (Fig 6.5 (E)). The exception in the south of the

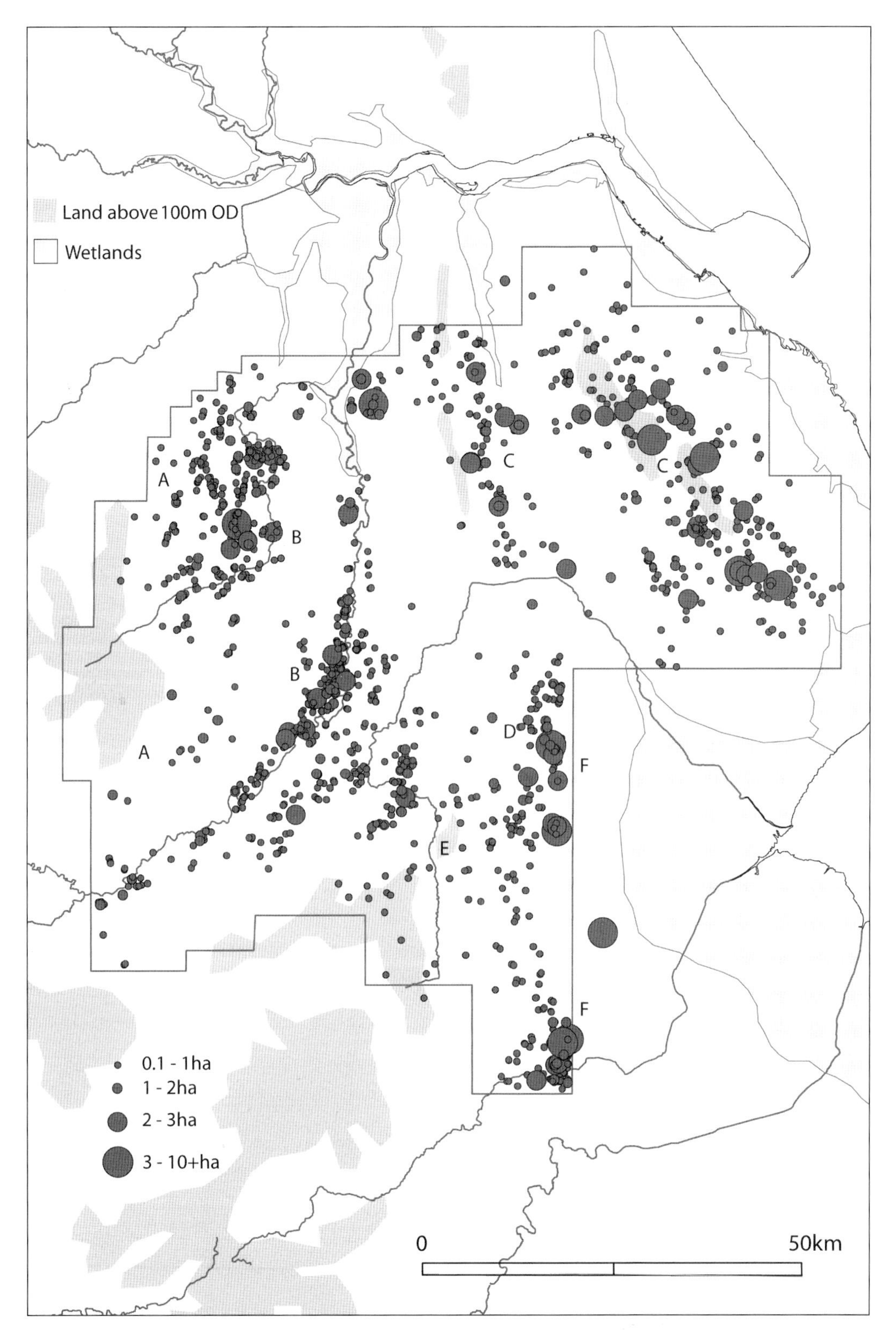

Figure 6.5 Distribution map of dispersed and nucleated rural settlement recorded in the Nottinghamshire/ Lincolnshire survey (letters refer to different settlement zones discussed in the text)

survey is the large number of nucleated linear system settlements along the western edge of the East Anglian Fenland (Fig 6.5 (F)). These appear to be a continuation of the well-established pattern, known from earlier surveys in the Fenland itself (eg Hallam 1970; Fincham 2002), of nucleated settlements that reached their peak of development by the late Roman period. Elsewhere, the numbers of sites recorded through aerial photography were too limited to adequately assess possible settlement patterns. This should not, however, be taken as an indication of an absence of settlement, as substantial numbers of probable sites were recorded as artefact scatters or through excavation and evaluation in the clay vale of Lincolnshire and on the Coal Measures of Nottinghamshire during the national survey.

Table 6.1 The number of settlements recorded by the Roman rural settlement project national survey and the NMP case study. The proportions of each as part of the total record are shown in brackets

MCD settlement class	National survey (%)	NMP case study (%)
Unenclosed	36 (2.2)	83 (4.3)
Enclosed	507 (30.9)	1314 (67.6)
Linear systems	114 (7)	273 (14)
Unclassified or possible field system	982 (59.9)	273 (14)
Total	1639	1943

Table 6.1 shows the total number of settlements for each survey, recorded by class. The results are not directly comparable, as the national survey data includes all of Lincolnshire while the case study results exclude the Fenland. Despite this, the total numbers are higher for the case study than the national survey. This is perhaps not surprising as the NMP data for Nottinghamshire had not been included in the SMR at the time of the national survey and NMP surveys consistently increase the numbers of recorded settlements in a region. More important are some of the other major differences between the two surveys. The first of these is the far higher proportion of settlements that could be characterised in the case study. This was to be expected given the obvious potential of aerial photographic results for morphological classification, but was nevertheless rewarding to see. The implications for the extension of the characterisation of Roman rural settlements to other areas where NMP surveys have been completed are obvious. Using the simple criteria adopted by the Roman rural settlement project's national survey it may on this evidence be possible to increase the national total of characterised settlements from over 12,000 to nearer 20,000–24,000.

The balance between the proportion of settlement forms recorded from the different surveys is also interesting. Unenclosed settlements, as was noted above, remain rare in both cases, although there are more in the NMP survey. This stems from the greater ease with which it was possible to classify such sites using the systematically recorded information in MORPH2 records, rather than the often simpler, or more inconsistently used, terms found in SMRs. Few unenclosed sites have been excavated but those that have appear to represent settlements of middle to late Iron Age, rather than Roman, date. Records of enclosed settlement rose substantially with the case study. In part this reflects the high visibility of this form in aerial survey and thus the ease with which they are recognised. It also, however, reflects the way MORPH2 records enclosure as one of its basic morphological types. Many of these records are then subsequently noted as possible settlements, though experience, especially in Nottinghamshire, has shown that on excavation some are simple stock enclosures rather than settlements. As a consequence, the SMRs have tended to be rigorous in insisting that an enclosure only be considered a settlement when there is further supporting evidence; they may thus under-represent enclosures as a settlement form.

Linear system settlements are also far more commonly recorded by the case study, confirming a potential problem recognised in the national survey. Many of the additional linear system settlements were recorded across Lincolnshire, where the use of generalised terms such as 'settlement' or 'farmstead' by the SMR has prevented more detailed characterisation of many settlements in the national survey. The way complex settlement forms are recorded for the Roman period is a common problem in Britain. While simple enclosed settlements are easily recognised and classified, the absence of a useful terminology for linear system settlements has led to the confusing adoption of a plethora of borrowed terms, such as 'village'; localised terms, such as 'ladder settlement'; and generalised terms, such as 'settlement complex'.

While the total numbers of characterised settlements varied significantly between the two surveys, the balance between mapped forms and sizes shows a more consistent picture. The ratio of enclosed to linear system settlements remains reasonably stable (at 4.4:1 for the national survey and 4.8:1 for the case study). Furthermore, enclosed settlements were still predominantly found in those areas where they were thought to be dominant in the national survey, although they became a far more significant proportion of the total settlement record in Lincolnshire. Thus the sandstones of north-west Nottinghamshire were still an area with a high ratio of enclosed to linear system settlements, while the Wolds and Lincoln Edge were still clearly areas with a more mixed pattern. The ability of the NMP survey to characterise a far higher proportion of all settlements and to record their size allows more confidence in the degree to which the characterised sites can be treated as a representative guide to the total rural settlement landscape. Thus the different character of rural settlement recorded by the NMP case study in different parts of the region is, in fact, a far more accurate picture than might have been thought before. The case study also allows us to investigate the degree of settlement nucleation and dispersal in more detail. In this case study it is noticeable that, of the enclosed settlements which dominate in the west of the region, the vast majority are dispersed in nature. Likewise, it is possible to suggest more confidently that while linear system settlements are relatively common in both the Trent valley and much of Lincolnshire, they show a greater degree of nucleation in the latter.

Comparing the kinds of relatively simple national and regional characterisation made possible by the national survey (Figs 4.2 and 4.3) with the more detailed and nuanced view provided by regional and local case studies (eg Fig 6.5), it is increasingly possible to investigate the balance between settlement class and size. There are, of course, problems with the NMP data, stemming mainly from its reliance on aerial photography and the methodology used for classification and recording. Many of these issues are being addressed by the NMP itself (P Horne pers comm) but here it is worth concluding with some comments on specific issues relating to the national survey.

The NMP data was, of course, only effective in enhancing our picture of settlement in areas with generally good cropmark formation (or earthwork survival) and, preferably, long histories of reconnaissance. It adds little or nothing to our picture of settlement in the clay vale of Lincolnshire and on the Coal Measures of Nottinghamshire, therefore leaving gaps in our understanding across the region. In these areas the national survey SMR data, drawing particularly on excavation and artefact scatters, shows that settlements were still common (see Figs 4.1 and 6.1), and these types of evidence provide our best chance to characterise the nature of the rural landscape.

Second, the NMP data provides relatively poor chronological information about recorded settlements. This stems from the way MORPH2 has recorded date – under simple 'Iron Age', or 'Roman' headings – and the large number of otherwise undated sites. As a consequence important chronological differences in the development of different settlement forms across the region tend to be lost, a problem that was also encountered in the national survey but for rather different reasons.

Third, the hierarchical nature of MORPH2 records, in which sites may simply be recorded as Sites, but also pulled together into related Groups, leads to problems in determining just how many separate settlements are being assessed. It was, for example, time-consuming to identify unenclosed settlements within MORPH2, as individual hut circles or buildings are recorded as a Site but these are not always grouped to indicate whether they are part of enclosed or linear system settlements or clustered into nucleated unenclosed groups. This can be remedied through recourse to the original maps: a slow and not always simple process.

The Salisbury Plain/Danebury Environs survey

The second case study incorporated the overlapping areas of the Salisbury Plain Training Area (SPTA) and the Danebury Environs surveys (Fig 6.6). The former was mapped by the NMP in 1994 and its results summarised in 2000 (Crutchley 2000). The Danebury Environs survey mapping was carried out by Roger Palmer and published as a separate volume in the Danebury series (Palmer 1984). Both areas have also been subject to detailed ground-based survey and excavation projects (Entwhistle *et al* 1993; 1994; McOmish *et al* 2002; Cunliffe 2000; 2003a; 2003b; Fulford *et al* 2006). Together these provided an intensively surveyed region with sometimes very good, but more typically mixed, survival of archaeological remains of the period. As a result of this work the extent to which variable preservation and recording might affect recorded settlement character could be assessed, and the results of surveys using similar but distinct methods of recording and classification could be compared in order to see whether these methods could be adapted to characterise settlement in a systematic way more widely across the Wessex chalkland.

More significantly, for the purposes of the current project, the area lay within a region that, according to the national survey, had a high incidence of linear system settlements. The results of the national survey suggested that the presence of such sites reflected regions with potentially mixed, nucleated, and dispersed rural settlement patterns, and this case study

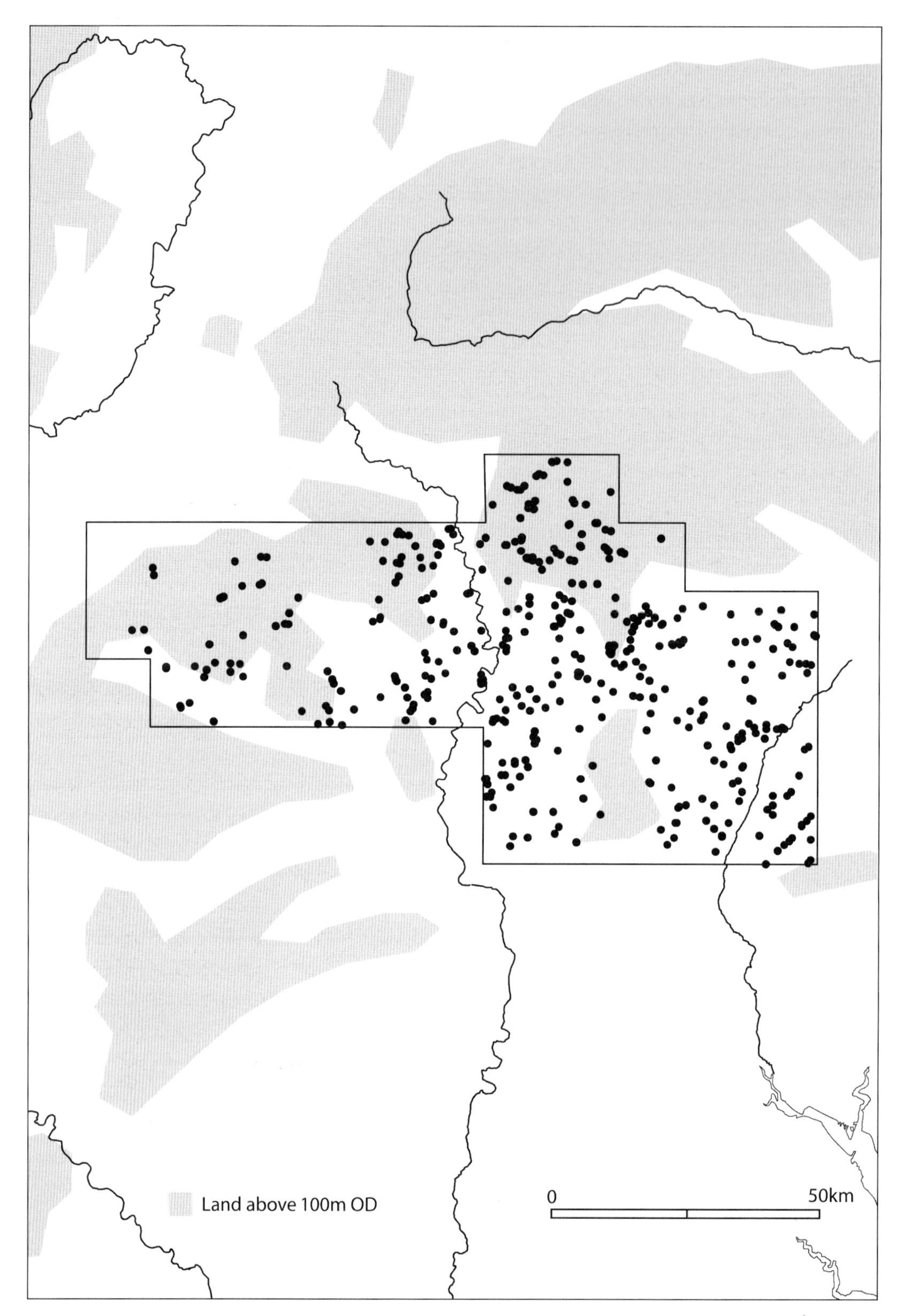

Figure 6.6 The location and extent of the SPTA/Danebury Environs survey area, showing all sites mapped in the case study

provided an opportunity to investigate comparative settlement size. Large nucleated linear system settlements were already known to exist within the SPTA, and the use of the SPTA and Danebury surveys made it possible to assess whether these settlements were characteristic of rural settlement in the region as a whole, or were distinctive to this limited area. Significant and ongoing ground-based investigation and excavation in this area allowed more accurate dating of the development of different forms of settlement and thus the kinds of investigation of settlement dynamics that were impossible within the national survey or the Nottinghamshire/Lincolnshire survey (above) could be carried out here.

As with the first case study, both map overlays and digital data sets from the MORPH2 database (in the form of Access records) held by the NMP for the SPTA survey were acquired. These were then used to reclassify the results of the NMP data according to the methodology used in the national survey. For the Danebury Environs survey Palmer's (1984) published catalogue and maps of the aerial photographic evidence were used and, where necessary, updated using the information published by Bewley in Cunliffe (2000). Both data sets were then mapped within the current project and assessed in conjunction with available published and unpublished reports on excavations and field surveys in the area to compare Iron Age and Roman settlement patterns derived from the two sources.

A total of 457 sites was recorded by the case study across the two survey areas, although this figure included 133 examples of field systems (Fig 6.6). Of the remaining 324 sites, 229 were recorded as enclosures, 41 as linear systems, and 28 as possible unenclosed settlements. Of these sites, 69 could be dated to the Iron Age and 83 to the Roman period; 309 remained as uncertain late prehistoric or Roman sites.

Figure 6.7 shows the distribution of Iron Age settlement forms. It can be seen that enclosed settlements were common, alongside a smaller number of hillforts. Excavations at Danebury, Bury Hill (Cunliffe 2000), and Woolbury (Cunliffe and Poole 2000a) have revealed that hillforts in the area underwent radical change in the 1st century BC which led to their abandonment or, in the case of Woolbury, conversion to smaller settlements. Linear system settlements are comparatively scarce and of a kind Cunliffe (1991; 2000) has referred to as 'clustered enclosure settlements'. All date to the 1st centuries BC and AD and they seem to have been an increasingly common form by the end of the Iron Age. Across much of the survey region, though predominantly east of the river Avon, simple and bivallate curvilinear enclosed sites have been recognised from excavation, as at Chisenbury Field Barn (Entwhistle *et al* 1993), Coombe Down (underlying the large linear system settlement), Boscombe Down West (Richardson 1951), Suddern Farm (Cunliffe 2000); these sites date from the middle–late Iron Age, with the use of some extending into the early Roman period, and several have earlier histories of occupation. In the late Iron Age many are characterised by the comparatively large size of their enclosing earthworks and their size, many enclosing an area of between 1 to 2.5ha. These are accompanied by smaller curvilinear enclosed settlements, some in the form of banjo enclosures, as on Mancombe Down (Crutchley 2000), at Nettlebank Copse (Cunliffe and Poole 2000b), and at Grately South (Cunliffe 2003a; pers comm). Few if any of these sites appear to survive in this form beyond the mid-1st century AD.

During the Roman period (Fig 6.8) enclosed settlements became increasingly scarce and were mainly early in date. At Netheravon, in the Avon valley, a large polygonal enclosure (*c* 8ha) of late Iron Age date was the focus for the development of a villa in the Roman period (Graham and Newman 1993). Villas are now more common than was once thought around Salisbury Plain, and in the Avon valley there are at least two near Netheravon and a third at Compton. The Compton villa also appears to sit within an enclosure but here it is of the more common double-ditched kind (1ha+) dated elsewhere to the late Iron Age (McOmish *et al* 2002). At Balksbury a plateau enclosure originally of late Bronze Age date was also reused in the Roman period, when the interior was occupied by a small linear system settlement that in the late Roman period had a substantial rectilinear building at its heart (Wainwright and Davies 1995). To the east, in the Danebury area, a further villa associated with a nearby mill has been recorded within a rectilinear enclosure of *c* 0.9ha at Fullerton. A cautionary tale about the Roman dating of such enclosures, however, comes from Flint Farm and Rowbury Farm, where rectilinear enclosures integrated with field systems were dated by excavation (Cunliffe 2003b; pers comm) to the early Iron Age, though the Rowbury enclosure was later reoccupied from the late Iron Age through to the 2nd century AD, probably for stock management (although, given the limited area excavated, it could have been a settlement).

The major change in the Roman period is the widespread development of linear system settlements (Fig 6.8). Size varies significantly, but most were larger than 1ha. On Salisbury Plain several of these settlements, such as Charlton Down (covering 26ha, making it larger than many so-called small towns), are massive, but others, such as Coombe Down and Knook East, cover only some 2ha and 3.5ha respectively. In scale the latter sites are far more akin to settlements of the kind found in the Danebury survey area (to the east of the region covered by the case study), where no site of the size of Charlton was recorded.

Roman-period village excavation on Salisbury Plain is limited but the evidence to date suggests that they reach a peak in the 3rd to 4th centuries AD (Entwhistle *et al* 1993; 1994; McOmish *et al* 2002). Several of

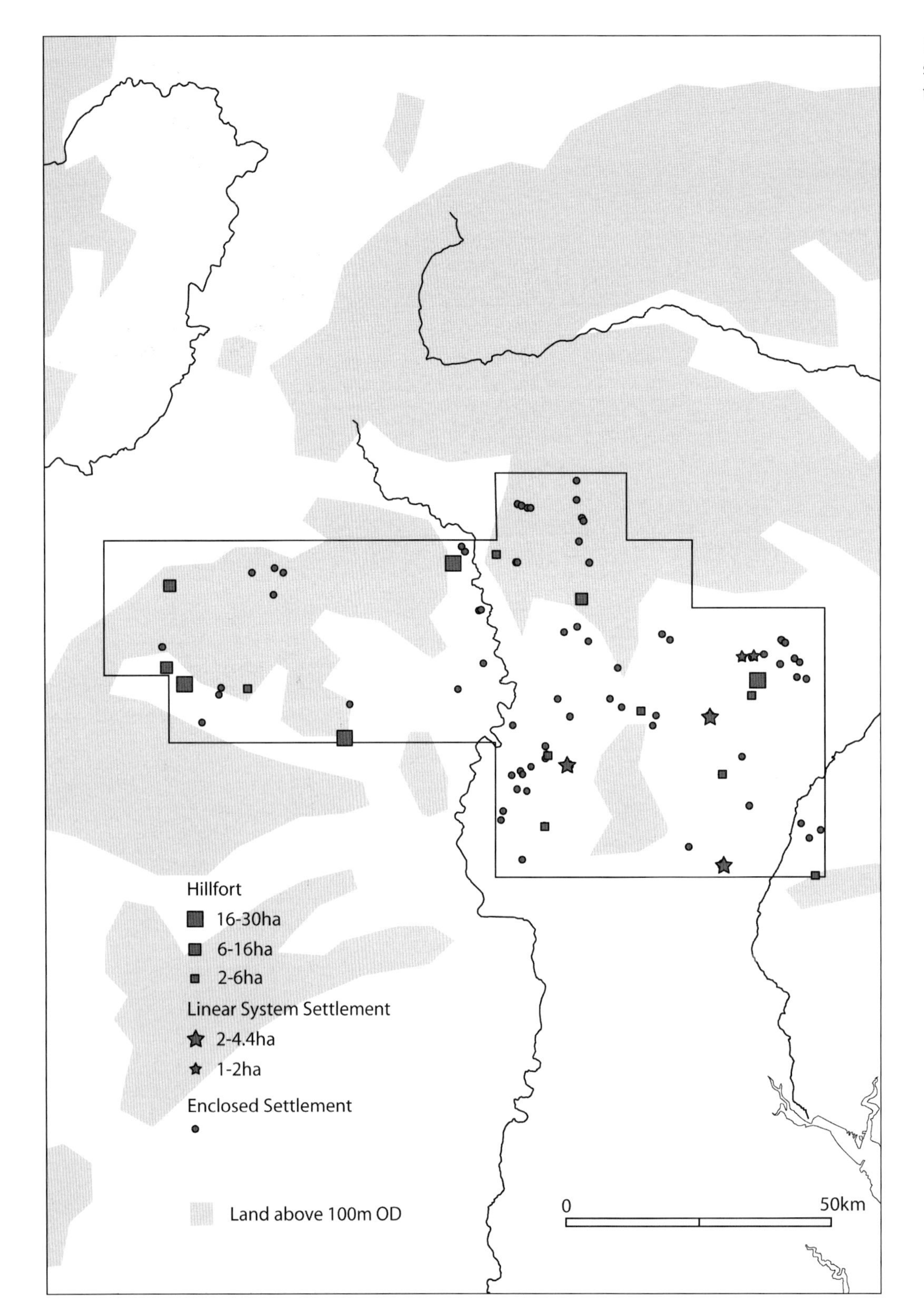

Figure 6.7 Iron Age settlement forms in the SPTA/Danebury case study

these sites overlie the late Iron Age enclosures noted above and there is some suggestion of a period of marked restructuring of these sites in the late 1st or 2nd centuries AD. Within the Danebury area larger complex sites at Grately South and Houghton Down provide an interesting contrast to the Salisbury Plain settlements. At Houghton Down a late Iron Age enclosure complex (of *c* 1.6ha) forms the framework for the subsequent development of a Roman settlement of similar size that incorporated a minimum of one to three separate houses at any one time and which in its later phases developed as a villa (Cunliffe 2003a). Grately South, in contrast, was preceded by a banjo enclosure with attendant paddocks in the late Iron Age. At some point in the subsequent period large-scale reorganisation took place, creating a linear

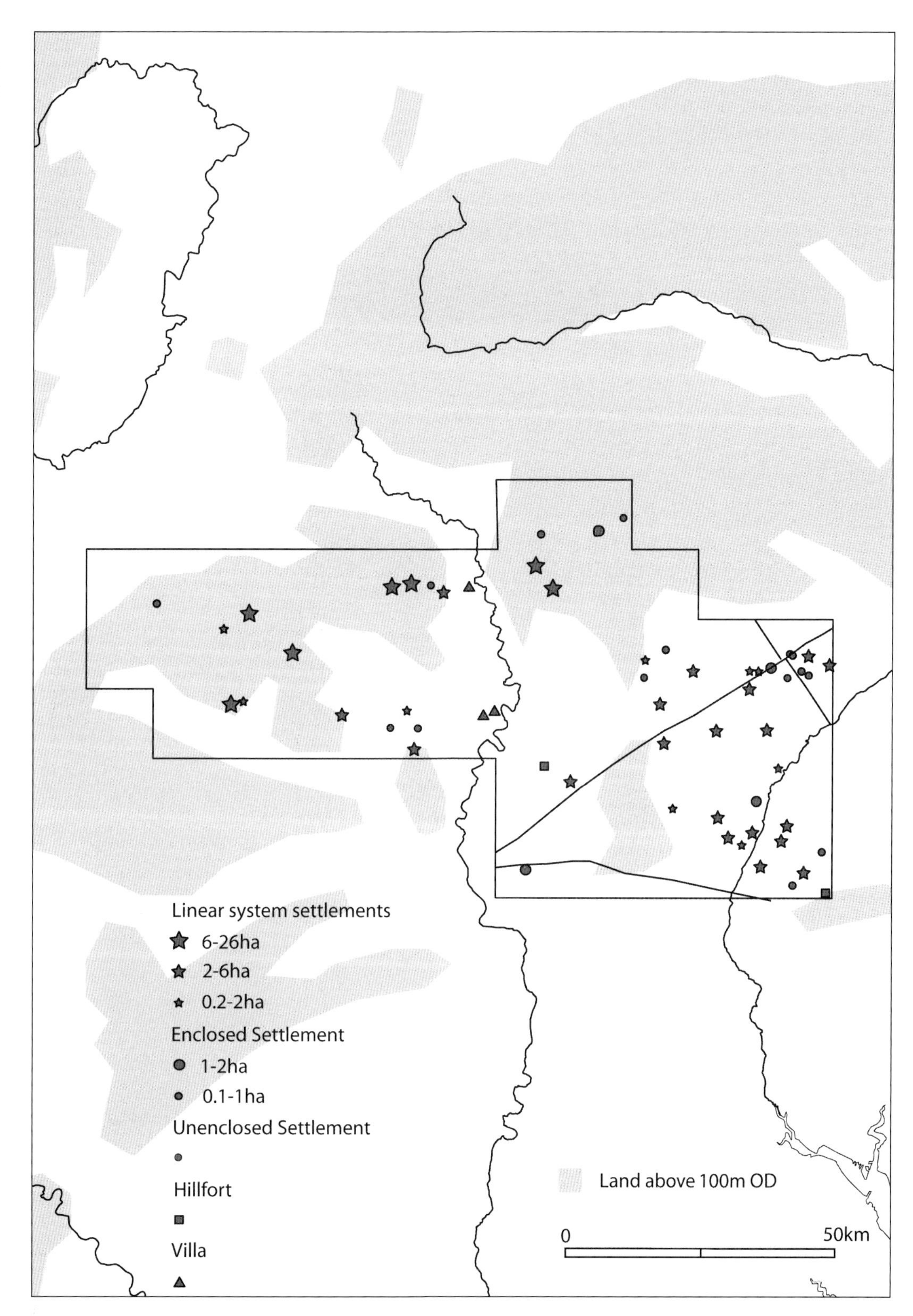

Figure 6.8 Roman settlement forms in the SPTA/Danebury case study

system of enclosures (covering *c* 2.3ha) within which we see the development of a settlement of timber and then masonry buildings. At present, though the site is extensive, these buildings seem to represent a single complex with, at any one time, only one or possibly two houses. By the 3rd century AD it was associated with a number of agricultural buildings for crop processing. Comparison of the layout of the linear system settlements would suggest that several of those in the Danebury area differ significantly from the sites on Salisbury Plain. In particular, the Danebury settlements often develop as complex curvilinear forms that borrow elements of pre-existing enclosed or enclosure-cluster settlements of the late Iron Age, while several of the Salisbury Plain villages are more regular and rectilinear in form, arranged, as at Chisenbury, perpendicular to an existing trackway or, as at Charlton, in clusters within rectilinear enclosure plots in a surrounding and probably pre-existing field system.

At its simplest the Salisbury Plain/Danebury Environs case study has helped to confirm some of the broad patterns of rural settlement for the area observed in the national survey. It mapped the complex, mixed pattern of enclosed, linear system, and potentially unenclosed settlements noted for this area in the national survey, and highlighted the presence of a significant hierarchy based upon settlement size. The quality of both aerial photographic and supporting excavated data, however, has enabled us to draw out some of the underlying geographical and chronological complexity behind this pattern. Chronologically, it is clear that the majority of enclosed settlements recorded are likely to date to the Iron Age (or even the Bronze Age), but that some of the large curvilinear and polygonal enclosures were still significant foci well into the 1st century AD, if not a little beyond. Some ultimately develop into late Roman villas, but morphology appears no guide to status, as some linear system settlements are also associated with villas.

The majority of Roman-period settlements took the form of linear systems of small enclosures and paddocks of both rectilinear and curvilinear form. Geographical distinctions can be drawn between the areas to the west and east of the Avon; while nucleated forms develop in both areas only those on the central and western belt of the chalk dipslope of Salisbury Plain, west of the Avon, become very large (exceeding 6ha in each case). Several, while borrowing elements of the pre-existing landscape in their form, seem to develop during the period from the 2nd to the 4th century AD into large villages not immediately associated with attendant villas. Villas here are found off the chalk of the Plain itself down in the Avon valley and, where evidence is currently best, they are seemingly situated within pre-existing substantial enclosures of Iron Age date.

To the east of the Avon and across the Danebury Environs survey area, linear system settlements take on a rather different form, apparently developing, within an existing curvilinear pattern of clustered enclosures, into larger farmsteads and villas, or 'hamlet'-sized settlements (between 1 and 3ha) that in several cases develop into villas. Thus, while both areas are characteristic of the complex patterns of settlement suggested by the national survey there are important local distinctions between them in terms of chronological development, morphology, size, and relative status. This localised variability within a complex mixed dispersed and nucleated pattern would appear to be a characteristic of the wider region. To the south-west of the Salisbury Plain survey area, for example, Corney (1989; 2001) identified a locally distinctive pattern of late Iron Age banjo enclosures associated with multiple dyke systems, which were replaced by nucleated linear system settlements in the Roman period.

The Solway Plain

The final aerial photographic case study focused on a region within the national survey seemingly dominated by enclosed settlement. Here the intentions behind the case study were straightforward. First, the validity of the impression given by the national survey regarding enclosed settlement was to be checked. Second, the sizes of such settlements were to be assessed in order to ascertain the extent to which the rural landscape was characterised by dispersed rather than nucleated settlement forms. Finally, the limited but nevertheless useful data generated by trial excavations carried out on these sites were to be used in order to determine whether any chronological pattern in these settlements' development could be discerned. To these ends, Bewley's (1994) published survey of the cropmark evidence was used in conjunction with a database of reports on trial excavations carried out on a number of the sites by Bewley and other authors. Map overlays and accounts from Higham and Jones' earlier published work (1975; 1985) were also drawn upon for the purposes of comparison.

Bewley's work highlights the overwhelming significance of enclosed settlement in this area. Although excavations have identified some open settlements, these appear to be rare and are dated to the Iron Age. Additionally, the recent excavations of open sites such as that at Carlisle mean that some of the ring ditches recorded by Bewley as probably Bronze Age barrows might be elements of surviving open Iron Age settlements. Linear system settlements were, as suspected, very rare and all associated with military communities in the form of *vici* or extramural occupation around known forts.

Analysis of the size of these settlements shows that they range from small dispersed settlements of less than 0.3ha up to nucleated sites of as much as 3.9ha (Fig 6.9). The overall size distribution of these sites is, however, heavily weighted towards the lower end of the scale. In fact, over 80% of all the recorded sites

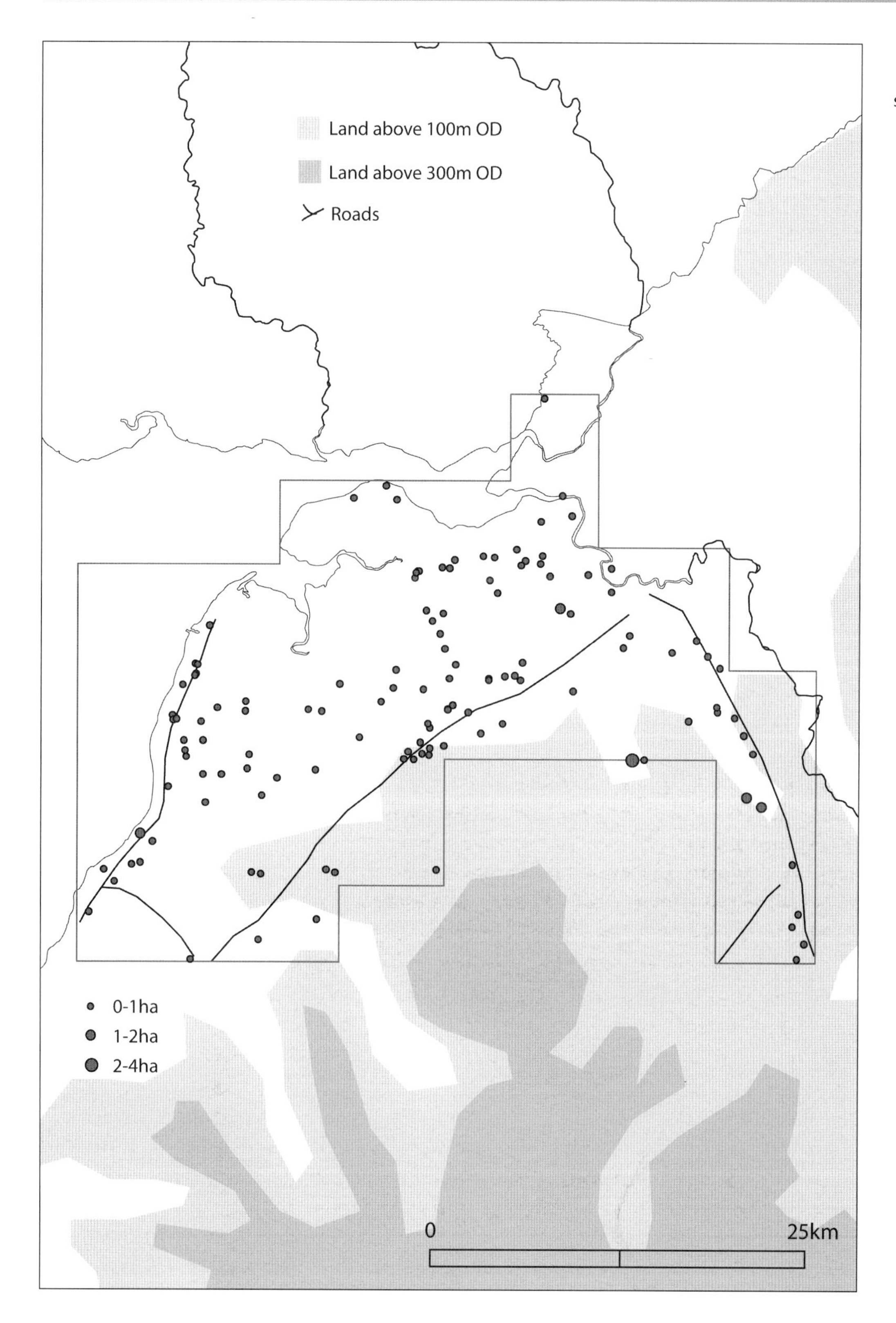

Figure 6.9 Distribution map of rural settlements recorded in the Solway Plain

were less than 0.5ha in area, suggesting a rural settlement pattern dominated by small farmsteads, with only a comparatively small number of larger farms and enclosed farm clusters or 'hamlet'-scale settlements.

Dating of these sites has long been problematic because of the scarcity of material culture associated with them and the relatively small scale of excavation that has been carried out. That said, a campaign of trial excavation has been undertaken on several sites by Bewley (eg 1986; 1992; 1993), building upon earlier work predominantly by Higham and Jones (1983). The small number of artefact scatters associated with these sites were interpreted alongside the results of the trial excavations to give estimated dates for 41 of the sites. Of these, 12 were considered to be of Iron Age date and 35 were probably Roman.

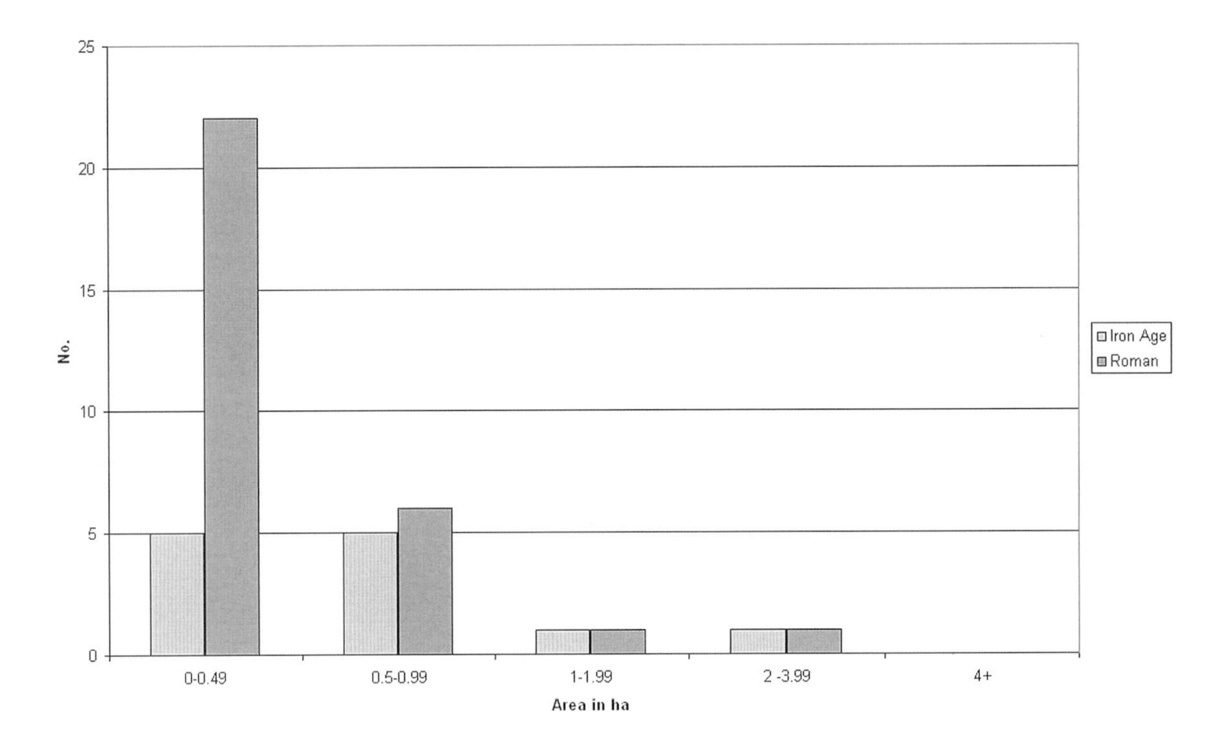

Figure 6.10 Number of dated Iron Age and Roman settlements in each size range within the Solway Plain survey

Analysis of such a small sample – the Iron Age sites in particular – makes any conclusions regarding changing patterns of settlement through time tentative, but Figure 6.10 provides some potential insights. The most obvious characteristic is the significant difference between the Iron Age and Roman periods in the proportion of sites that are less than 0.5ha. The results for the small group of Iron Age sites suggests that the settlements from this period were more evenly distributed between small farmsteads, larger farmsteads, and small nucleated sites. During the Roman period the number of recorded settlements rose dramatically, something that Jones (Higham and Jones 1983) took as a sign of the positive effects of the new economic demands and relative peace afforded by the Roman garrison. Bewley (1994), however, highlighted the problems of dating sites through small-scale trial excavation in an area with an almost aceramic Iron Age, cautioning us against taking this pattern at face value. At least some of the Roman sites may have been occupied in the Iron Age, given that undated phases of activity have been recorded in several cases. Consequently, this difference in settlement size range between the two periods may be exaggerated. Even so, the pattern for the Roman period is striking, suggesting that rural settlement in the vicinity of the Roman military communities along Hadrian's Wall was overwhelmingly focused on dispersed enclosed farms (alongside the communities of the *vici*), with few of the larger sites that might indicate a more diverse settlement hierarchy.

Comparison of this picture with the evidence discussed by Gregory (2001) north of the Solway highlights some interesting similarities and contrasts. Gregory notes the long chronological lifespan of many forms of settlement through the pre-Roman and Roman Iron Age, but also suggests that rectilinear enclosed settlements and small curvilinear enclosed sites of *c* 0.3ha or less seem to belong to the late pre-Roman Iron Age and Roman periods. Alongside this extensive network of dispersed enclosed settlements were significant, but lower, numbers of small unenclosed sites, and one or two larger and more monumentally enclosed settlements that continued to be occupied. The latter had been a more common characteristic of the pre-Roman Iron Age landscape but several, such as Burnswark Hill, appear to have been reoccupied in the Roman Iron Age by smaller settlements.

Summary

These case studies considered aspects of the morphological distinctions between settlements that could be analysed via aerial photographic data in conjunction with other sources, and were considered to be one of the most practical ways to assess some of the marked regional variation of settlement form found across the country. Though clearly simplistic, they drew out major distinctions in the way settlement space was defined in different areas that in some respects confirmed the broader picture suggested in the national survey. The significance of this is discussed further below, after consideration of a second series of case studies that make use of a very different source of data.

Case studies 2: fieldwalking surveys

Up to now, of necessity, the case studies have focused primarily on simple morphological characteristics of settlement broadly datable to the Roman period. These incorporate two significant, if largely unavoidable, limitations with the evidence which are also present in much of the national survey. First, even using the simple morphological classification employed by the national survey, a large proportion (55%) of the settlements recorded within the SMRs had to be excluded from analysis. In some cases this was due to the limitations on interpretation imposed by the use of generic descriptors such as 'settlement' or 'occupation', even when further information about size, form, and potential detail were available from the original survey data. In many instances, however, morphological information was absent because of the nature of the evidence available, such as records of finds scatters collected through fieldwalking or metal detecting. Second, the simplistic and often generic way such information was recorded precluded any attempt to gain a diachronic perspective on the development of Roman-period settlement across the landscape at a national scale.

The aim of the following case studies was to address the second of these issues by attempting to use surface survey data to map diachronic patterns in rural settlement on a regional scale. This section draws on the results of a series of surface surveys conducted in different parts of England. In keeping with the rest of the current survey it takes a comparative approach, in that it concentrates less on any one project than on the broader pattern of settlement history in different parts of the province.

A total of ten projects providing relatively intensive and systematic coverage of ten parishes or groups of parishes across England was chosen for detailed examination in order to gauge the potential of field survey data in rural settlement characterisation beyond that recorded within the SMRs. Figure 6.1 and Table 6.2 present the locations and names of the principal surveys used. They were chosen partly on the pragmatic grounds that their data were available for analysis, but also partly to attempt to provide as broad a geographical coverage across England as possible. A caveat is in order here, however. Examination of Figure 6.1 reveals a clear central southern and eastern bias in the distribution of the selected projects. In part this is a genuine reflection of a bias in the distribution of field surveys carried out, but it also mirrors those parts of the province in which durable material culture was used on rural sites to the extent that sufficient survives to be identified via survey (see Fig 3.4 for some sense of this). The combination of predominantly pastoral land use, and the lack of surviving surface artefactual material reflecting the presence of settlement of the Roman period in much of the west and north mean that with a small number of notable exceptions (such as the Wroxeter Hinterland Project and the Durham survey) few such projects have been attempted in these regions.

An advantage in using the fieldwalked data was that several of the surveys covered significant areas of clayland soils that are generally not conducive to cropmark formation. Consequently, they provided information on landscapes where aerial photography is of less general use and where field scatters may represent the predominant, or only, source of evidence for rural settlement characterisation. This situation was one commonly encountered in many clayland areas of England during the national survey, where artefact scatters were often recorded but where the use of non-specific and uninformative general descriptors such as 'finds scatter' or 'occupation' provided insufficient evidence to characterise settlement more accurately.

While the specific methodologies for the ten surveys used varied (see Table 6.2) it was hoped that the results of each could be compared at a qualitative level to assess simple aspects of the development of rural settlement across different parts of the country. In each case the national survey looked for evidence of relative settlement size and overall pattern through time, but not total settlement density, as this was considered too problematic an issue given the very different and sometimes poorly quantified extent of field coverage within each survey. This was followed by a case-by-case analysis of evidence for apparent settlement continuity and discontinuity through time,

Figure 6.11 Rural settlement patterns in the Shapwick survey

noting any trends that became apparent. Finally, any evidence for variability in possible status or function was checked and cross-referenced with other trends to identify and evaluate any potential links between size, date and apparent status.

The chronological time frame focused upon here was the late Iron Age and the Roman period and, importantly, subdivisions within them. Here we encounter a common problem regarding the use of different chronological horizons by different projects. In order to overcome this, a simplified standard framework was chosen that allowed the different detailed

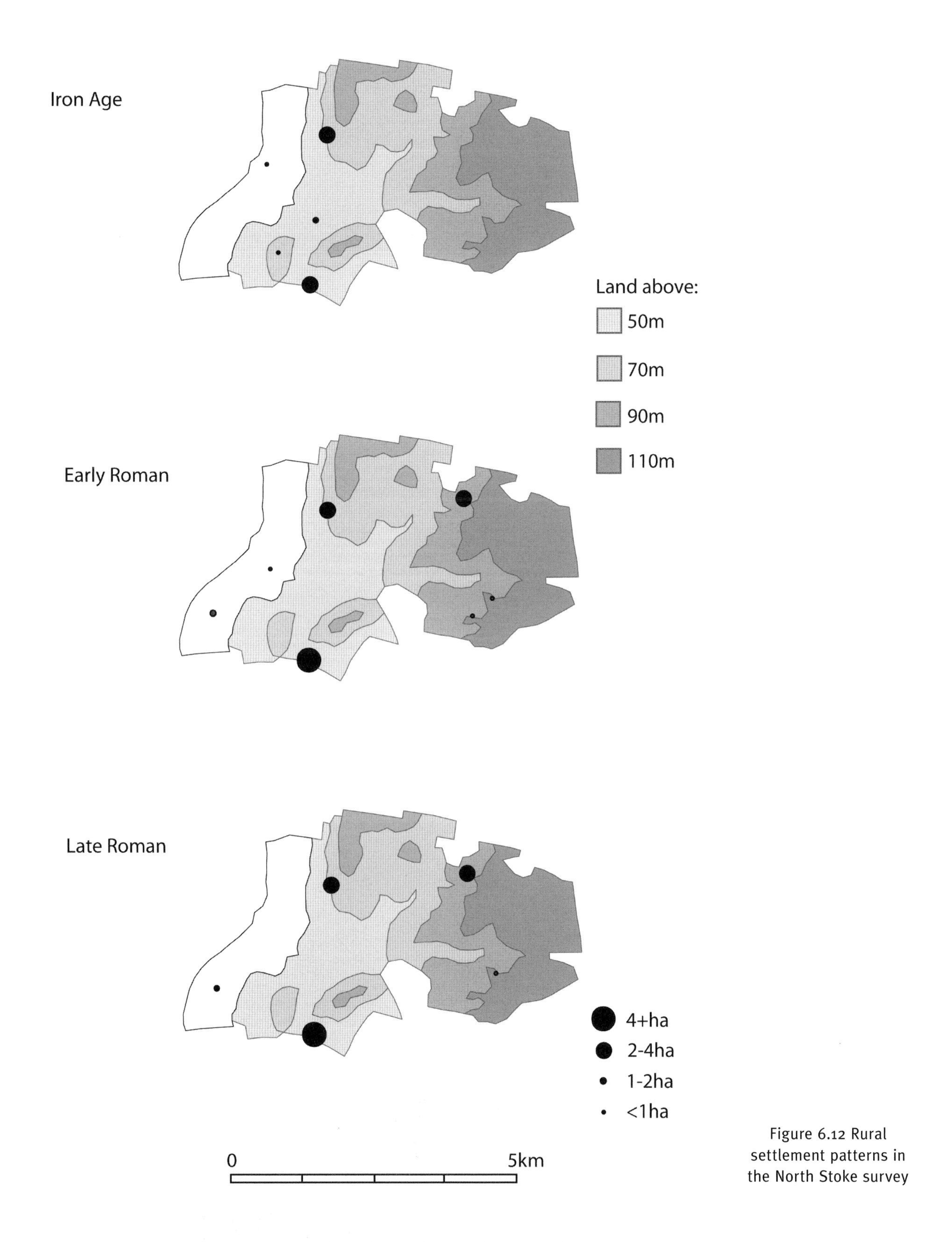

Figure 6.12 Rural settlement patterns in the North Stoke survey

periodisations used to be approximated with each other. This created a simple threefold chronological division of the material into late Iron Age (predominantly 4th century BC to mid-1st century AD), early Roman (1st to mid-2nd century AD), and late Roman (predominantly 3rd to 4th century AD). The absolute dates cited are, of course, fairly arbitrary, as in some cases more sensitive chronologies were used, with better-defined patterns thus presented, while in others the chronological boundary between what constituted, for example, early and late Roman material varied to some degree. While the data from several of the

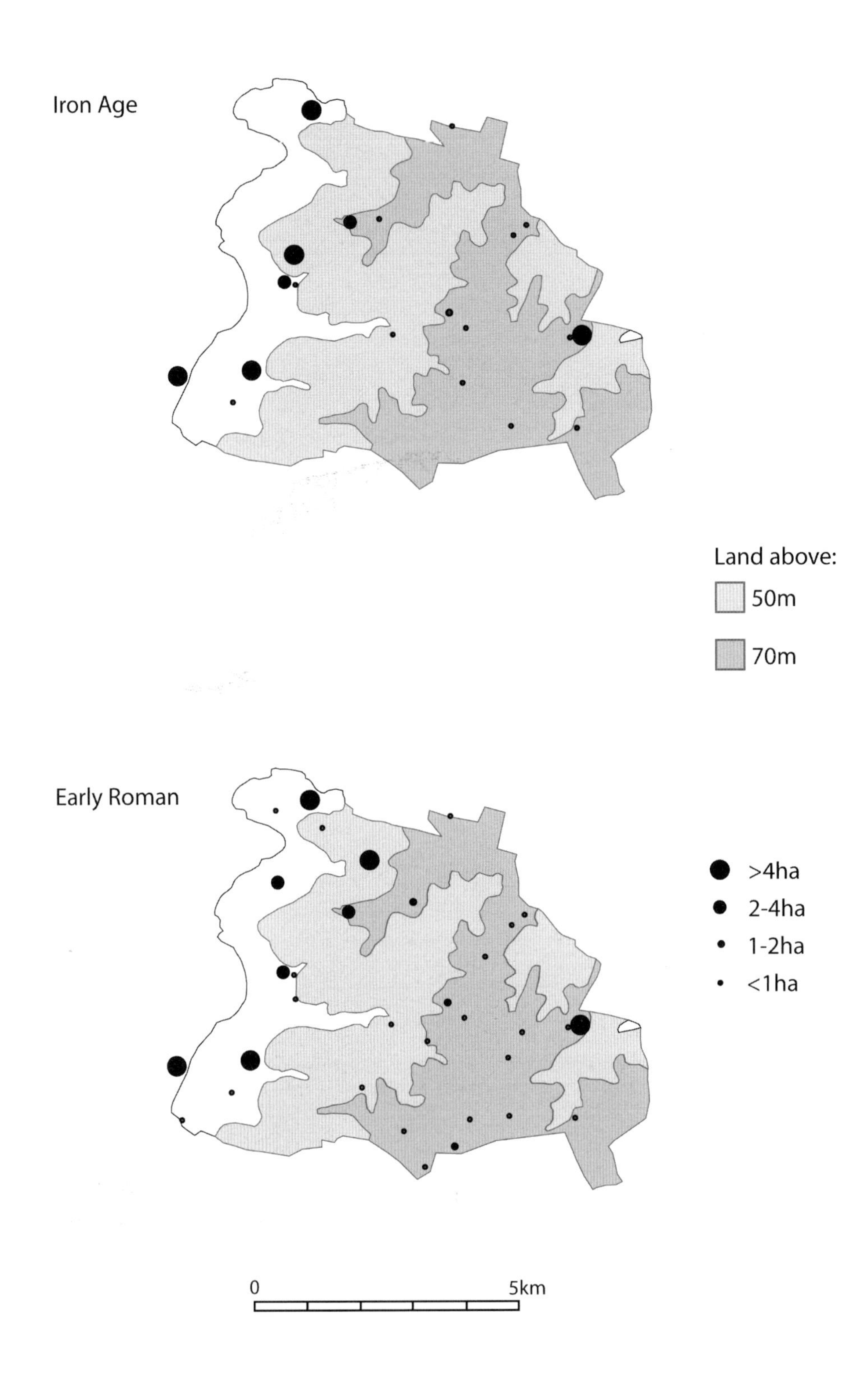

Figure 6.13 Iron Age and early Roman rural settlement patterns in the Raunds Area survey

surveys can be (and indeed has been) broken down into finer period divisions, the boundaries outlined above were chosen to ensure that they can be widely replicated in survey data across much of southern and eastern Britain, even in areas where local ceramics are often less chronologically diagnostic or where surface artefact survival is poor. Consequently, they helped provide some indication of broad changes through time and could also be systematically compared with similar chronological phases in other surveys nationally.

The analysis will begin with a brief survey-by-survey summary of settlement patterns before going on to compare this with the evidence from other, more

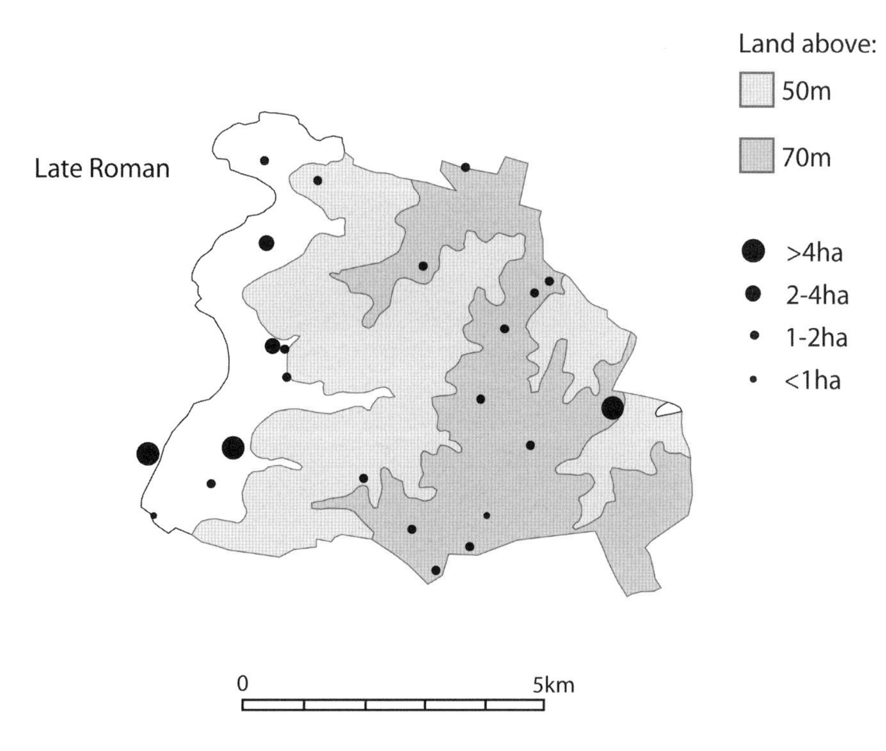

Figure 6.14 Late Roman settlement pattern in the Raunds Area survey

extensive surveys. Several of these projects await publication and will undoubtedly alter in detail as a consequence, but some distinctive general patterns in the data are clearly apparent. Only the main trends will be discussed here. The chapter will conclude with a broader interpretation designed to provide a wider context for each of the surveys.

The Shapwick project was a detailed integrated survey and excavation project looking at the development of a medieval parish in Somerset, which covered both the edge of the Somerset Levels and the north slope of the Polden Hills (Gerrard forthcoming). It is clear that in the later Iron Age the area saw a reasonably dense pattern of settlements along the northern slopes of the Polden ridge and close to the edge of the wetlands to the north (Fig 6.11). The early Roman period saw a large degree of stability, with evidence for settlements of the period being found at all six of the late Iron Age locations, supporting the wider assertions made by Leech (1982, 217) that there is little evidence for settlement abandonment in Somerset in the 1st and 2nd centuries AD, with the exception of

Table 6.2 The names and survey methodology used for the ten fieldwalking surveys

Survey	Methodology used	Reference
Barton Bendish	Intensive line walk, metal detecting	Rogerson *et al* 1997
Holme-on-Spalding Moor	Intensive line walk, aerial photography and some trial excavation	Halkon and Millett 1999
Loddon	Intensive line walk	Davison 1990
Medbourne	Intensive line walk and some grid walked	Liddle 1994; Condliffe 2004
North Stoke	Intensive line walk	Ford and Hazell 1991
Raunds	Intensive line walk, geophysical surveys, trial excavation	Parry in press
Shapwick	Intensive line walk, geophysics and test excavation	Gerrard forthcoming
Wharram	Intensive line walk, extensive survey, geophysical survey	Hayfield 1987
Whittlewood	Intensive line walk	Jones and Page 2006
Wreake Valley	Intensive line walk	Johnson 2005

Figure 6.15 Iron Age and early Roman settlement patterns in the Medbourne Area survey

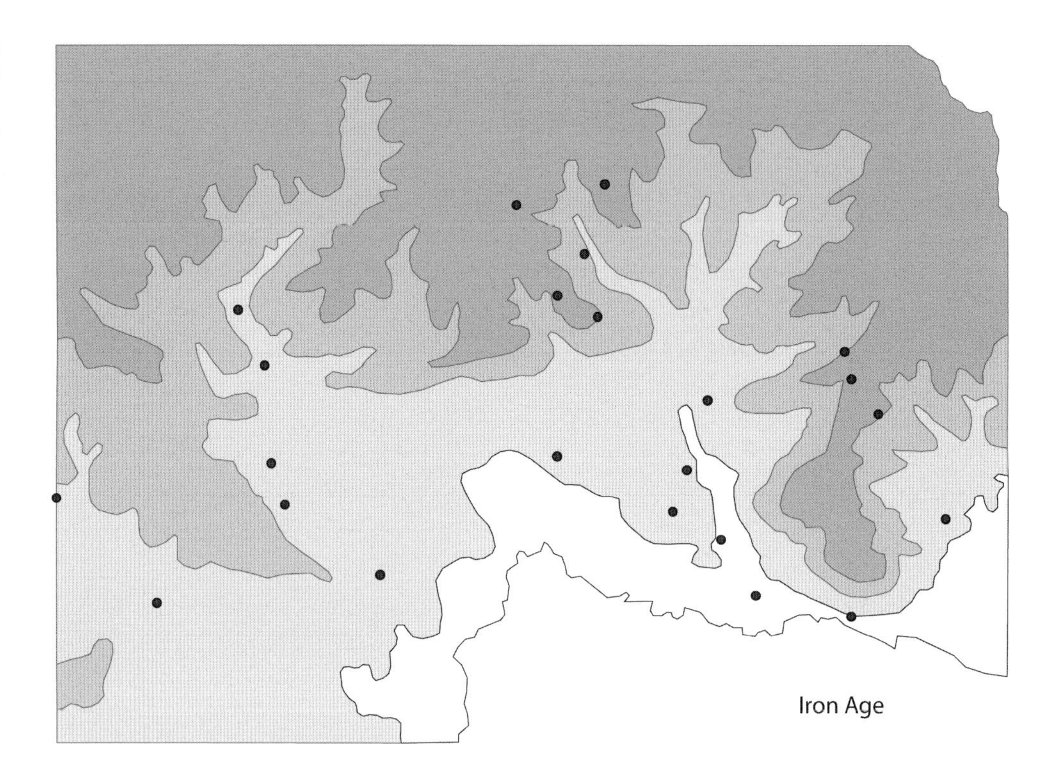

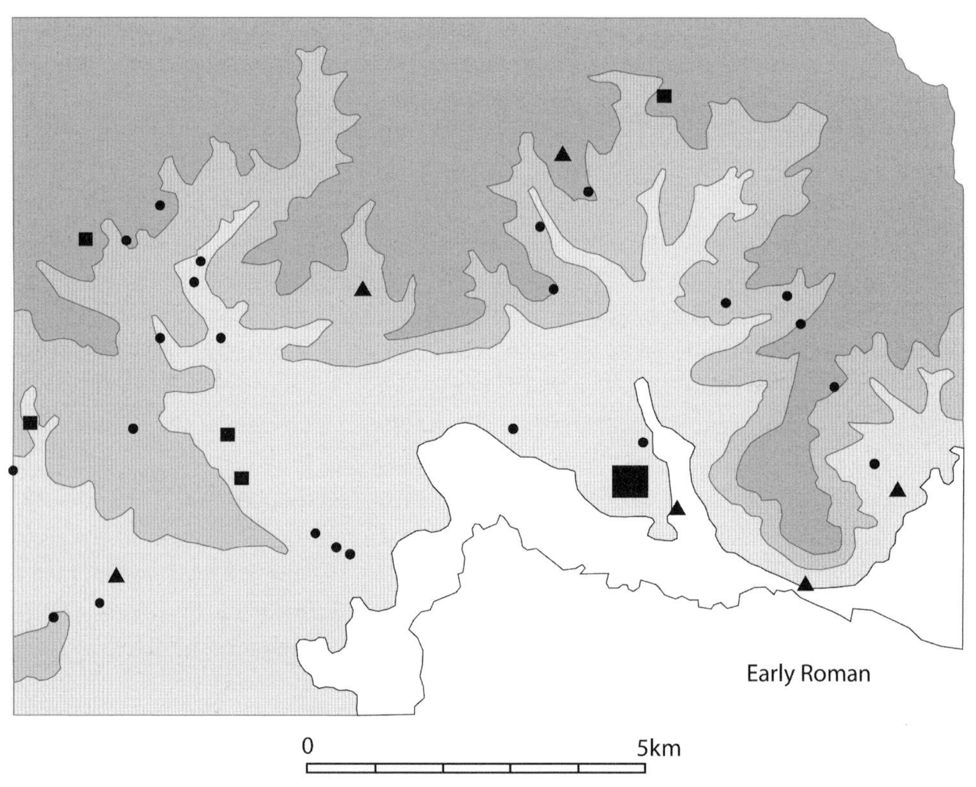

some of the hillforts of the region. The early Roman period, however, also saw the foundation of two further settlements that fill out the existing settlement pattern at the western end of the parish. This pattern seems to have formed the framework for settlement throughout the 2nd century, but by the late Roman period the abandonment of a small number of sites in the 3rd and early 4th centuries sees a decline in site numbers back to the level of the late Iron Age by the mid-4th century AD.

Further to the north-east, in the Thames valley, field survey of a block of land 6km by 4km around North Stoke, 3km south of Wallingford, covered the eastern side of the Thames, running from the floor of the valley up onto the chalk scarp of the Chilterns (Ford and Hazell 1991). Here Iron Age occupation was extensive and five sites lay evenly spaced along the gravels and Lower Chalk soils of the lower valley sides (Fig 6.12). There was little evidence of settlement on the plateau gravels and Middle Chalk of the Chiltern scarp to the east. During the early Roman period there is a marked shift in this pattern, with abandonment, localised settlement shift, and new settlement being founded on the gravels and Lower Chalk, leading to an equally densely occupied but rather differently structured landscape by the 2nd century AD. This is accompanied by evidence for the establishment of two small and one large site on the previously unoccupied landscape of the Chiltern scarp. This pattern remains the basis for the late Roman settlement pattern, although by the 4th century there is evidence to suggest a slight decline in the number of sites, from seven in the early Roman period to five.

North of the Thames in the East Midlands there is a useful cluster of field survey projects, some of which are both extensive and of a high standard. The southernmost of these is the Whittlewood survey, which focused on a large sample fieldwalk of some 993ha of the total survey area, supported by large-scale test pitting and trial excavation. The aim was to look at the evolution of the medieval and post-medieval rural settlement pattern, but earlier material was collected during systematic fieldwalking. While much of the medieval material has now been fully assessed and published (Jones and Page 2006) only a sample of the earlier pottery has been fully analysed. Iron Age material in the analysed assemblages was scarce and so, as yet, the pattern of Iron Age settlement in the area is difficult to assess. By the early Roman period, however, it is clear that much of this landscape was occupied with settlement areas associated with extensive manuring scatters on both clayland and lighter soils. This possible expansion seems to continue into the 2nd century AD, but by the late Roman period this trend is reversed and numbers of settlements drop to 1st-century levels, although they are now in a somewhat different configuration across the landscape.

The Raunds Area project, in contrast, focused on a detailed and systematic multi-period survey of three parishes in Northamptonshire, providing a cross section of topographical contexts from the valley floor and gravels to the extensive boulder-clay areas across the watershed between the Nene and Ouse valleys (Parry in press). Here the intensive survey methodology, backed up by geophysical survey and trial excavations, and the deliberate focus on both prehistoric and historic-period archaeology, meant that evidence for Iron Age settlement was extensive, and therefore the rural settlement pattern in the middle and late Iron Age is comparatively well understood. Settlement in the early Iron Age was largely restricted to the valley, but by the late Iron Age it had expanded onto the boulder clays of the watershed (Fig 6.13). During the early Roman period settlement was closely linked to this pre-existing pattern with apparent continuity at most locations. This was accompanied, however, by the appearance of many new settlements, so that by the 2nd century there was a dense spread across the entire landscape. Gradual reorganisation of this landscape in the later 2nd and 3rd centuries saw the emergence of a rather different late Roman pattern, with smaller numbers of settlements on the boulder-clay plateau accompanied by continued occupation of the main settlements in the valley (Fig 6.14).

An ideal comparison for the Raunds Area material comes from a long and ongoing campaign of systematic fieldwalking in south-east Leicestershire, in and around the parish of Medbourne (Liddle 1994; Condliffe 2004). This project has seen the detailed and extensive fieldwalking of fourteen parishes along the northern side of the Welland valley, again covering land from valley floor to upland areas of boulder clay on the watershed. Evidence for Iron Age occupation is extensive, with 25 recorded sites spread across the valley and boulder-clay areas, showing a distinct preference for locations close to the main tributary streams (Fig 6.15). Densities of settlement seem higher in the valley than on the higher land and clay-capped interfluves. In the period after the Roman conquest the Medbourne area saw apparent continuity of occupation of existing late Iron Age sites alongside expansion of settlement onto the open land between the tributary streams. This development occurs alongside the establishment and rise of a Roman small town at Medbourne itself, and by the mid-2nd century AD the rural landscape is densely settled. Significant change occurs during the course of the 3rd century, so that by the late Roman period we see a contraction of settlement across the higher ground, predominantly on the boulder clay, accompanied by broad stability in rural settlement in lower-lying areas of the valley and the continued occupation of the small town at Medbourne (Fig 6.16).

The final survey in this East Midlands group is an ongoing study (using the same methodology as the Medbourne survey) of parishes along the Wreake valley in Leicestershire (Johnson 2005). Survey here is at an earlier stage and consequently coverage and the number

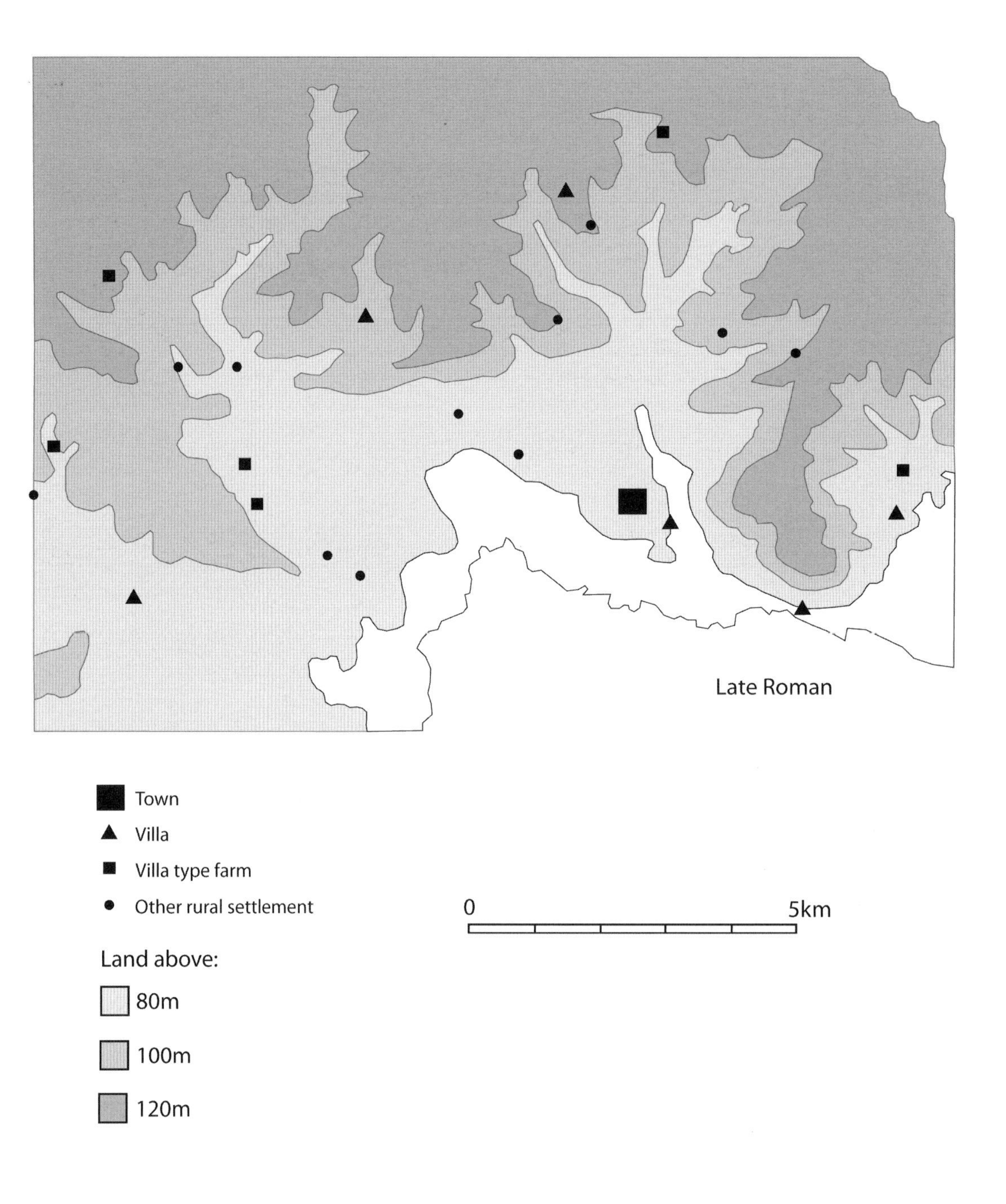

Figure 6.16 Late Roman rural settlement pattern in the Medbourne Area survey

of recorded sites is much lower, but sufficient is already known to suggest a picture of settlement. The majority of the evidence so far comes from three parishes, Barkby Thorpe, Kirby Bellars, and Brooksby, that lie in rather different landscape contexts along the Wreake valley. Kirby Bellars and Brooksby lie close to the Wreake valley and run from the gravel terrace of the river valley at about 65m AOD up onto boulder-clay valley-side and ridge-top deposits around tributary streams at about 80m AOD. Barkby Thorpe lies rather further from the main valley, high up a tributary stream that eventually joins the main valley close to the confluence of the Wreake and Soar. Here the land consists of gentle rolling boulder-clay hills and narrow valleys at a height of between 75–95m AOD. The somewhat contrasting landscapes of the three parishes seem to be reflected in their settlement histories. In Brooksby and Kirby Bellars evidence for middle to late Iron Age settlement is extensive, with a string of sites lying along the top of a narrow ridge parallel to and overlooking the Wreake valley. In contrast, evidence for Iron Age settlement in the Barkby Thorpe area is scarce, with only a single possible site identified. In Brooksby and Kirby Bellars the early Roman period saw continuity of occupation at the same sites along the ridge, although in Kirby Bellars the two separate Iron Age foci seem to coalesce into a major nucleated settlement – possibly a small town – by the middle of the 2nd century AD. In Kirby Bellars and Brooksby this pattern of stability continues into the late Roman period and it is notable that all three late Roman sites are also associated with early to middle Saxon pottery. The Barkby Thorpe landscape in the early Roman period, however, is seemingly transformed with the establishment of three sites across the later parish. None appears to have been occupied in the Iron Age and the only pre-existing site seems to have been abandoned by this date, suggesting both an expansion in settlement across this area and absence of continuity across it. By the late Roman period this pattern alters slightly, with the abandonment of one of the three sites by the 4th century AD.

To the east of the Fenland two smaller-scale surveys suggest interesting contrasts in the possible nature of Roman settlement in different parts of northern East Anglia. The first covered the parish of Barton Bendish in south-west Norfolk (Rogerson *et al* 1997). The survey area lay on well-drained chalky soils in undulating countryside between 5m and 25m AOD. Evidence for Iron Age settlement was abundant across the whole parish, with a total of 21 recorded sites being found. Of these, fifteen could be dated to the middle to late Iron Age; these are found across all parts of the landscape with the exception of the wet valley bottoms (Fig 6.17). Despite the dating of early Roman material being somewhat problematic in this area, twelve settlements of the period are recorded across the parish. Interestingly, however, only five of these indicate apparent continuity of settlement location, with the remainder being established in new locations. Once established, this pattern remained remarkably stable through the Roman period, with the addition of a single site leading to a dense pattern of thirteen settlements across the parish by the late Roman period.

The second East Anglian example investigated was a survey of the parishes of Hales, Loddon, and Heckingham, in south-east Norfolk (Davison 1990). These parishes lie within a low-lying part of the county drained by the rivers Waveney and Yare. These rivers and their tributaries create a low peninsula separated from neighbouring areas of the region by the very low-lying and marshy ground of the river valleys. The three parishes studied here lie on the southern side of the Chet, a tributary of the Waveney, on ground

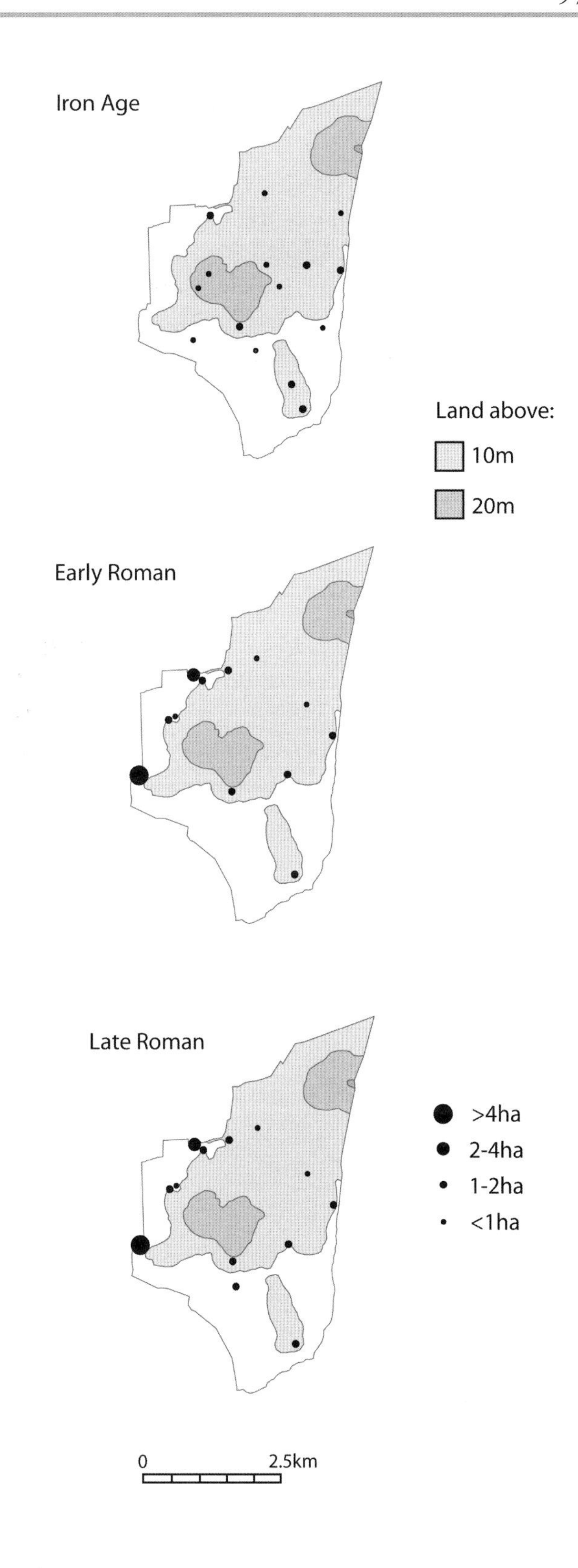

Figure 6.17 Rural settlement patterns recorded in the Barton Bendish survey

sloping gently from 40m AOD in the south-west to 5m AOD in the valley itself. The landscape between is dissected into a series of small valleys by northward-running streams, with boulder-clay soils to the south giving way to glacial sands and sandy clays further north. The evidence for Iron Age occupation here appears more limited than at Barton Bendish and was focused on a central belt of land around and between the two main tributary streams (Fig 6.18). In the early Roman period the significance of this central area remains, with a large proportion of sites apparently continuously occupied, but there is some evidence of settlement expansion elsewhere across the landscape. By the late Roman period this pattern has changed somewhat and site numbers across the central belt of the survey had declined whilst overall numbers remained steady.

Available surveys further north and west were unfortunately in short supply but two examples from East Yorkshire provided a further area to study settlement development. The Holme survey (Halkon and Millett 1999) focused on fieldwalking, aerial photography, and trial excavation of sites across a block of land 8km by 8km in the formerly marginal wetlands to the north of the Humber estuary. In the Holme area datable Iron Age material from fieldwalking was in very short supply, though excavation and radiocarbon dating successfully confirmed the presence of both settlement and iron production sites of this period. In part this situation would seem to be due to a genuine scarcity of Iron Age ceramics, as none was found in the excavation of the Iron Age settlement at Bursea Grange (Halkon and Millett 1999). This meant that patterns of Iron Age settlement could not be reliably recorded through fieldwalking, although the aerial-photographic survey carried out as part of the project apparently shows a pattern of relatively extensive settlement on the higher, drier, sandy ridges of this marginal wetland zone by the late Iron Age. Pottery use and survival is much greater in this area during the Roman period and it is possible to see a relatively stable settlement pattern with evidence of a slight expansion in numbers that continues through the late 2nd and possibly into the 3rd century. This is followed by a slight decline by the 4th century back to levels of settlement similar to those of the late 1st century.

Located only a comparatively short distance to the north-east, the Wharram survey was situated within a very different landscape setting (Hayfield 1987). Here the survey of several parishes on the upland chalk of the Yorkshire Wolds recorded a complex and long-utilised landscape that was extensively settled by the late Iron Age. The Wharram survey used a mixed methodology, recording settlement through fieldwalking in several different ways, some more intensive and systematic than others. Consequently, the number of settlements recorded was perhaps lower than it should have been given the area covered by the survey, and its comparability with other surveys discussed here is thus less certain. That said, the analysis of recorded material was reasonably thorough and systematic and thus the dating of occupation at individual sites appears fairly robust. At Wharram the available evidence suggests that the early Roman period saw expansion around existing settlements and continuing occupation of late Iron Age sites. This process, as at Holme, appears to continue well into the 2nd century AD and in this respect the Yorkshire surveys differ from their more southerly counterparts in seeing continued expansion later into the Roman period. This was followed by a stable pattern of occupation through into the late Roman period.

At this point it is useful to consider to what degree these apparent changes can be taken as genuine rather than as an artefact of survey. Are, for example, the empirical patterns in site numbers in large part a reflection of the relative visibility of sites at different times? One of the greatest worries in interpreting many such surveys is that dating is reliant on a very small number of fine wares. This tends to be a problem characteristic of many earlier field surveys that only selectively collected and analysed surviving material, an action which assumes equal access to such material across past rural populations, and access in sufficient quantity through time to survive and be retrieved in quantifiable amounts by surface survey. This strategy obviously runs the risk of identifying only settlements and phases of occupation within settlements where such conditions applied. Linked to this problem is the continuing difficulty of dating common coarse wares when their forms and fabric change little over time. In order to minimise these potential problems care was taken in the current case to focus on surveys that collected and analysed as wide a variety of material as possible.

The tricky relationship between surface and subsurface material is a further consideration in the interpretation of these surveys. An extensive literature on the subject now exists and there are many instances where individual studies testing the relationship have shown it to be complex and not always entirely reliable. Particularly problematic is the survival of pottery which is less well fired and more friable, typical of the kind found in many later prehistoric or early medieval contexts. This material may well survive in buried archaeological contexts but, once disturbed and

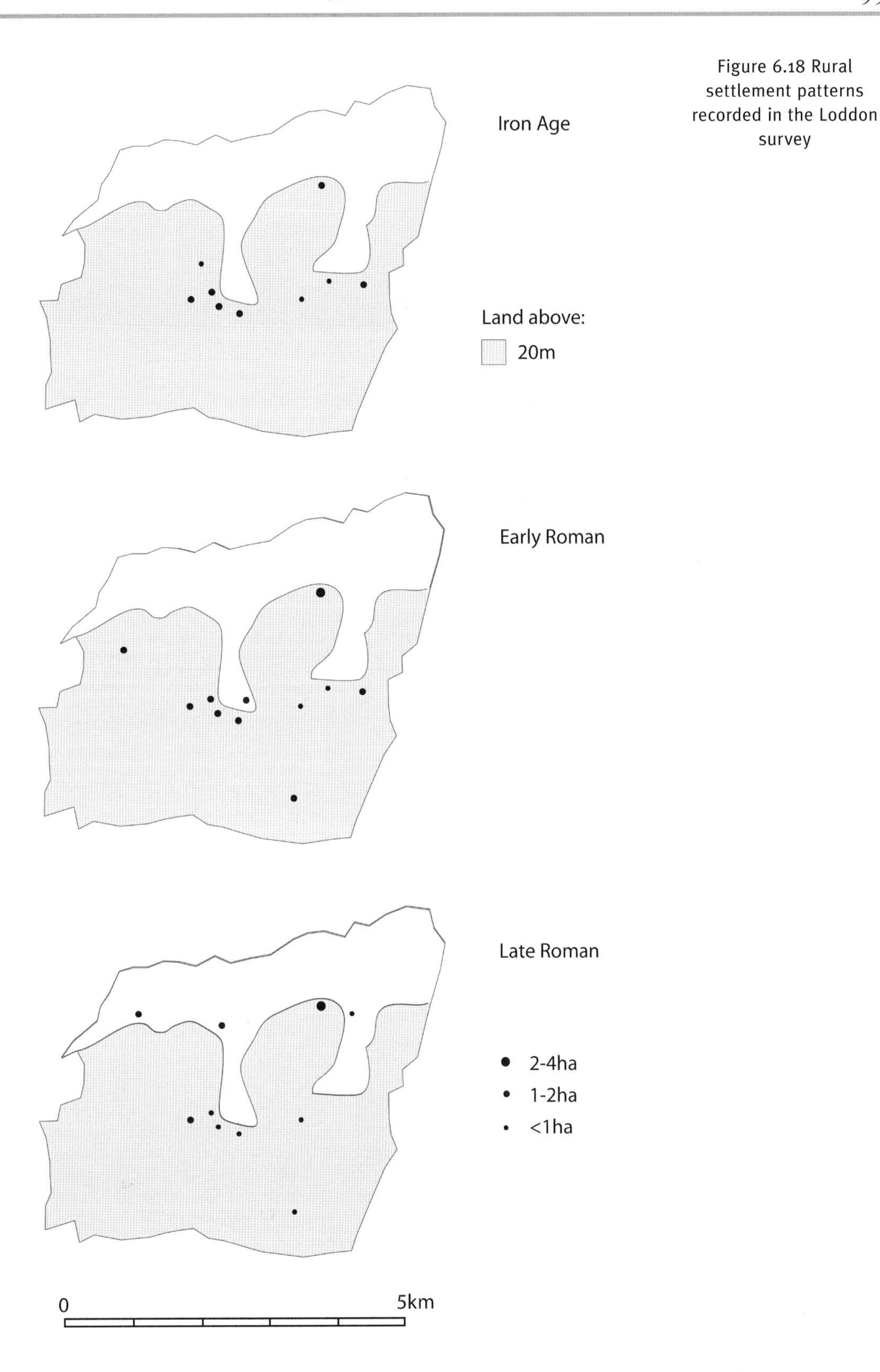

Figure 6.18 Rural settlement patterns recorded in the Loddon survey

exposed to the harsher physical and chemical environment of cultivated topsoils, it is quickly broken down, leaving little or no trace on the surface. This problem is not easily resolved by surface survey alone but several of the current projects, especially Shapwick, Raunds, and Medbourne, and to some extent Whittlewood and Holme upon Spalding Moor, used test pitting or trial excavation to test a number of sites; their findings were incorporated within the discussion here.

In general, although several surveys found individual instances where the surface material did not correspond well to that from excavation (especially for late Iron Age occupation), most instances of trial excavation helped confirm the broad chronological patterns

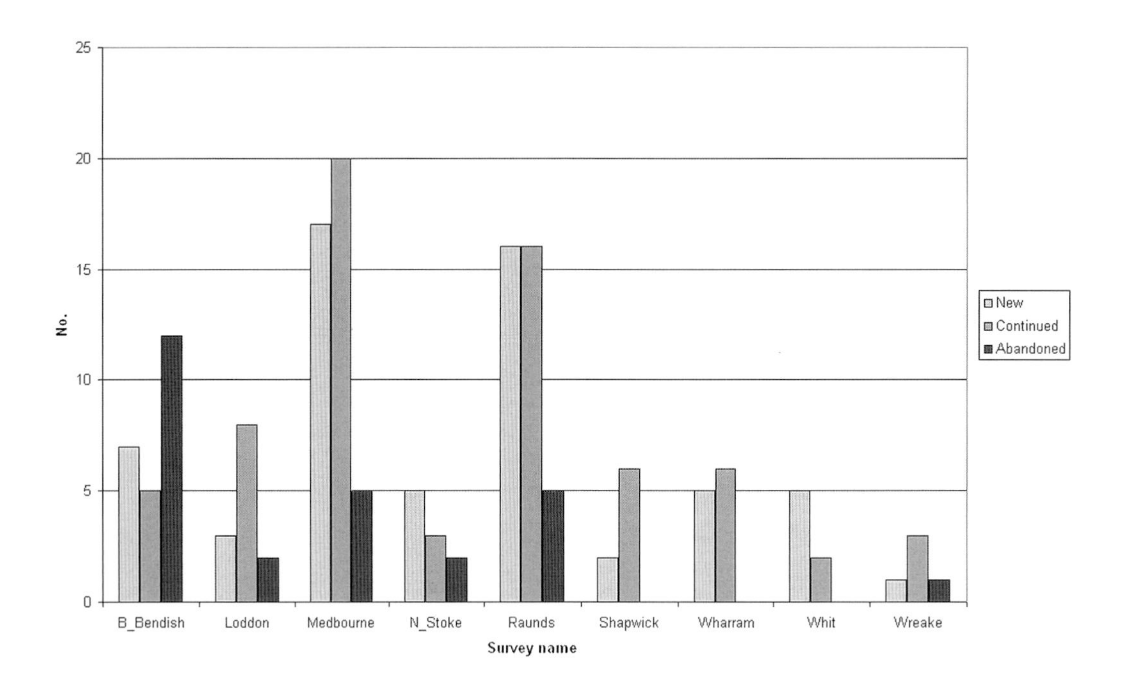

Figure 6.19 Chart summarising patterns of settlement continuity and discontinuity from the Iron Age into the early Roman period for the ten fieldwalking surveys

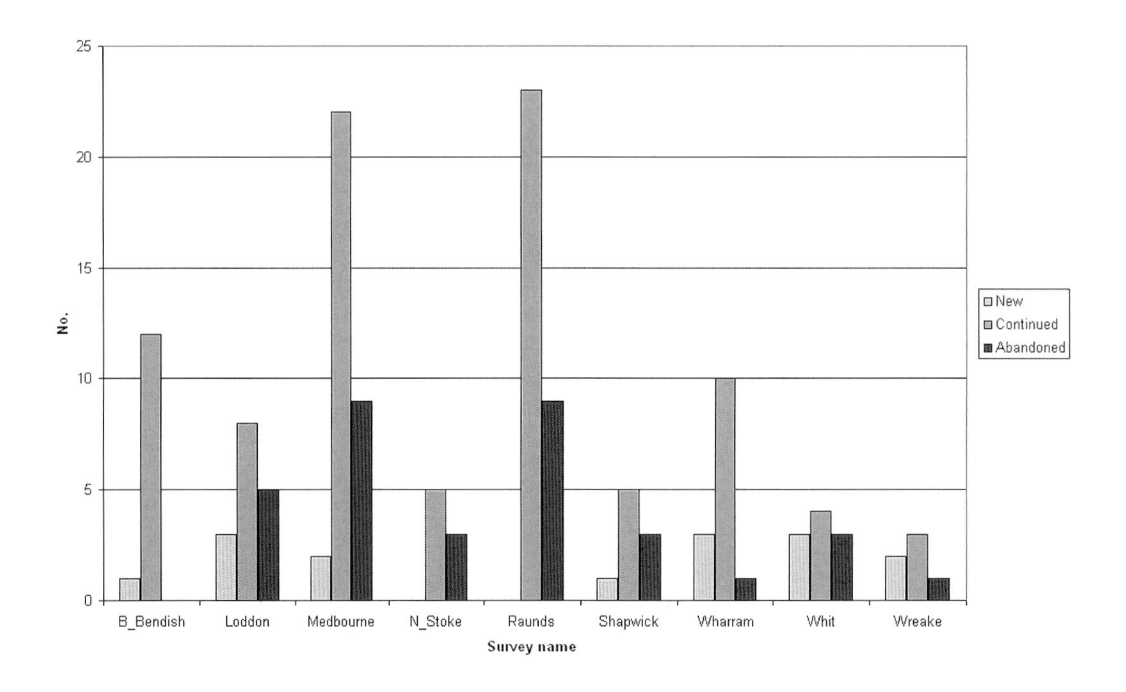

Figure 6.20 Chart summarising patterns of settlement continuity and discontinuity from the early Roman to the late Roman period for the ten fieldwalking surveys

of development recorded from the survey as a whole. Perhaps one of the lessons of this work is that, while individual site histories cannot always be trusted, the overall impression of trends that surface survey produces usually suffices to give a reasonable overview of wider patterns in settlement history.

Considered together, these surveys form a useful body of local summaries of settlement development over a wide range of different landscapes in central and southern England. The very active nature of the late Iron Age landscape in most of the surveyed areas is noticeable, as is the significant degree of stability in settlement numbers, and in places the significant expansion of settlement in the early Roman period. In the late Roman period this pattern often appears to have changed, for while several areas still show relatively stable settlement populations many witness a decline.

Studying variability in rural activity through survey data can at least give us insights into changes in the organisation of the agricultural landscape and broad patterns of land use, if not the detailed patterns of land-holding and ownership. At a simple level the numbers of recorded settlements through time provides us with one source of evidence but in order to build up a more complex picture of rural settlement development, other aspects of settlement must be considered, as is explored below.

Locational continuity and discontinuity

Evidence for patterns of apparent continuity or discontinuity in site occupation can be used to determine whether there were changes in the patterns of settlement that might imply shifts in the distribution of rural populations. Such disruption, as Alcock (1993, 56) has noted, may suggest changes in patterns of land organisation or ownership. A significant degree of continuity from the late Iron Age into the early Roman period has already been noted in the survey summaries outlined above, suggesting that site numbers in most areas did not see a dramatic decline or increase. Continuity or discontinuity in occupation of a specific locale, however, offers a further and potentially more useful indicator. A high degree of site continuity may imply stability in rural settlement and land-holding patterns, while high levels of discontinuity may imply variability in land-holding and exploitation.

Figure 6.19 and Table 6.3 summarise the overall patterns of continuity and discontinuity from the late Iron Age into the early Roman period for those fieldwalking surveys deemed to have had sufficiently high-quality data. Surveys with few new sites and few sites abandoned, such as Loddon, Shapwick, and the Wreake valley, suggest a pattern of relative settlement stability. Those such as Medbourne, Raunds, Whittlewood, and Wharram, where there was a significant level of settlement continuity alongside the foundation of a high number of new sites, suggest instead expansion or dispersion of settlement. Together these two rural settlement patterns – stable continuity, and continuity with expansion – account for the majority of the case studies. One example, North Stoke, sees notable discontinuity in settlement location but is similar to many of the other surveys in being associated with settlement expansion or dispersal. The only true exception to the pattern above is Barton Bendish, where the post-conquest period sees marked discontinuity of settlement location and a decline in overall numbers that may represent settlement contraction or nucleation. Interestingly, this pattern appears to be repeated elsewhere in western Norfolk, with results from the survey of the parish of West Acre indicating a similarly great degree of discontinuity in settlement in the post-conquest period (Davison 2001).

At this point, the evidence from the admittedly small number of surveys discussed here would tentatively suggest that many established late Iron Age settlements continued into the early Roman period in most areas, but that this was often associated with the establishment of new rural settlements during the 1st and 2nd centuries AD. The latter development suggests, albeit crudely, that in the majority of areas incorpora-

Table 6.3 Summary of settlement numbers and continuity or discontinuity from the ten fieldwalking surveys

Survey	Iron Age–early Roman	Early–late Roman
Barton Bendish	Discontinuity/contraction?	Stability
Holme	Stability?	Stability
Loddon	Stability/expansion?	Stability/contraction?
Medbourne	Expansion	Contraction
North Stoke	Discontinuity/expansion?	Contraction
Raunds	Expansion	Contraction
Shapwick	Stability	Stability/contraction?
Wharram	Expansion	Stability
Whittlewood	Expansion	Discontinuity
Wreake Valley	Stability	Stability

tion within the Roman province led to a significant alteration of the pattern of rural land occupation and use, but that this occurred within and around an established framework of settlement.

A very different picture emerges from the evidence for continuity or discontinuity from the early to late Roman periods (Fig 6.20 and Table 6.3). Overall, levels of settlement continuity are again high, but now all surveys indicate the relatively low incidence of new site foundation. In the case of the Barton Bendish and Wharram surveys, and probably also the Wreake valley survey, this is accompanied by very little site abandonment, suggesting a marked rural stability through the period. At Medbourne, North Stoke, Raunds, and, to a lesser degree, Shapwick and Loddon, there are noticeable numbers of abandoned sites that suggest settlement contraction or nucleation by the late Roman period. Only the Whittlewood survey records a pattern of comparatively high levels of discontinuity but no overall contraction in site numbers, although it must be remembered that only a sample of the full number of surveyed sites were studied here and these may not be representative of the wider pattern.

Again, drawing wider conclusions on the basis of this small and geographically constrained group of surveys is a tentative exercise but the overall impression gained from these surveys is that continuity was a significant element of rural settlement from the early to late Roman period. Alongside this pattern, however, is evidence from many areas for a steady decline in settlement numbers that may have been associated with a genuine contraction of rural settlement population or may reflect settlement nucleation as the same rural populace inhabited a smaller number of larger sites. It is also notable that many areas that saw the most dramatic pattern of settlement expansion and reordering in the early Roman period are those that saw the most marked levels of settlement contraction or nucleation by the late Roman period. Those that witnessed a great degree of continuity in the early Roman period often have the same characteristic in the late Roman period.

Site size

The second variable worth assessing here is artefact scatter size as a proxy guide to settlement size. Surface scatters are, of course, particularly susceptible to depositional and post-depositional factors that can obscure their visibility, and diminish or spread their apparent extent (eg papers in Haselgrove *et al* 1985; Schofield 1991; Francovich and Patterson 2000). Furthermore, surface scatters represent a palimpsest of material of all dates throughout the history of occupation, and few surveys have recorded the material in sufficient detail to be able to define site size within any specific period of occupation. Despite this, most surveys recorded the extent of the entire surface scatter and, though coarse, size change relative to different periods (Alcock 1993, 58) is nevertheless a useful if potentially biased way of assessing changing settlement size through time. This evidence, compared with patterns in overall site numbers and continuity/discontinuity of settlement, provides invaluable insights into the possible processes behind the observed changes, in that it may clarify whether apparent contractions, expansions or restructurings of sites relate to decline or rise in settlement, or are evidence for rural settlement dispersal, nucleation or restructuring.

Based on the criteria adopted for the national survey, rural settlements were divided into four size groups: the first two (less than 1ha and 1–2ha) represent different scales of dispersed settlement, and the last two (2–4ha and greater than 4ha) different scales of nucleated settlement. In this case study, however, our primary source of evidence is the artefact depositional 'signature' left by a former settlement. There is, of course, no reason to assume that this indication of settlement activity should necessarily reflect the full extent of settlement as derived from structural evidence. Here, however, the aim was to check whether the fieldwalked data provided a second useful guide to the relative size of settlements that could ultimately be compared with the crude patterns of settlement suggested during the national survey on other grounds.

Analysis of the overall size of artefact scatters within the case studies (Fig 6.21 and Table 6.4) confirms the impression from the national survey that even within regions of mixed enclosed and linear system settlement (within which lay virtually all the case study surveys), small dispersed settlements were the predominant form. While not in itself surprising it does help confirm the observation made elsewhere in this volume that nowhere in Roman Britain do we seem to see a landscape dominated by 'villages' as we do in some areas in the medieval period. That said, the evidence available from the field surveys indicates a general upward trend in average site size through time (Fig 6.21). Variability in the recording of Iron Age ceramics and their relative paucity in comparison to numbers

Table 6.4 The number of settlements in each size category for the ten fieldwalking surveys

Survey area	Small dispersed settlement (<1ha)	Larger dispersed settlement (1–2ha)	Nucleated settlement (2–4ha)	Large nucleated settlement (4+ha)
Barton Bendish	6	5	0	2
Holme	10	2	0	0
Loddon	11	5	1	0
Medbourne	21	9	4	1
North Stoke	5	2	2	1
Raunds	12	12	4	4
Shapwick	4	1	3	0
Wharram Percy	7	3	1	2
Whittlewood	6	1	2	1
Wreake Valley	3	2	0	1

for the Roman period make quantifying the size of sites of this period difficult. There are, however, clear indications from a number of the surveys that where nucleation existed it was at least partly in place by the time of the conquest. At Raunds, for example, several sites, such as Stanwick and Ringstead, are known from excavation to have been extensive complexes by the late Iron Age.

Comparison of the relative size of settlements between the early and late Roman periods (Fig 6.21) shows the apparent increase in average settlement size is in large part caused by a high rate of loss of the small dispersed sites that would normally be thought of as farmsteads. This process is noticeable in almost all of the survey areas, although far more so in the Loddon, Medbourne, North Stoke, and Raunds surveys than others. While a significant decline that clearly affected the balance of rural settlement between the early and late Roman periods, it is important to note that dispersed settlement was still a common, if not always dominant, characteristic of the late Roman landscape. It would be foolish to speculate on the specific relationship between this evidence for rural settlement form and particular land-holding patterns,

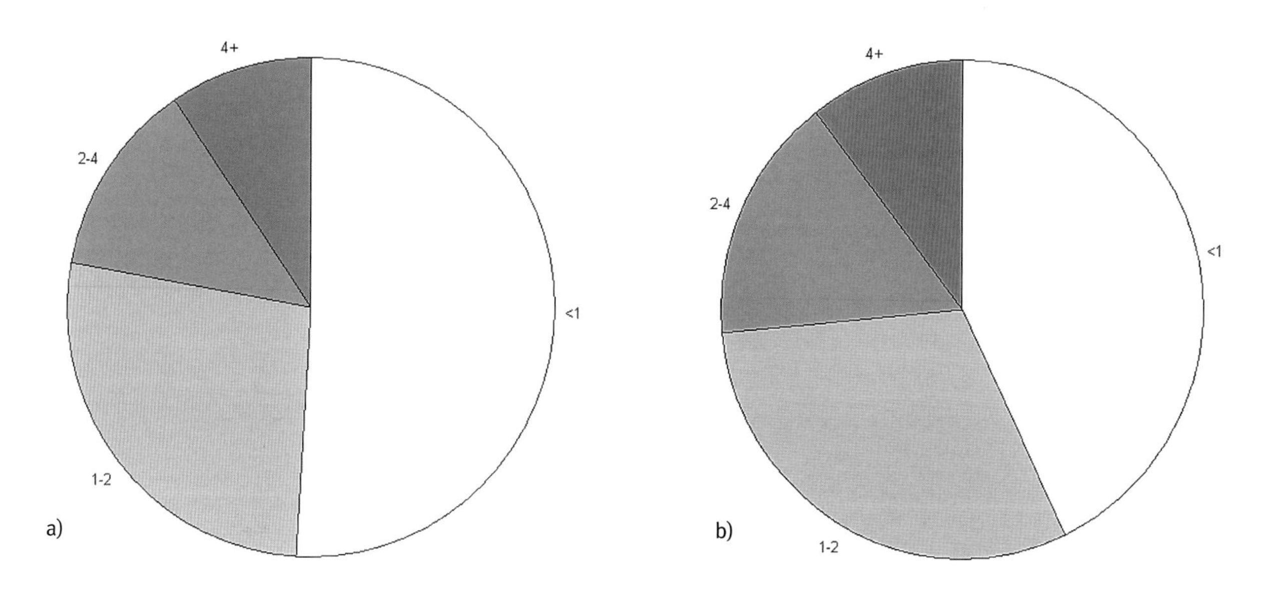

Figure 6.21 Site size for all settlements recorded in the ten fieldwalking surveys in a) the early Roman period and b) the late Roman period

although Alcock (1993, 60–2) has suggested that patterns of dispersed settlement in Greece may be indicative of small-scale proprietors intent on the intensive cultivation of consolidated holdings rather than the extensive use of dispersed and fragmented holdings. It would seem reasonable, however, to suggest that such a significant scale of change, at least in some of the survey areas, must have been commensurate with equally significant changes in land tenure and exploitation in the Roman period.

Given that this survey data does not enable us to judge period-by-period variability in site size within an individual site, we are left with several possibilities for the interpretation of the character of nucleated sites. First, large sites may be a higher proportion of the late Roman settlement pattern than of the early Roman simply because they survive the vicissitudes of the rural economy better. Second, the greater longevity of large sites may in fact represent a pattern of localised settlement 'shuffle'. In this case the sites recognised by field scatters are not nucleated settlements at all but rather small sites whose overall footprint appears large due to their slight relocation at different points through their long lives. Finally, while these sites appear to be nucleated settlements they may only have been so during one phase of their history. If, for example, the perceived fall in the number of small sites is indicative of a genuine decline in rural population it is quite possible that a number of the nucleated sites may themselves have declined in size by the late Roman period. In the majority of cases it is not possible to distinguish between these possibilities, but there is some evidence from trial excavation and intra-site analysis of finds from Raunds, the Wreake valley, and Medbourne that the larger sites are genuinely representative of nucleated settlements. At Shapwick, however, similar work seemed to indicate that sites in the middle of the size range (*c* 1–3ha) are in part the result of localised settlement shift of smaller sites over time.

Site function/status

In addition to ceramics, other forms of artefactual and structural remains recorded by surveys provide the opportunity to further characterise settlements. Defining a site's function on the basis of surface finds is undoubtedly a problematic exercise given that the most useful evidence of such activities is only likely to be recoverable by excavation. Most useful for our purposes are characteristics such as the presence of carved stonework, flue tiles, roof tiles, painted wall plaster, and tesserae that give some indication of the architectural status of buildings on each settlement. This at least enables a distinction to be drawn between settlement size and possible settlement status on the basis of a simple threefold division between:

- Villa buildings – sites where flue tiles, painted wall plaster and/or tesserae were recorded;
- Villa-type buildings – sites where stonework and roof tiles were recorded;
- Other rural settlements – sites where none of the above were recorded.

Figure 6.22 summarises the results of this analysis and demonstrates some useful basic patterns in the Roman settlement data. If the presence of villa or villa-type architecture on a site can be taken as indicative of relative status among the Roman settlements it does not appear to be a factor of settlement size alone. Villa architecture was found on a higher proportion of nucleated settlements (6 of 27) than on dispersed sites (9 of 113), but examples are found associated with settlements of all sizes. The vast majority of sites with indications of villa architecture also survive into the late Roman period, irrespective of settlement size (14 of 15). On the one hand this evidence could indicate that while a greater proportion of nucleated sites are foci for rural status display, smaller sites could become and remain significantly wealthy settlements into the late Roman period. On the other, it helps demonstrate the important distinction that was made in the national survey between potential indications of status and consumption on the one hand (such as villa architecture) and the size and layout of settlements on the other.

Through the evidence from the surveys for site patterns, continuity, size, and status indicators, a clear if sometimes gradual transformation in rural settlement can be noted during the course of the Roman period. When combined, these individual patterns can suggest several trends in rural settlement organisation at this time that can be summarised as follows:

- A common and widespread pattern of relative stability or expansion in the numbers of rural settlements in the early Roman period within frequently already densely occupied late Iron Age landscapes. Only during the course of the middle to late Roman period was this pattern reversed, and this mostly occurred in areas that had seen early Roman expansion.

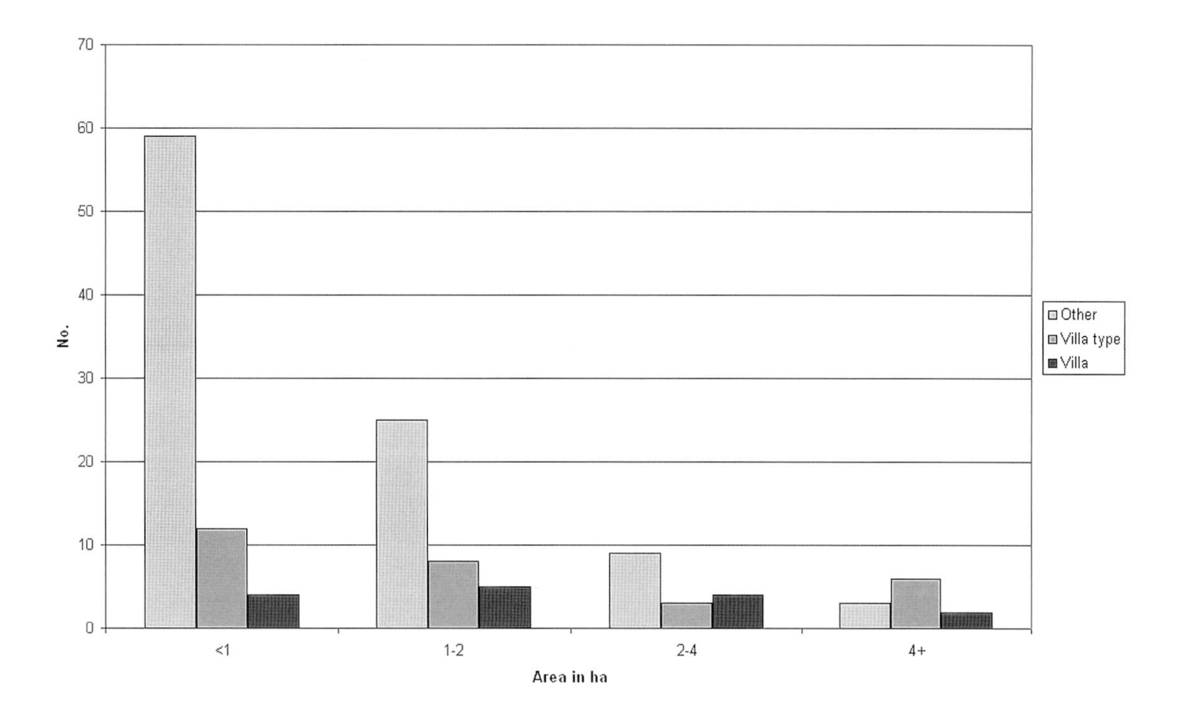

Figure 6.22 A comparison of settlement status as recorded through the presence of evidence for architectural elaboration and site size

- Common but far from universal stability in site occupation from the late Iron Age into the early Roman period that, following Alcock (1993), might arguably be taken to indicate the same for systems of land tenure. Settlement continuity was still relatively high from the early to late Roman periods, but was now affected by a variable process of settlement abandonment.
- The decline in settlement numbers by the late Roman period was overwhelmingly due to the loss of dispersed settlements that would usually be thought of as individual farms.
- Average site size increased through the Roman period (this, in some areas, may have been a process begun in the late Iron Age), so that by the late Roman period nucleated sites formed a significant minority of the total pattern. This is largely as a consequence of the demise of many dispersed sites and the marked continuity of larger ones.
- The greater longevity of these larger sites may represent an increasing preference for nucleated rural settlement and/or the better survival of larger rural foci, be they nucleated settlements or larger rural estate foci for the processing and redistribution of produce, by the late Roman period.
- Material wealth in the form of architectural elaboration is found on a substantial minority of rural settlements. While frequently associated with larger settlements, this trend is far from universal, suggesting the presence of rural ostentation across the range of different forms of rural settlement.
- The presence of architectural elaboration on a greater proportion of surviving settlements by the late Roman period may indicate increasing rural social stratification by this time.

Together, these points help summarise the kinds of analysis that fieldwalking data such as this can demonstrate. Now it is useful to return to the broader results of both sets of case studies in order to briefly summarise what they can tell us within the context of the national survey.

The aerial photographic and field survey case studies in a national context

The three aerial photographic case studies discussed above provided very contrasting pictures of the scale, complexity, and chronological development of rural settlement in their respective regions. Each was in part

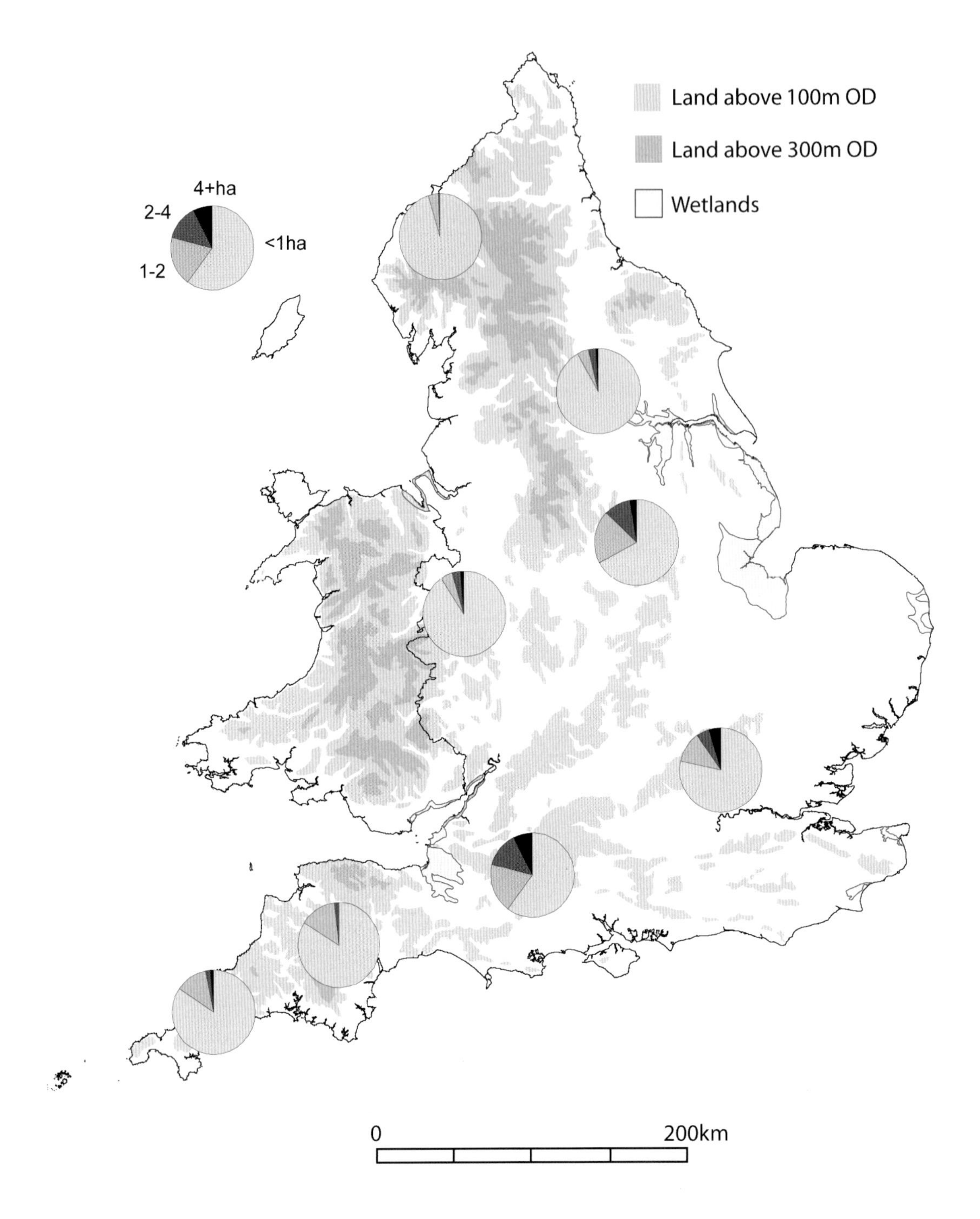

Figure 6.23 Summary map of rural settlement size from the aerial photographic data

affected by the quality of the available evidence and the scale and purpose of the original surveys, but together they significantly fill out our emerging understanding of the probable nature of Roman rural settlement across the country.

Furthermore, during the course of the national survey discussed in Chapter 4, it was possible to draw together some easily accessible SMR data on the morphology and scale of settlements from five of the counties studied (Cornwall, Devon, Shropshire, Hertfordshire and West Yorkshire) that also helped to provide an initial overview of potential differences in rural settlement. By linking these with the evidence from the three aerial photographic case studies it is possible to provide a fuller and more comprehensive view of potential settlement size ranges across the country, based on aerial-photographic and earthwork survey evidence (Fig 6.23).

Figure 6.24 Summary map of Roman rural settlement size from the ten fieldwalking surveys

First, it is clear that the national pattern suggestive of a twofold divide between an overwhelmingly dispersed enclosed pattern of rural settlement in the far north, the west, and south-west of England, and a far more mixed dispersed and nucleated linear system and enclosed settlement landscape in the Midlands and south-east, is reinforced. Within this general picture, however, the detailed evidence available from the case studies points to a series of more localised contrasts in the character of rural settlement. In the dispersed settlement landscapes of the north and west, for example, it would seem that enclosed settlements in Cornwall and Devon show far greater variability in size then those to their north. A significant minority (12–14%) of sites are between 1ha and 2ha. This, as Rose and Preston-Jones (1995, 56) have suggested, raises the possibility that we are looking at settlements akin to enclosed farm groups or hamlets rather than single farms. The proportion of such larger dispersed settlements noticeably decreases as we progress northward, with the Solway landscape of Cumbria overwhelmingly characterised by individual farms of less than 1ha and usually less than 0.5ha.

In the more mixed settlement regions we see markedly different scales of nucleation. In parts of Wessex nucleated settlements form as much as 20% of the recorded pattern, but a more common situation is probably reflected in the examples from the Nottinghamshire/Lincolnshire case study and from Hertfordshire, where the figure is nearer 8–10% and where the rural landscape of the Roman period is more commonly characterised by smaller linear system settlements of between 0.5ha and 1.5ha.

Extending this simple approach to the results of the field survey case studies provides a second source of evidence related, though not directly comparable, to the above (Fig 6.24). Here the surveys generally provide more localised but comprehensive pictures of rural settlement scale and distribution through time. They are also predominantly located within that part of the province thought to have been characterised by mixed patterns of settlement. These too, however, provide insights into the scale and degree of this mixed pattern and, importantly, do so in areas where aerial photographic survey is often of less help.

The cumulative results of these surveys seem to indicate a pattern of significant rural settlement nucleation that ran from the Yorkshire Wolds south through Lincolnshire to the East Anglian Fenland and then on south-westward across the Thames as far as Somerset. Noticeable, however, is that either side of this band, evidence for nucleation is either less certain or less pronounced. In Yorkshire, for example, while settlement nucleation on the Wolds appears pronounced, to the west, in the Holme area, nucleation is absent. This rapid transition from mixed to dispersed settlement patterns is supported by the results of the aerial photographic data from West Yorkshire and the brickwork-plan field-system areas on the north Nottinghamshire and South Yorkshire sandstones.

To the east of this zone, in East Anglia, evidence for a less clearly nucleated pattern is suggested by the results of the Loddon survey in east Norfolk. Unfortunately, no other case studies were drawn from this region for this project but some suggestion that this pattern may be more widespread across East Anglia comes from other partially published surveys or interim survey results. Newman (1994; 2005), reporting on the evidence from the Deben valley in Suffolk, notes that Roman settlement is characterised by a dispersed pattern of small farm or hamlet-type sites and only a single larger nucleated settlement at Burgh. Williamson (1984; 1987b; 1988), summarising his work on the chalky boulder clays of north-west Essex, recorded some 35 probable settlements; on the plateau clays dispersed settlements of *c* 0.5ha were usual, while in the tributary and main river valleys sites ranged from 0.5ha to 1.5ha. Again, this evidence suggests a mixed but largely dispersed pattern of probable farms and possible hamlets rather than larger nucleated villages. Williamson also notes (1988, 76), however, that a few of the sites formed clusters that might represent larger settlements only loosely gathered together.

The wider implications of these results, in conjunction with some of the other data discussed earlier in this volume, are many; in the final chapter, some of these implications are highlighted in conjunction with evidence from other sources in a discussion of the wider significance and meaning of this material.

CHAPTER 7
CONCLUSIONS: SOME EMERGING TRENDS IN A SEA OF COMPLEXITY

A survey such as this can present only a fraction of the archaeological evidence available for Roman rural settlement, yet even the relatively brief review of this evidence given in the preceding chapters makes plain the remarkable diversity of these settlements in terms of form and scale. While the regional and national scale of this study has, of necessity, simplified a much more complex picture, it has nevertheless drawn out important trends in the development of rural settlements and landscapes. Furthermore, the archaeology, when viewed in its totality, points to some important differences between regions within the province and through time, including the simple but important observations that:

- Roman Britain was overwhelmingly a landscape of farms and hamlets, but within this general pattern there were regions that saw the development of nucleated rural settlements which became home to a significant component of the rural population from the 2nd century AD.
- Across the country there are distinctions in the basic architectural form of rural settlements, between landscapes of primarily enclosed settlement and those of complex patterns of open, enclosed, and linear systems settlements consisting of integrated enclosures and paddocks.
- These patterns in settlement are to some degree reflected in the wider systems of rural land allotment and boundary definition of which they were a part. Enclosed dispersed settlements lie at the heart of rural landscapes characterised by individual or local aggregate holdings often with access to nearby unenclosed or potentially wooded lands. The mixed traditions of settlement are found predominatly in regions with far more extensive field systems, integrated via long droves and tracks into complex bounded agricultural landscapes.
- The architecture of buildings within these settlements reflects similar patterns of change, between those sites that saw the adoption of rectilinear building traditions, in part inspired by continental parallels, and those where new forms of building develop from pre-existing Iron Age traditions within their vicinity.
- While the nature of the evidence used here and its often very incompletely or poorly recorded form does not permit us to point with certainty to the specific causes that lay behind these changes, a picture may be emerging that allows us to provide a foundation for the wider development of Roman Britain in which the diverse development of these landscapes played an integral part rather than acted as a backdrop to wider events.

The intention in this chapter is not to attempt to develop a thematic study of these issues or to write a brief history of the role of rural society in the developing province but rather simply to reiterate some apparent trends evident from this survey that are deserving of wider consideration in future debate.

The architecture and role of settlement space

Frequently a matter of debate within later prehistory, the potential significance of the conception and manipulation of space within rural settlements has seen comparatively little consideration in Roman archaeology. This is despite the fact that much of the province was characterised by regions with very conservative patterns of enclosed settlement that had a long history of development during the first millennium BC, if not earlier. Enclosed settlement, in a variety of forms, was a form that remained common to many areas of Roman Britain. While this form emphasised a clear distinction between an inside and outside world, it were paradoxically often internally open and undifferentiated. While multiple houses are often found within these settlements there is rarely any sense of spatial segregation between them. Some areas, as in parts of north-east England and Cumbria, see some change towards more internal division within enclosed settlements in the Roman period, but the wider significance of this to the study of changing attitudes toward intra-communal relations has seen little consideration.

Elsewhere previous traditions of open and enclosed settlement of the Iron Age were generally superseded by complex linear systems in which settlement boundaries are not easily distinguished from the surrounding field enclosures and paddocks of which they were a part. This pattern of increasing internal demarcation and the differentiation of space may reflect changing cultural attitudes towards land or property and/or the spatial specificity of activities and the necessity for them to be located in particular places. What does seem apparent is a trend toward increasing spatial segregation of activity and buildings within settlements that parallels a similar pattern within much domestic architecture of the period (*cf* Taylor 2001).

Trends in rural settlement: continuity and discontinuity, expansion and contraction

A common and seemingly widespread pattern suggested by the survey case studies was one of relative stability or gradual expansion in rural settlement during the 1st and 2nd centuries AD. Many rural settlement loci that had existed before the conquest continued or were gradually restructured during the 1st century AD, often alongside the appearance of new foundations in previously less densely occupied locations in the landscape. Exceptions, where the early years of the Roman province appear to have seen dramatic change, are apparent, as was evident in the west Norfolk case studies, but these seem comparatively rare. The early years of the province seem to have had a less dramatic impact on these aspects of rural settlement than the middle and later years. While many areas still saw significant continuity of settlement and relative stability in numbers, some saw a process of decline or nucleation by the 3rd and 4th centuries. This evidence is, of course, biased towards the east and the Midlands in landscapes of mixed settlement, as fieldwalking is generally not well suited to the pattern of modern land use and the nature of the archaeological record further west and north.

As one way of addressing this issue, resort to the expanding corpus of excavated evidence from these latter areas may help. While absolute numbers of sites investigated are much lower and dating often still a problem, this evidence at least provides some way of checking if the perceived pattern is similar to that seen in the rest of province. As a start, two data sets, from Cornwall and north-west England, are used by way of illustration here (Tables 7.1–7.3).

Analysis of the Cornish excavations shows a very similar pattern to that seen in many of the survey case studies, in which the transition from the late Iron Age to the 1st century AD saw marked continuity of existing settlement alongside evidence for the expansion of settlement through new foundations (Table 7.2). This pattern of continuity and expansion continues and possibly even accelerates into the 2nd century AD, after which settlement dynamics in the region shift. By the 3rd century new settlement appears to have ceased and while continuity was still high the rate of abandonment of existing sites began to rise. This pattern continued into the 4th century, and by the end of the Roman period settlement numbers had seemingly returned to the levels recorded in the late Iron Age.

In the Mersey Basin the dating of excavated sites is more problematic but here again the evidence to date suggests an expansion in settlement numbers in the first two centuries AD (Nevell 2004, 12; Table 7.3). That said, this expansion seems to have taken place within a context of less settlement continuity than often seen elsewhere. Together these patterns may suggest marked restructuring of the rural landscape in this period as local rural society came to terms with the presence of large Roman garrisons at Chester and elsewhere in the region. While the detailed dating of several sites is still in doubt, however, the later Roman period, again, seems to have witnessed a marked decline in settlement back to numbers similar to those seen in the late Iron Age.

Table 7.1 Numbers of excavated rural sites occupied from the late Iron Age to the late Roman period in Cornwall and the Mersey Basin

	Cornwall (after Quinnell 2004)	Mersey Basin (after Nevell 2004)
Late Iron Age	10	11
Early Roman (1st–2nd AD)	19	17
Late Roman (3rd–4th AD)	14	7

Table 7.2 The pattern of continuity, abandonment and new settlement through time for excavated rural sites in Cornwall

	Continued	Abandoned	New foundation
LIA–1st century AD	10	1	4
1st–2nd century AD	12	2	7
2nd–3rd century AD	14	5	0
3rd–4th century AD	9	5	0

Table 7.3 Trends in settlement continuity, abandonment and new foundation through time for excavated sites in the Mersey Basin

	Continued	Abandoned	New foundation
LIA–early Roman	6	3	9
Early–late Roman	8	8	1

In large part these results mirror those noted from the Cumbrian case study in Chapter 6, where the combined excavated and field-survey data for the Solway Plain, though providing poor chronological resolution, suggested a similar increase in settlement numbers in the early Roman period. Higham and Jones (1985; Jones 1999), Matthews (1999), and Nevell (2004) have all suggested this may have been due to the impact of the supply needs of the Roman army on the rural populace in the north-west. The results of other surveys summarised in Chapter 6, however, suggests that this is part of a much wider phenomenon across the province that may well have extended back into the Iron Age in many areas.

Settlement size: nucleation and dispersal

The distinctions seen in settlement morphology are, to some degree, paralleled by variations in the size of rural settlements across the province. On the one hand we have regions of enclosed settlement that consisted overwhelmingly of dispersed farmsteads and small hamlets. Where reasonable chronological evidence is available from excavation, as in the north-western and Cornish examples above, there is little suggestion of a major change in this pattern through the Roman period. In Cornwall, though excavations of cliff castles and hillforts are in fairly short supply, the indications so far are that these sites were either no longer occupied or acted as major nucleated foci by the end of the Iron Age. Within a Roman landscape overwhelmingly characterised by dispersed settlement there is little evidence to suggest that larger enclosed farms/hamlets became any more or less common over time (Table 7.4). This picture of a comparatively stable and 'flat' rural settlement hierarchy (by size at least) throughout the Roman period was also evident in the Solway case study results in Chapter 6.

Nevell (2001; 2004) has suggested a similar situation in the Mersey Basin, but places this within the wider settlement context of contemporary *vici*, roadside settlements, and towns. Noticeable within both the north-western studies and the Cornish material is a gap in the overall size of settlements between the main population of small rural settlements and the smaller number of roadside settlements and *vici*. Rural settlements between around 3ha and 6ha (what we might think of as hamlets or smaller villages) are by and large missing, as are evidently wealthy rural

Table 7.4 The proportion of excavated settlements occupied through time in Cornwall by size

	Small dispersed settlement (<1ha)	Large dispersed settlement (1–2ha)	Total
LIA	8	2	10
1st century AD	12	2	14
2nd century AD	17	2	19
3rd century AD	13	1	14
4th century AD	9	0	9

settlements in the form of villas. This would seem to mirror the evidence from the wider aerial photographic survey evidence discussed in Chapter 6 (Fig 6.23) for the absence of nucleated rural settlements over much of the west and north of the province. While the reasons for this might be varied it is nonetheless tempting to speculate that this pattern might reflect relatively socially autonomous rural communities in these landscapes grouped into comparatively small societies with little overt evidence for social stratification.

Elsewhere, in central, southern, and eastern England, were regions with more mixed patterns of rural settlement. In some we have clear evidence for late Iron Age precursors of the nucleated rural settlements found, but in others the appearance of nucleated settlements was a predominantly mid–late Roman (ie 2nd to 4th century) phenomenon. This rise in nucleated rural settlements is seemingly paralleled by a decline in smaller farmsteads, though the evidence from the surveys in Chapter 6 suggests this was only ever part of the story. Further support for this view comes from more extensive field surveys of the Fenland (Hallam 1970) and by David Hall in Northamptonshire (Taylor 1996). Both Hallam and Hall's work (Fig 7.1) show a gradual but nevertheless significant shift towards nucleated settlement becoming a more significant part of the rural landscape by the 3rd and 4th centuries AD. In Northamptonshire much of this trend built upon pre-existing Iron Age settlement (as was noted with the Raunds survey), while in the wetlands of the Fenland it can be seen to be a result of the transforma-

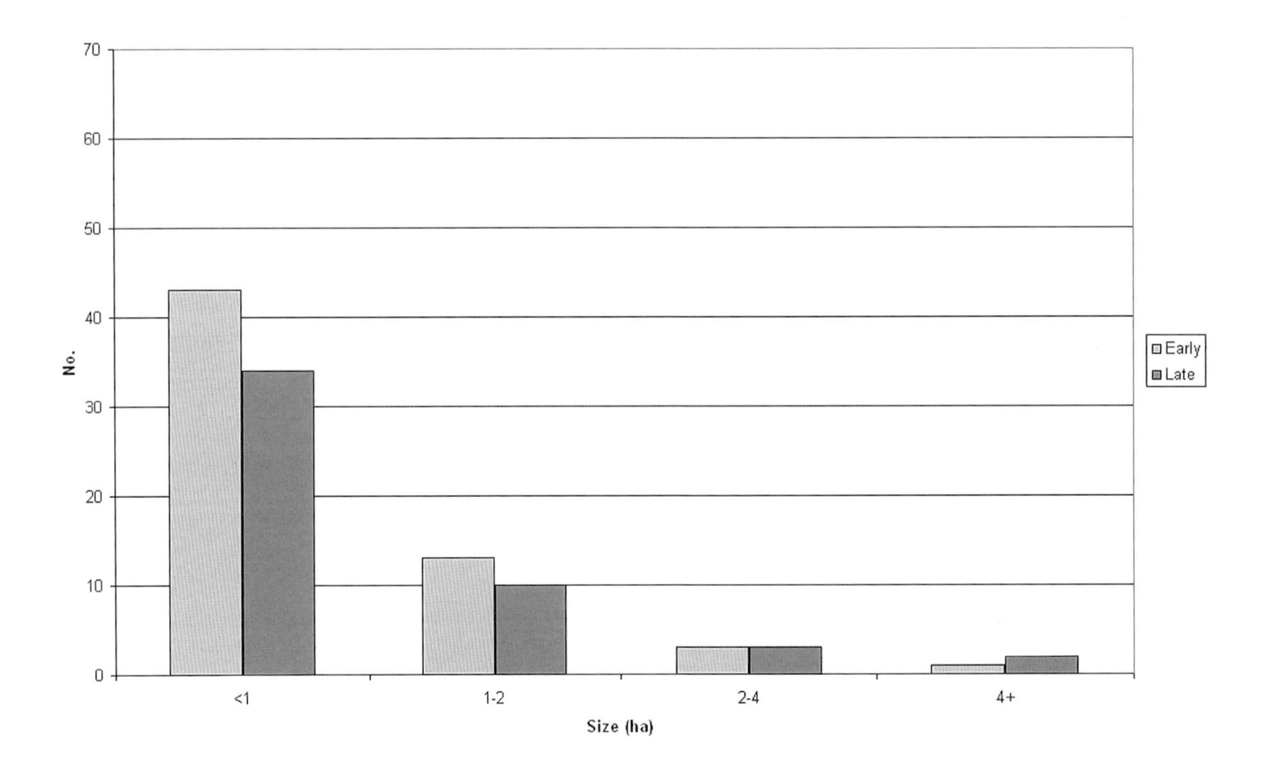

Figure 7.1 Chart showing changing site size in the Northamptonshire extensive survey

tion of a settlement pattern first fully established through significant colonisation of marginal land during the later 1st and 2nd centuries AD (Taylor 2000b).

Together the evidence from these regions suggests that the Roman period saw a shift – sometimes marked but more commonly gradual – to rural populations living in a mixture of larger nucleated settlements (larger hamlets and villages), alongside a declining number of smaller farms. Some of the larger settlements became the centres of later Roman villa estates but equally some of the surviving smaller settlements were prosperous enough to be transformed into small villas from the 2nd century AD. The relationships between these different communities are not easy to access from archaeological evidence alone but do help to show the complex, probably competing, and sometimes very unequal and hierarchical rural social milieu that probably existed within these regions.

Settlement status and architecture

Again here we see two if not more worlds operating within the province. Eastern and central Britain saw the introduction of a wide range of new architectural traditions drawing upon influences and forms from the near continent and occasionally further afield within the empire. Rectilinear traditions of architecture held sway in both timber and stone by the 2nd and 3rd centuries AD (Figs 4.8 and 4.9). Here we see the development of the familiar forms of 'villa' architecture that have been the focus of so much work in Roman Britain, but it should also be realised that this developed within a much more widespread adoption of new forms in timber. Indeed, in many areas of the south and east where local building stone was scarce, such as Norfolk and Suffolk, timber-framed buildings were the norm. In scale and sophistication many, such as building 416 at Great Holts, Farm, Essex (Germany 2003), rival more traditionally identified stone-built villas. In other words, an entirely new architectural vocabulary was being developed over a substantial part of the province, of which the commonly identified villas are just the most obvious and heavily studied part.

In much of the north and west, in contrast, Iron Age traditions of roundhouse architecture and variants upon it held sway for at least the first two centuries AD. Rectilinear traditions rarely extended beyond the confines of the military bases and the major urban foundations, at least until the 3rd and 4th centuries. That is not, however, to suggest that architectural forms here remained stagnant; rather, they developed along their own trajectories with little apparent call on influences from the near continent or even other parts of Britain. In the development of courtyard houses, ovoid or boat-shaped houses, and others in Cornwall, for example, we instead see a seemingly distinctive and more internally driven social discourse.

Settlement and land use: field systems

The broader landscape context of rural settlements demonstrates a very wide range of different and locally distinctive land allotment and land-use patterns. In much of the north and west, and in upland areas of the central Pennine spine of Britain, these systems were commonly characterised by localised settlement-focused patterns of enclosure with significant areas of unbounded land in the wider landscape (Fig 5.2 (1–4)). These landscapes also happen to be those dominated by dispersed patterns of settlement (Fig 7.2). While it is impossible to understand the precise tenurial relationships of such communities on the basis of the archaeological evidence alone, drawing on wider medieval and anthropological parallels we might suggest they constituted rural communities where the immediate enclosed lands around individual farms were held in severalty or in mixed patterns of severalty alongside more complex communal rights, especially in the often unenclosed or partially bounded land beyond. Often these wider upland or wetland areas show little evidence for wholesale restructuring of their field systems during the Roman period, suggesting that gradual or piecemeal change was the norm.

The more extensively and continuously bounded landscapes characteristic of the south and Midlands frequently incorporated long-distance trackways and droves (many of which had developed during the later part of the Iron Age or before) which were now clearly bounded and demarcated, linking rural settlements into extensive networks (Fig 5.2 (5–9)) sometimes over many kilometres. Extensive field systems or demarcated pasture lands often lay between these settlements. While frequently building upon a much older

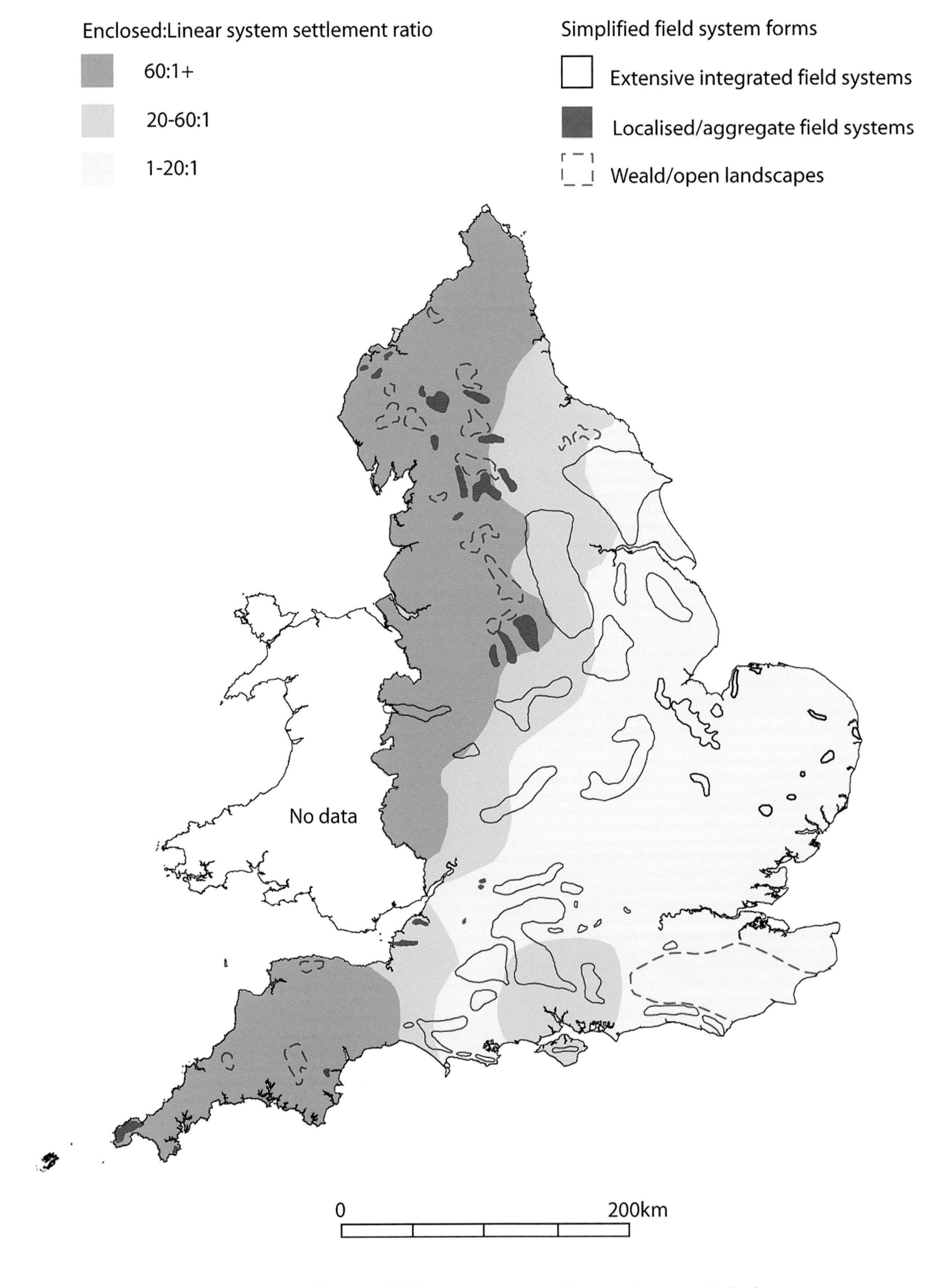

Figure 7.2 Simplified map of field systems against settlement ratios across England

landscape structure, individual field systems and settlements themselves were often restructured into new layouts and it is surely no coincidence that these landscapes also see the rise of complex hierarchical rural settlement patterns (Fig 7.2). While the end results of this process were many and varied across different landscapes, one thing they often appear to have in common is the creation of complex patchworks of land allotment that were integrated via trackways and roads to allow use of different parts of the landscape for more specialised agricultural production and, critically, the infrastructure to transport any surpluses produced.

Rural landscapes that saw wholesale reorganisation in the aftermath of the conquest were comparatively rare but have been found predominantly in formerly marginal lands (especially wetlands such as the Wentlooge levels) and, at more local scale, in the vicinity of emerging urban foci, although this restructuring never approached the kinds of centuriated or fundamentally restructured landscape seen around some urban centres on the continent.

Settlement and agriculture

The study of agricultural practice itself was not a focus of this study although it is clearly a critical element in understanding processes of wider social change in the countryside of Roman Britain. Even so, it is worth at least suggesting some indications of the changes at work. In the bounded landscapes of mixed rural settlement across much of central and southern England we see evidence for the development of agricultural production strategies designed to create a significant surplus, indicated by:

- the development of a specialised architecture and technology of storage and crop processing, such as mills, granaries, and corn driers (Fig 7.3);
- the continued extension of cultivation onto previously uncultivated lands and palynological evidence for continued pressure on surviving woodland;
- the drainage and management of wetlands, noted above, that opened up formerly marginal land to more systematic agricultural exploitation;
- evidence for an increasing emphasis on arable cultivation linked to cattle husbandry as part of what we might call a 'corn and cattle' culture, in which cattle became a larger proportion of domestic farm animals and were valued both as a resource in their own right and as a major source of traction for cultivation;
- the introduction of exotica, especially certain fruits and legumes.

Similar evidence for these changes in the regions of dispersed enclosed settlement is generally lacking. In the case of the botanical and zoological evidence to support the analysis of the last two points above this is in large part a problem of survival and the comparative lack of excavation, but in the context of the remaining trends is not. In these regions there is scant evidence for such things as so-called corn driers (taken as an indication of the specialised processing of a significant arable surplus: Fig 7.3) or attempts to drain or 'improve' wetlands for agricultural use.

Rural industry

There is, again, a major contrast in our evidence for rural industry across the province. In the south and east the later 1st to 2nd centuries saw the emergence of many large and sometimes specialised industries at many locations. Especially evident is the expansion of pottery, iron, and salt industries that sometimes had late Iron Age precursors (Fig 7.4). While all of these industries involved mineral extraction there is little overt evidence for imperial control of the process itself, which was instead located within the working lives of local rural (and sometimes urban) populations. Interestingly, we do not see the development of these industries in the west and north on anything like the same scale, even though in some cases the resources themselves are widely available in these regions. Why, for example, do we see the extraordinary situation of the significant transport of Black Burnished Ware pottery from Dorset to Hadrian's Wall rather than the establishment on a significant scale of more localised production in, say, Cheshire?

In the north and west craft and industry in the Roman period were still comparatively localised,

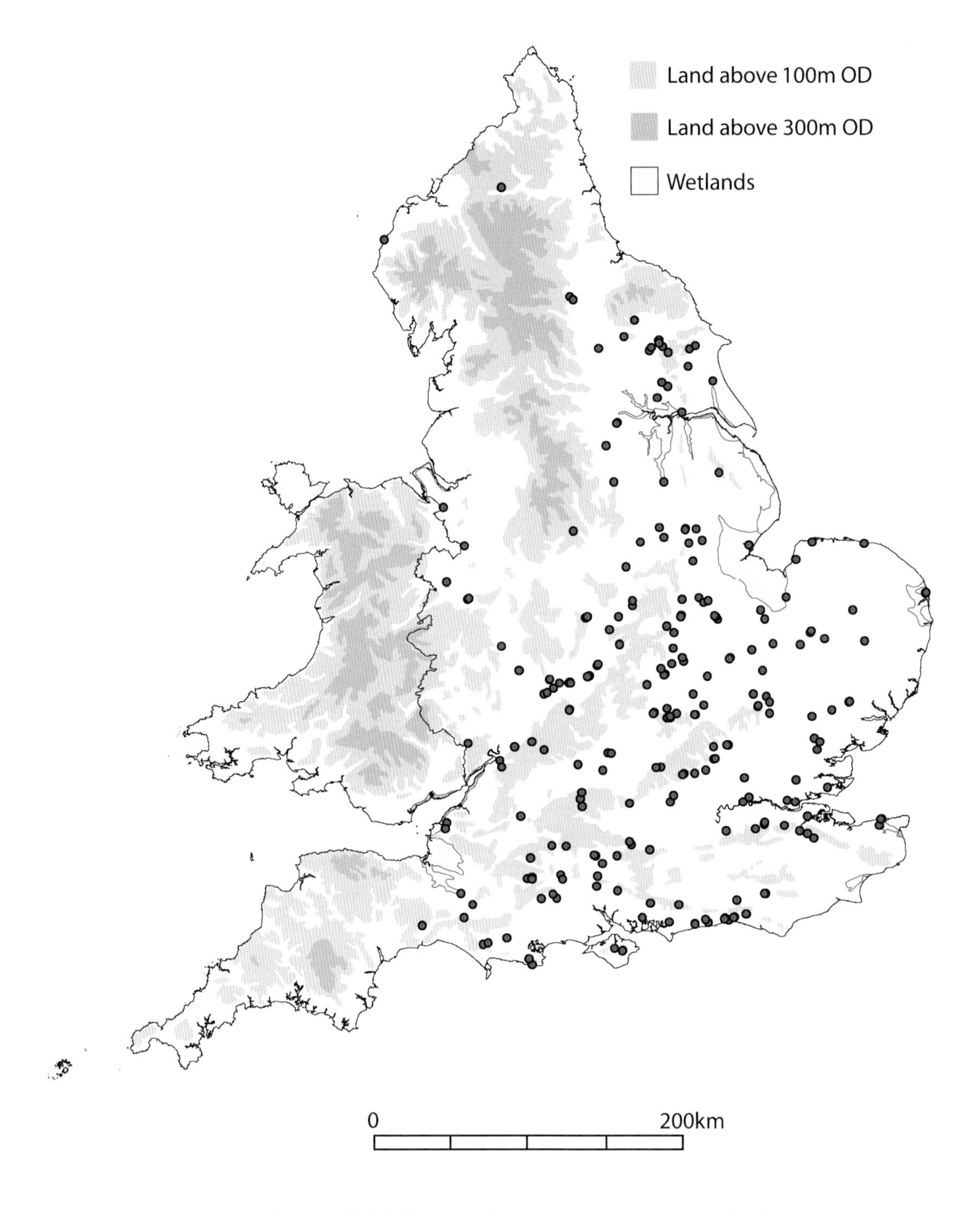

Figure 7.3 National distribution map of Roman corn driers recorded in the survey

dispersed and small-scale, or absent except in the few instances where we have seemingly deliberate foundations for the comparatively short-term supply of pottery to existing garrisons/towns, as at Wilderspool. When we encounter evidence for industries in this region they are more obviously involved with the extraction of mineral wealth, such as gold, lead, and silver, and they were seemingly carried out with more overt state intervention in the form of military communities and/or the establishment of associated specialised settlements, as at Dolaucothi and Charterhouse. Here, the involvement of wider rural communities in the vicinity of these industries is far less obvious (other than possibly as being on the end of acts of land appropriation or as a supply of labour for the mines and the local industrial centres themselves). Interestingly, there is little evidence in these cases for the development of wider local rural landscapes of craft specialisation associated with the specific materials.

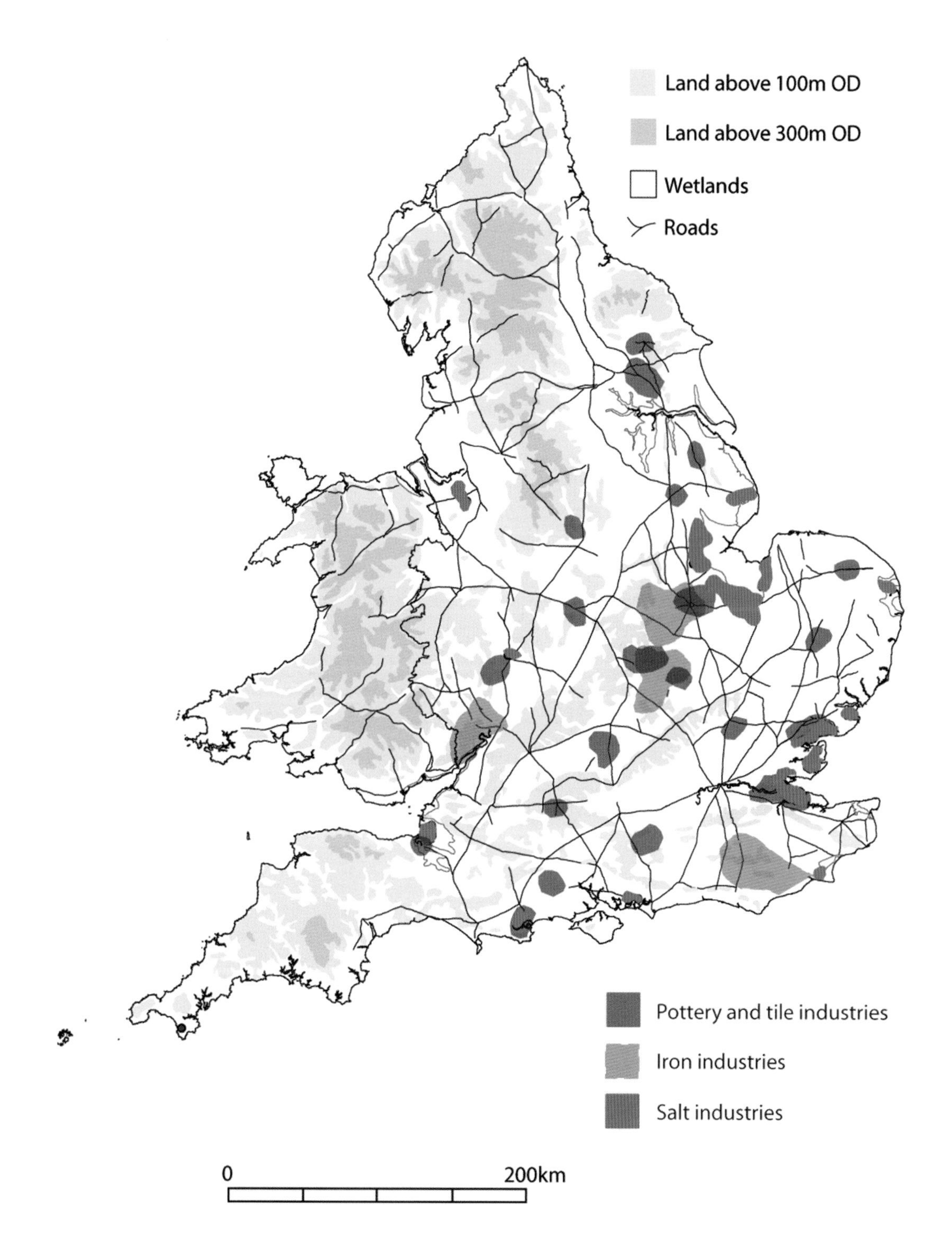

Figure 7.4 Summary map showing main landscapes of rural industry in Roman Britain

Rural economic integration and the rise of towns

A final parallel to note is the striking link between the development and extent of the complex hierarchical rural landscapes of southern and eastern England noted here and the evidence we have for both major and minor urban foci across the province. While major towns are comparatively rare but spaced widely across the province, probably reflecting the major geopolitical aims of the imperial and provincial administration, the evidence for the smaller market centres, religious foci, and industrial settlements that develop around them is far more irregular. Their distribution tends to parallel that of the mixed rural settlement landscape, and they are comparatively rare beyond this zone. In the north-west, for example, while such sites are found as far north as the Mersey, they rarely survive beyond unless as *vici* tied directly to the fortunes of their neighbouring military communities. It is, I would suggest, reasonable to argue that while the presence and survival of the major towns to some degree reflected the imperial and provincial need for governance and at least some theatre for 'proper' social life, the so-called small towns are a better indication of the development of an economy in which rural surplus production could be mobilised for exchange. In effect they are one indicator of the degree to which rural societies in different parts of the province were integrating with wider provincial economic and social life.

The nature of urbanism in Roman Britain, and its form, as John Creighton has noted (2006), were very much influenced by the experiences and desires of the 'stakeholders' in it. Their visions of urban life varied as much as ours, but for such institutions to develop and be sustained it is imperative to remember that a large proportion of those 'stakeholders', especially away from the small number of major urban centres, were likely to have been indigenous Britons whose roots had been firmly based within rural societies before the conquest, and continued to be after. The choices they made and the specific rural social and economic context within which they were based will have had a fundamental effect on whether urban life and the development of a cash-orientated market for rural surpluses, for example, ever had a chance to thrive.

Ultimately this work has shown that the picture emerging from the huge range of evidence from rural contexts potentially lies at the heart of our whole understanding of the nature of the Roman province. Rural communities and their agricultural landscapes were not a background to the development of towns, to the rise of villas or even to the ultimate location of military garrisons and frontiers, but were integral to them. Understanding the chronology of these developments and their local manifestations within a national context should serve to help us understand the nature of *Britannia* as a province of the Roman Empire.

It is clear that Britain, both before and after the Roman conquest, was a very diverse place. Here I have tended to draw out major distinctions between what we might think of as two Roman Britains, but on closer inspection, of course, we can see more. It is important, therefore, that we try to get a better understanding of this 'cultural bricolage', as Terrenato memorably called it, as it provides us with insights into why Britain within the Roman Empire developed in the way it did.

Bibliography

Adams, C & Laurence, R, 2001 *Travel and geography in the Roman Empire*. London: Routledge

Alcock, S, 1993 *Graecia Capta: the landscapes of Roman Greece*. Cambridge: Cambridge University Press

Allen, T G, Darvill, T C, Green, L S & Jones, M U, 1993 *Excavations at Roughground Farm, Lechlade, Gloucestershire: a prehistoric and Roman landscape*, Thames Valley Landscapes **1**. Oxford: Oxford University Committee for Archaeology for Oxford Archaeological Unit

Annis, R, 1996 Bonny Grove Farm and Dixon's Bank: two Romano-British settlement sites in Cleveland, *Durham Archaeol J*, **12**, 41–60

Applebaum, S, 1972 Roman Britain, in H P R Finberg (ed) *The agrarian history of England and Wales*. Cambridge: Cambridge University Press, 3–277

Aston, M & Iles, R, 1987 *The archaeology of Avon: a review from the Neolithic to the Middle Ages*. Bristol: County of Avon, Public Relations and Publicity Department

ASUD, 2000 Quarry Farm, Ingleby Barwick, Stockton-on-Tees. Unpubl report, Durham University

Baker, A, 1992 Air Archaeology in the Valley of the River Severn. Unpubl PhD thesis, University of Southampton

Baker, S, 2002 Prehistoric and Romano-British landscapes at little Whittenham and Long Whittenham, Oxfordshire, *Oxoniensia*, **67**, 1–28

Barber, L, Gardiner, M & Rudling, D, 2002 Excavations at Eastwick Barn, in D Rudling (ed) *Downland settlement and land-use, the archaeology of the Brighton bypass*. London: Archetype Publications, 107–40

Barnatt, J & Smith, K, 1997 *Peak District: landscapes through time*. London: Batsford

Barrett, J C, 1997 Romanisation: a critical comment, in D Mattingly (ed) *Dialogues in Roman imperialism: power, discourse and discrepant experience in the Roman Empire. J Roman Archaeol*, Supplement **23**, 51–64

Barrett, J C, Bradley, R & Hall, M (eds), 1991 *Papers on the prehistoric archaeology of Cranborne Chase*. Oxford: Oxbow Books

Basford, H V, 1980 *The Vectis Report: a survey of Isle of Wight archaeology*. Newport: Isle of Wight County Council

Bassett, S R, 1990 The Roman and medieval landscape of Wroxeter, in P Barker (ed) *From Roman Viroconium to medieval Wroxeter*. Worcester: West Mercian Archaeological Consultants, 10–12

Bedwin, O, 1983 The development of prehistoric settlement on the West Sussex coastal plain, *Sussex Archaeol Collect*, **121**, 31–44

Bedwin, O & Pitts, M, 1978 Excavation of an Iron Age settlement at North Bersted, Bognor Regis, West Sussex, 1975–76, *Sussex Archaeol Collect*, **116**, 293–346

Bedwin, O & Place, C, 1995 Late Iron Age and Romano-British occupation at Ounces Barn, Boxgrove, West Sussex: excavations 1982–83, *Sussex Archaeol Collect*, **133**, 45–101

Bell, A, Gurney, D & Healey, H, 1999 *Lincolnshire salterns: excavations at Helpringham, Holbeach St Johns and Bicker Haven*, East Anglian Archaeology **89**. Heckington: Heritage Trust of Lincolnshire

Bell, M, 1990 *Brean Down excavations 1983–1987*. London: HBMCE

Benson, M & Miles, D, 1974 *The upper Thames valley: an archaeological survey of the river gravels*, Oxfordshire Archaeological Unit **2**. Oxford: Oxfordshire Archaeological Unit

Bevan, B, 2003 The upper Derwent: long-term landscape archaeology in the Peak District. Unpubl PhD thesis, Department of Archaeology, University of Sheffield

Bevan, B, 2005 Peaks Romana: the Peak District Romano-British Rural Upland Settlement Survey, 1998–2000, *Derbyshire Archaeol J*, **125**, 26–58

Bewley, R H, 1986 Survey and excavation in the Solway Plain, Cumbria, *Trans Cumberland Westmorland Antiq Archaeol Soc*, Series 2, **86**, 20–39

Bewley, R H, 1992 Excavations on two crop-mark sites in the Solway Plain, Cumbria. Ewanrigg settlement and Swarthy Hill 1986–1988, *Trans Cumberland Westmorland Antiq Archaeol Soc*, Series 2, **92**, 23–47

Bewley, R H, 1993 Survey and excavation at a crop-mark enclosure, Plasketlands, Cumbria, *Trans Cumberland Westmorland Antiq Archaeol Soc*, Series 2, **93**, 1–18

Bewley, R H, 1994 *Prehistoric and Romano-British settlement in the Solway Plain, Cumbria*. Oxford: Oxbow Books

Bewley, R H, 1995 A national mapping programme for England. *Forschungen zur Archeologie im Land Brandenburg*, **3**, 83–92

Bewley, R H (ed), 1998 *Lincolnshire's archaeology from the air*, Occasional Papers in Lincolnshire History and Archaeology **11**. Lincoln: The Society for Lincolnshire History and Archaeology

Bird, D G, 1996 The London region in the Roman period, in J Bird, M Hassall & H Sheldon (eds) *Interpreting Roman London: papers in memory of Hugh Chapman*. Oxford: Oxbow Books, 217–32

Bird, D G, 2000 The environs of Londinium: roads, roadside settlements and the countryside, in I Haynes, H Sheldon & L Hannington (eds) *London under ground: the archaeology of a city*. Oxford: Oxbow Books, 151–74

Bird, D G, 2004 Surrey in the Roman period: a survey of recent discoveries, in J Cotton, G Crocker & A Graham (eds) *Aspects of Archaeology and History in Surrey*. Guildford: Surrey Archaeological Society, 65–76

Boutwood, Y, 1998 The physical landscape of Lincolnshire, in R Bewley (ed) 1998, 23–8

Bowden, M, Ford, S & Mees, G, 1993 The date of the ancient fields on the Berkshire Downs, *Berkshire Archaeol J*, **74**, 109–33

Bowen, H C & Fowler, P J, 1978 *Early land allotment*, BAR Brit Ser **48**. Oxford: British Archaeological Reports

Bradley, R, 1984 *The social foundations of prehistoric Britain*. London: Longman

Bradley, R, Entwhistle, R & Raymond, F, 1994 *Prehistoric land divisions on Salisbury Plain*. London: English Heritage

Branigan, K, 1977 *Gatcombe: the excavation and study of a Romano-British villa estate, 1967–1976*, BAR Brit ser **44**. Oxford: British Archaeological Reports

Branigan, K, 1985 *The Catuvellauni*. Gloucester: Sutton

Branigan, K, 1991 Civilian development in a military zone: the Peak AD43–400, in R Hodges & K Smith (eds) *Recent developments in the archaeology of the Peak District*. Sheffield: Sheffield University Press, 57–68

Branigan, K & Miles, D (eds), 1988 *The economies of Romano-British villas*. Sheffield: Department of Archaeology and Prehistory, University of Sheffield

Burnham, B C, Collis, J, Dobinson, C, Haselgrove, C & Jones, M, 2001 Themes for urban research, c.100 BC to AD 200, in S James & M Millett (eds) 2001, 67–76

Carter, A, 1998 The contribution of aerial survey, in R Bewley (ed) 1998, 96–104

Chadwick, A, 1999 Digging ditches but missing riches? Ways into the Iron Age and Romano-British cropmark landscapes of the north midlands, in B Bevan (ed) *Northern exposure: interpretative devolution and the Iron Ages in Britain*. Leicester: School of Archaeological Studies, University of Leicester, 149–72

Champion, T, 2007 Settlement in Kent from 1500 to 300 BC, in C Haselgrove & R Pope (eds) 2007, 293–305

Chapman, H, Fenwick, H, Head, R, Fletcher, W & Lillie, M, 1999 The archaeological survey of the rivers Aire, Ouse, Wharfe and Derwent, in R van de Noort & S Ellis (eds) *Wetland heritage of the Vale of York, an archaeological survey*. Kingston upon Hull: University of Hull, 205–41

Clarke, S, 1990 The social significance of villa architecture in Celtic north west Europe, *Oxford J Archaeol*, **9**, 337–53

Clarke, S, 1998 Social change and architectural diversity in Roman period Britain, in C Forcey, J Hawthorne & R Witcher (eds) *TRAC97: The seventh theoretical Roman archaeology conference 1997*. Oxford: Oxbow Books, 28–41

Clarke, S, 1999 Contact, architectural symbolism and the negotiation of cultural identity in the military zone, in P Baker, C Forcey, S Jundi & R Witcher (eds) *TRAC98: proceedings of the eighth annual theoretical Roman archaeology conference, Leicester 1998*. Oxford: Oxbow Books, 36–45

Cleere, H & Crossley, D, 1985 *The iron industry of the Weald*. Leicester: Leicester University Press

Cleverdon, F, 1995 Survey and excavation in the Manifold valley, *Staffordshire Archaeol Stud*, **5**, 12–36

Coates, G, 2002 *A prehistoric and Romano-British landscape. Excavations at Whitemoor Haye Quarry, Staffordshire, 1997–1999*, BAR Brit Ser **340**. Oxford: British Archaeological Reports

Coggins, D, 1986a *Upper Teesdale: the archaeology of a north Pennine valley*, BAR Brit Ser **150**. Oxford: British Archaeological Reports

Coggins, D, 1986b Early settlement in Upper Teesdale, in T G Manby & P Turnbull (eds) *Archaeology in the Pennines. Studies in honour of Arthur Raistrick*, BAR Brit Ser **158**. Oxford: British Archaeological Reports, 195–203

Collingwood, R G & Richmond, I A, 1969 *The archaeology of Roman Britain*. London: Methuen

Condliffe, J, 2004 The evolution of a south east Leicestershire landscape. Unpubl MA dissertation, University of Leicester

Cornell, T J & Lomas, K (eds), 1994 *Urban society in Roman Italy*. London: UCL Press

Corney, M, 1989 Multiple ditch systems and Late Iron Age settlement in central Wessex, in M Bowden, D Mackay & P Topping (eds) *From Cornwall to Caithness: some aspects of British field archaeology. Papers presented to Norman V Quinnell*, BAR Brit Ser **209**. Oxford: British Archaeological Reports, 111–28

Corney, M, 2000 Characterising the landscape of Roman Britain, in D Hooke (ed) *Landscape, the richest historical record*, Soc Landscape Stud Suppl Ser **1**.

Amesbury: Society for Landscape Studies, 33–45
Corney, M, 2001 The Romano-British nucleated settlements of Wiltshire, in P Ellis (ed) *Roman Wiltshire and after. Papers in honour of Ken Annable*. Devizes: Wiltshire Archaeological and Natural History Society, 5–38
Cowell, R W & Philpott, R A, 2000 *Prehistoric, Romano-British and medieval settlement in lowland North West England*. Liverpool: National Museums and Galleries on Merseyside
Crawford, G M, 1982 Excavations at Wasperton: second interim report, *W Midlands Archaeol*, **25**, 31–44
Crawford, G M, 1983 Excavations at Wasperton: third interim report, *W Midlands Archaeol*, **26**, 15–28
Crawford, G M, 1984 Excavations at Wasperton: fourth interim report, *W Midlands Archaeol*, **27**, 44–53
Creighton, J, 2000 *Coins and power in Late Iron Age Britain*. Cambridge: Cambridge University Press
Creighton, J, 2006 *Britannia: the Creation of a Roman province*. Abingdon: Routledge.
Crowson, A, Lane, T & Reeve, J (eds), 2000 *Fenland Management Project excavations 1991–1995*, Lincolnshire Archaeology and Heritage Reports Series **3**. Sleaford: Heritage Trust of Lincolnshire
Crutchley, S, 2000 Salisbury Plain Training Area. A report for the National Mapping Programme, Aerial Survey Reports AER/3/2000. Swindon: English Heritage internal report
Cunliffe, B W, 1973 Chalton, Hants: the evolution of a landscape, *Antiq J*, **53**, 173–90
Cunliffe, B W, 1977 The Romano-British village at Chalton, *Proc Hampshire Fld Club and Archaeol Soc*, **33**, 45–67
Cunliffe, B W, 1991 *Iron Age communities in Britain*. London: Routledge
Cunliffe, B W, 2000 *The Danebury Environs Programme: the prehistory of a Wessex landscape. Volume 1, Introduction*. Oxford: English Heritage and Oxford University Committee for Archaeology
Cunliffe, B W, 2003a Roman Danebury, *Curr Archaeol*, **188**, 344–51
Cunliffe, B W, 2003b *The Danebury Environs Roman Project 7. Rowbury Farm excavations 2003, interim report*. Oxford: Danebury Trust, Institute of Archaeology
Cunliffe, B W, 2004 *Flint Farm 2004*. Oxford: Danebury Trust, Institute of Archaeology
Cunliffe, B W & Poole, C, 2000a *The Danebury Environs Programme: the prehistory of a Wessex landscape. Volume 2, Part 1, Woolbury and Stockbridge Down, Stockbridge, Hants, 1989*. Oxford: Institute of Archaeology
Cunliffe, B W & Poole, C, 2000b *The Danebury Environs Programme: the prehistory of a Wessex landscape. Volume 2, Part 5, Nettlebank Copse, Wherwell, Hants, 1993*. Oxford: Institute of Archaeology
Dark, K & Dark P, 1997 *The landscape of Roman Britain*. Stroud: Sutton
Davenport, C, 2003 The late pre-Roman Iron Age of the West Sussex coastal plain: continuity or change?, in D Rudling (ed) *The archaeology of Sussex to AD2000*. Kings Lynn: Heritage Marketing and Publications, 101–10
Davison, A, 1990 The *Evolution of Settlement in three parishes in South-East Norfolk*. East Anglian Archaeology **49**. Norwich: Norfolk Archaeoloy Unit.
Davison, A, 2001 The archaeology of the parish of West Acre. Part 1: field survey evidence, *Norfolk Archaeol*, **43.4**, 202–21
Deegan, A, 1999 *The Nottinghamshire Mapping Project: a report for the National Mapping Programme*. Swindon: RCHME
Deegan, A, 2001 Aerial photographs, in I Roberts *et al* 2001, 13–28
Deegan, A, forthcoming *The Northamptonshire Mapping Project*
Didsbury, P, 1990 Exploitation in the Lower Hull Valley in the Roman period, in S Ellis & D Crowther (eds) *Humber perspectives: a region through the ages*. Kingston upon Hull: University of Hull, 199–210
Dobney, K, 2001 A place at the table: the role of vertebrate zooarchaeology within a Roman research agenda, in S James & M Millett (eds) 2001, 46–59
Drewett, P, Rudling, D & Gardiner, M, 1988 *The South East to AD1000*. London: Longman
Drury, P, 1976 Braintree: excavations and research 1971–6, *Essex Archaeol Hist*, **8**, 1–141
Duncan-Jones, R, 1982 *The economy of the Roman Empire: quantitative studies*. Cambridge: Cambridge University Press
Eddison, J, 2000 *Romney Marsh: survival on a frontier*. Stroud: Tempus
Edwards, D, 1978 Air photography and early fields, in H C Bowen & P J Fowler (eds) 1978, 99–102
Ellis, P, 1984 *Catsgore 1979, further excavation of the Romano-British village*, Western Archaeological Trust Excavation Monograph **7**. Gloucester: Alan Sutton for the Western Archaeological Trust
Ellis, P, Evans, J, Hannaford, H, Hughes, G & Jones, A, 1994 Excavations in the Wroxeter Hinterland 1988–1990: the archaeology of the A5/A49 Shrewsbury bypass, *Trans Shropshire Archaeol Hist Soc*, **69**, 1–119
Elsdon, S M, 1997 *Old Sleaford revealed*, Oxbow Monograph **91**. Oxford: Oxbow Books
Entwhistle, R, Fulford, M & Raymond, F, 1993 *Salisbury Plain Project 1992–93*. Reading: University of Reading
Entwhistle, R, Fulford, M & Raymond, F, 1994 *Salisbury Plain Project 1993–94*. Reading: University of Reading

Evans, C, 2003 *Power and island communities. Excavations at the Wardy Hill Ringwork, Coveney, Ely*, East Anglian Archaeology **103**. Cambridge: Cambridge Archaeological Unit

Fenner, V, 1994 The Thames Valley Project: a report for the National Mapping Programme. Swindon: RCHME internal report

Fenton-Thomas, C, 2003 *Late prehistoric and early historic landscapes on the Yorkshire chalk*, BAR Brit Ser **350**, Oxford: Archaeopress

Fenwick, H, Chapman, H, Head, R & Lillie, M, 1998 The archaeological survey of the Lower Trent Valley and Winterton Beck, in R van de Noort & S Ellis (eds) *Wetland heritage of the Ancholme and lower Trent valleys, an archaeological survey*. Kingston upon Hull: Humber Wetlands Project, Centre for Wetland Archaeology, University of Hull, 143–97

Fincham, G, 2002 *Landscapes of imperialism: Roman and native interaction in the East Anglian Fenland*, BAR Brit Ser **338**. Oxford: Archaeopress

Fitzpatrick, A P, Butterworth, C A & Grove, J, 1999 *Prehistoric and Roman sites in East Devon: the A30 Honiton to Exeter improvement DBFO, 1996–9*, Wessex Archaeology Report **16**. Salisbury: Trust for Wessex Archaeology

Fleming, A, 1988 *The Dartmoor reaves: investigating prehistoric land divisions*. London: Batsford

Fleming, A, 1998 *Swaledale: valley of the wild river*. Edinburgh: Edinburgh University Press

Ford, S, 1987 *East Berkshire archaeological survey*. Reading: Department of Highways and Planning, Berkshire County Council

Ford, S & Hazell, A, 1991 Prehistoric, Roman and Anglo-Saxon settlement patterns at North Stoke, Oxfordshire, *Oxoniensia*, **54**, 7–23

Fowler, P J, 1978 Pre-medieval fields in the Bristol region, in H C Bowen & P J Fowler (eds) 1978, 29–48

Fowler, P J, 1981 Later prehistory, in S Piggott (ed) *The agrarian history of England and Wales. Volume 1*. Cambridge: Cambridge University Press, 63–289

Fowler, P, 2000 *Landscape plotted and pieced: landscape history and local archaeology in Fyfield and Overton, Wiltshire*. London: Society of Antiquaries

Fowler, P & Blackwell, I, 1998 *The land of Lettice Sweetapple : an English countryside explored*. Stroud: Tempus

Francis, P D & Slater, D S, 1990 A record of vegetation and land use change from upland peat deposits on Exmoor, part 2: Hoar Moor, *Somerset Archaeol Natur Hist*, 134, 1–25

Francis, P D & Slater, D S, 1992 A record of vegetation and land use change from upland peat deposits on Exmoor, part 3: Codsend Moor, *Somerset Archaeol Natur Hist*, 136, 9–28

Francovich, R & Patterson, H (eds), 2000 *Extracting meaning from ploughsoil assemblages*. The archaeology of Mediterranean landscapes **5**. Oxford: Oxbow Books

Freeman, P, 1993 'Romanisation' and Roman material culture. Review of M Millett *The Romanisation of Britain*. *J Roman Archaeol*, **6**, 438–45

Frodsham, P (ed), 2004 *Archaeology in Northumberland National Park*, CBA Res Rep **136**. York: Council for British Archaeology

Fulford, M, 1989 The economy of Roman Britain, in M Todd (ed) *Research on Roman Britain 1960–89*, Britannia Monograph Series **11**. London: Society for the Promotion of Roman Studies, 175–201

Fulford, M G, Powell, A B, Entwhistle, R & Raymond, F, 2006 *Iron Age and Romano-British settlements and landscapes of Salisbury Plain*, Wessex Archaeology Report **20**. Salisbury: Wessex Archaeology

Fyfe, R M, Brown, A G & Rippon, S J, 2004 Characterising the late prehistoric, 'Romano-British' and medieval landscape, and dating the emergence of a regionally distinct agricultural system in South West Britain, *J Archaeol Sci*, **31**, 1699–714

Gaffney, V & Tingle, M, 1989 *The Maddle Farm Project: an integrated survey of prehistoric and Roman landscapes on the Berkshire Downs*, BAR Brit Ser **200**. Oxford: British Archaeological Reports

Gaffney, V L, White, R H & Buteux, S T E, forthcoming *Wroxeter, the Cornovii and the urban process: final work on the Wroxeter Hinterland Project and Wroxeter Hinterlands Survey, 1994–1999*

Gallant, L, Luxton, N & Collman, M, 1985 Ancient fields on the South Devon limestone plateau, *Devon Archaeol Soc Proc*, **43**, 23–37

Gardiner, M, 1990 The archaeology of the Weald – a survey and a review, *Sussex Archaeol Collect*, **128**, 33–53

Garnsey, P & Saller, R, 1987 *The Roman Empire: economy, society and culture*. London: Duckworth

Garton, D, 1987 Dunston's clump and the brickwork plan field systems at Babworth, Nottinghamshire: excavations 1981, *Trans Thoroton Soc Nottinghamshire*, **91**, 16–73

Garton, D, 2002 Walking fields in South Muskham and its implications for Romano-British cropmark landscapes in Nottinghamshire, *Trans Thoroton Soc Nottinghamshire*, **106**, 17–39

Gates, T, 1975 *The middle Thames valley: an archaeological survey of the river gravels*, Berkshire Archaeological Committee Publications **1**. Reading: Berkshire Archaeological Committee

Gates, T, 2000 The archaeology of the College Valley estate: an air photographic survey. Unpubl report, Northumberland National Park

Gates, T, 2004a Flying on the frontier. Recent archaeological air photography in the Hadrian's Wall corridor, in P Frodsham (ed) 2004, 236–45

Gates, T, 2004b The Hadrian's Wall landscape from Chesters to Greenhead: An air photographic survey. Unpubl report, Northumberland National Park

Gerrard, S, 1997 *Book of Dartmoor: landscapes through time*. London: Batsford

Germany, M, 2003 *Excavations at Great Holts Farm, Boreham, Essex, 1992–94*, East Anglian Archaeology **105**. Chelmsford: Essex County Council

Gerrard, C, forthcoming *The Shapwick Project, Somerset. A rural landscape explored*

Gingell, C J, 1992 The *Marlborough Downs: A Later Bronze Age Landscape and its Origins*. Wiltshire Archaeol Natur Hist Soc Monograph **1**. Stroud: Sutton

Graham, A & Newman, C, 1993 Recent excavations of Iron Age and Romano-British enclosures in the Avon Valley, Wiltshire, *Wiltshire Archaeol Natur Hist Mag*, **86**, 8–57

Grahame, M, 1998 Redefining Romanization: material culture and the question of social continuity in Roman Britain, in C Forcey, J Hawthorne & R Witcher (eds) *TRAC97: The seventh theoretical Roman archaeology conference 1997*. Oxford: Oxbow Books, 1–10

Grant, A, 1989 Animals in Roman Britain, in M Todd (ed) *Research on Roman Britain 1960–89*, Britannia Monograph Series **11**. London: Society for the Promotion of Roman Studies, 135–46

Gregory, R, 2001 Living on the frontier: Iron Age–Roman transitions in South-West Scotland, in N J Higham (ed) *Archaeology of the Roman Empire: a tribute to the life and works of Professor Barri Jones*. BAR Int Ser **940**, Oxford: Archaeopress, 35–49

Griffith, F, 1994 Changing perceptions of the context of prehistoric Dartmoor, *Devon Archaeol Soc Proc*, **52**, 85–99

Hadman, J A, 1978 Aisled buildings in Roman Britain, in M Todd (ed) 1978, 187–96

Halkon, P & Millett, M (eds), 1999 *Rural settlement and industry: studies in the Iron Age and Roman archaeology of lowland East Yorkshire*, Yorkshire Archaeology Monograph **4**. Leeds: Yorkshire Archaeology Society

Hall, D N, 1987 *The Fenland Project No. 2: fenland landscapes and settlement between Peterborough and March*, East Anglian Archaeology **35**. Cambridge: Fenland Project Committee

Hall, D N, 1992 *The Fenland Project No. 6: the south-western Cambridgeshire fenlands*, East Anglian Archaeology **56**. Cambridge: Cambridgeshire Archaeological Committee

Hall, D N, 1996 *The Fenland Project No. 10: Cambridgeshire survey, the Isle of Ely and Wisbech*, East Anglian Archaeology **79**. Cambridge: Cambridgeshire Archaeological Committee

Hall, D N & Coles, J, 1994 *Fenland survey. An essay in landscape and persistence*. London: English Heritage

Hallam, S, 1970 Settlement around the Wash, in C W Phillips (ed) 1970, 22–113

Hamerow, H, 2002 *Early medieval settlements: the archaeology of rural communities in northwest Europe, 400–900*. Oxford: Oxford University Press

Hanworth, R, 1987 The Iron Age in Surrey, in J Bird & D G Bird (eds) *The archaeology of Surrey to AD1540*. Guildford: Surrey Archaeological Society, 139–64

Harding, D W, 1979 Air survey in the Tyne-Tees Region, 1969–1979, in N J Higham (ed) *The changing past. Some recent work in the archaeology of Northern England*. Manchester: Department of Extra-Mural Studies, University of Manchester, 21–30

Harrison, S, 2002 Open fields and earlier landscapes: six parishes in south-east Cambridgeshire, *Landscapes*, **3.1**, 35–54

Hartley, B R, 1993 The Roman Period, AD70–410, in D A Spratt (ed) *Prehistoric and Roman Archaeology of North-East Yorkshire*, CBA Res Rep **87**. London: Council for British Archaeology, 155–66

Haselgrove, C C, 1997 Iron Age brooch deposition and chronology, in A Gwilt & C Haselgrove (eds) *Reconstructing Iron Age societies*. Oxford: Oxbow Books, 51–72

Haselgrove, C C, 2004 Society and polity in late Iron Age Britain, in M Todd (ed) *A Companion to Roman Britain*. Oxford: Blackwell, 12–29

Haselgrove, C C & Moore, T (eds), 2007 *The late Iron Age in Britain and beyond*. Oxford: Oxbow Books

Haselgrove, C C, Millett, M & Smith, I (eds), 1985 *Archaeology from the ploughsoil. Studies in the collection and interpretation of field survey data*. Sheffield: J R Collis

Haselgrove, C C & Pope, R (eds), 2007 *The earlier Iron Age in Britain and the near Continent*. Oxford: Oxbow Books

Hayfield, C, 1987 *Wharram: a study of settlement on the Yorkshire Wolds. Volume 5, an archaeological survey of the parish of Wharram Percy, East Yorkshire*, BAR Brit Ser **172**. Oxford: British Archaeological Reports

Henig, M, 2000 *Roman Oxfordshire*. Stroud: Sutton

Herring, P, 1998 *Cornwall's historic landscape. Presenting a method of historic landscape character assessment*. Truro: Cornwall Archaeological Unit and English Heritage, Cornwall County Council

Hesse, M, 1992 Fields, tracks and boundaries in the Creakes, north Norfolk, *Norfolk Archaeol*, **41**, 305–24

Hesse, M, 1998 Medieval field systems and land tenure in South Creake, Norfolk, *Norfolk Archaeol*, **43**, 79–97

Hey, G, 1996 Yarnton Floodplain, *South Midlands Archaeology* **26**, 63–7

Higham, N J, 1979 An aerial survey of the Upper Lune Valley, in N J Higham (ed) *The changing past. Some recent work in the archaeology of northern England.* Manchester: Department of Extra-Mural Studies, University of Manchester, 31–8

Higham, N J, 1993 *The origins of Cheshire.* Manchester: Manchester University Press

Higham, N J & Jones G D B, 1975 Frontier, forts and farmers. Cumbrian aerial survey 1974–75, *Archaeol J*, **132**, 16–53

Higham, N J & Jones G D B, 1983 The excavation of two Romano-British sites in northern Cumbria, *Britannia*, **14**, 45–72

Higham, N J & Jones G D B, 1985 *The Carvetii.* Stroud: Sutton

Hill, J D, 1995 The pre-Roman Iron Age in Britain and Ireland: an overview, *J World Prehistory*, **9**, 47–98

Hill, J D, 1999 Settlement, landscape and regionality: Norfolk and Suffolk in the pre-Roman Iron Age of Britain and beyond, in J Davies & T Williamson (eds) *Land of the Iceni: the Iron Age in northern East Anglia*, Studies in East Anglian History **4**. Norwich: Centre of East Anglian Studies, University of East Anglia, 185–207

Hingley, R, 1989 *Rural settlement in Roman Britain.* London: Seaby

Hingley, R, 1990 Domestic organization and gender relations in Iron Age and Romano-British households, in R Samson (ed) 1990b, 125–48

Hingley, R, 1991 Past, present and future: the study of the Roman period in Britain, *Scott Archaeol Rev*, **8**, 90–101

Hingley, R, 1996 Prehistoric Warwickshire: a review of the evidence, *Birmingham Warwickshire Archaeol Soc Trans*, **100**, 1–24

Hingley, R, 2000 *Roman officers and English gentlemen. The imperial origins of Roman archaeology.* London: Routledge

Hingley, R, 2004 Rural settlement in northern Britain, in M Todd (ed) *A companion to Roman Britain.* Oxford: Blackwell, 327–48

Hodges, R, 1991 *Wall-to-wall history: the story of Roystone Grange.* London: Duckworth

Horne, P D & MacLeod, D, 2004 The RCHME's Yorkshire Dales Mapping Project, in R F White & P R Wilson (eds) *Archaeology and historic landscapes of the Yorkshire Dales*, Yorkshire Archaeological Society Occasional Paper **2**, Leeds: Yorkshire Archaeological Society, 15–24

Inman, R, 1988 Romano-British settlement in the South Tees Basin, in J Price & P R Wilson (ed) *Recent research in Roman Yorkshire*, BAR Brit Ser **193**. Oxford: British Archaeological Reports, 219–34

James, S, 2001 Soldiers and civilians: identity and interaction in Roman Britain, in S James & M Millett (eds) 2001, 77–89

James, S & Millett, M (eds), 2001 *Britons and Romans: advancing an archaeological agenda*, CBA Res Rep **125**. York: Council for British Archaeology

Johns, C & Herring, P, 1996 *St Keverne historic landscape assessment: an archaeological and historical survey: a report to English Heritage and the Ministry of Agriculture, Fisheries and Food.* Truro: Cornwall Archaeological Unit

Johnson, L, 2005 Roman settlement in the Wreake valley, Leicestershire. Unpubl MA dissertation, University of Leicester

Johnson, M, 1993 *Housing culture: traditional architecture in an English landscape.* London: UCL Press

Johnson, N, 1994 *Bodmin Moor: an archaeological survey. Volume 1, the human landscape to c. 1800.* London: English Heritage and RCHME

Jones, A H M, 1974 *The later Roman Empire, 284–602: a social, economic and administrative survey.* Oxford: Blackwell

Jones, A M, 2001 The excavation of a multi-period site at Stencoose, Cornwall, *Cornish Archaeol*, **39–40**, 45–94

Jones, D, 1988 Aerial reconnaissance and prehistoric and Romano-British archaeology in northern Lincolnshire – a sample survey. *Lincolnshire Hist Archaeol*, **23**, 5–30

Jones, D, 1998 Romano-British settlements on the Lincolnshire Wolds, in R Bewley (ed) 1998, 69–80

Jones, D, in prep Romano-British settlement in the Vale of York: the aerial perspective, in D MacLeod (ed) *The Vale of York Project*

Jones, G D B, 1999 Conclusion: marginality, their fault or ours? A warning from the Cumbrian evidence, in M Nevell (ed) 1999, 90–6

Jones, M K & Miles, D 1979 Celt and Roman in the Thames valley: approaches to culture change, in B C Burnham & H B Johnson (eds) *Invasion and response: the case of Roman Britain*, BAR Brit Ser **73**. Oxford: British Archaeological Reports, 315–26

Jones, R & Page, M, 2006 *Medieval Villages in an English landscape: beginnings and ends.* Bollington: Windgather Press.

Kidd, S, 2004 Northamptonshire in the first millennium BC, in M Tingle (ed) *The Archaeology of Northamptonshire.* Northampton: Northamptonshire Archaeological Society, 44–62

King, A C, 1984 Animal bones and the dietary identity of military and civilian groups in Roman Britain, Germany and Gaul, in T F C Blagg & A C King (eds) *Military and civilian in Roman Britain: cultural relationships in a frontier province*, BAR Brit Ser **136**. Oxford: British Archaeological Reports, 187–217

Knight, D & Howard, A J, 2004a The later Bronze Age and Iron Ages: towards an enclosed landscape, in D Knight & A J Howard (eds) 2004, 79–114

Knight, D & Howard, A J (eds), 2004b *Trent valley landscapes*. Kings Lynn: Heritage Marketing and Publications

Knight, D, Howard, A J & Leary, R, 2004 The Romano-British landscape, in D Knight & A J Howard (eds) 2004b, 115–51

Lambrick, G & Allen, T, 2004 *Gravelly Guy, Stanton Harcourt: the development of a prehistoric and Romano-British community*, Thames Valley Landscapes Monograph **21**. Oxford: Oxford Archaeology

Lambrick, G & Robinson, M, 1979 *Iron Age and Roman riverside settlements at Farmoor, Oxfordshire*, CBA Res Rep **32**, Oxfordshire Archaeological Unit Report **2**. London: Council for British Archaeology, Oxford: Oxfordshire Archaeological Unit

Laurence, R, 1994 *Roman Pompeii: space and society*. London: Routledge

Laurence, R, 1999 *Roads of Roman Italy: mobility and cultural change*. London: Routledge

Leech, R, 1982 *Excavations at Catsgore 1970–3*, Western Archaeological Trust Excavation Monograph **2**. Bristol: Western Archaeological Trust

Lewis, C, Mitchell-Fox, P & Dyer, C, 1996 *Village, hamlet and field: changing medieval settlements in central England*. Manchester: Manchester University Press

Liddle, P, 1994 The Medbourne Area Survey, in M Parker Pearson & R T Schadla-Hall (eds) 1994, 34–6

Lobb, S J & Rose, P G, 1996 *Archaeological survey of the Lower Kennett Valley, Berkshire*. Salisbury: Wessex Archaeology

Lock, G & Gosden, C, 2001 *Hillforts of the Ridgeway Project: excavations at Alfred's Castle 2000*. Oxford: Institute of Archaeology

Lyne, M A B & Jefferies, R S, 1979 *The Alice Holt/Farnham pottery industry*, CBA Res Rep **30**. London: Council for British Archaeology

McOmish, D, Field, D & Brown, G, 2002 *The field archaeology of the Salisbury Plain Training Area*. London: English Heritage

Makepeace, G A, 1998 Romano-British settlements in the Peak District and north-east Staffordshire, *Derbyshire Archaeol J*, **118**, 95–138

Martin, E, 1999 Suffolk in the Iron Age, in J Davies & T Williamson (eds) *Land of the Iceni: the Iron Age in northern East Anglia*. Studies in East Anglian History **4**. Norwich: Centre of East Anglian Studies, University of East Anglia, 45–99

Matthews, K, 1999 Rural settlement in Roman Cheshire: a theoretical view, in M Nevell (ed) 1999, 27–34

Maude, K, 1999 The very edge: reappraising Romano-British settlement in the central Pennines; the Littondale experience, in M Nevell (ed) 1999, 42–6

May, J, 1984 Major settlements of the Late Iron Age in Lincolnshire, in F N Field & A J White (eds) *A prospect of Lincolnshire*. Lincoln, 18–22

May, J, 1996 *Dragonby: report on excavations at an Iron Age and Romano-British settlement in north Lincolnshire*, Oxbow Monograph **61**. Oxford: Oxbow Books

Meadows, I, 1995 Wollaston: the Nene Valley, a British Moselle?, *Curr Archaeol*, **150**, 212–15

Metzler, J, Millett, M, Roymans, N & Slofstra, J (eds), 1995 *Integration in the early Roman West*, Luxembourg: Musee National

Miles, D (ed), 1982 *The Romano-British countryside: studies in rural settlement and economy*, BAR Brit Ser **103**. Oxford: British Archaeological Reports

Miles, D, 1989 The Romano-British countryside, in M Todd (ed) 1989, 115–26

Miles, D, Palmer, S, Lock, G, Gosden, C & Cromarty, A M, 2003 *Uffington White Horse and its landscape: investigations at White Horse Hill, Uffington, 1989–95, and Tower Hill, Ashbury, 1993–4*. Oxford: Oxford Archaeology

Miles, D, Palmer, S, Smith, A & Jones, G P, 2006 *Iron Age and Roman settlement in the upper Thames valley: excavations at Claydon Pike and other sites within the Cotswold Water Park*. Oxford: Oxford Archaeology

Millett, M, 1985 Field survey calibration: a contribution, in C C Haselgrove, M Millett & I Smith (eds) 1985, 31–7

Millett, M, 1990 *The Romanization of Britain*. Cambridge: Cambridge University Press

Millett, M, 1991 Pottery: population or supply pattern? The Ager Tarraconensis approach, in G W W Barker & J Lloyd (eds) 1991, 18–26

Millett, M, 2001 Approaches to urban societies, in S James & M Millett (eds) 2001, 60–6

Millett, M (ed), 2006 *Survey and excavation of a Roman roadside settlement at Shiptonthorpe, East Yorkshire*, Yorkshire Archaeological Society Monograph **5**

Morris, M & Wainwright, A, 1995 Iron Age and Romano-British settlement, agriculture and industry in the Upper Bulbourne Valley, Hertfordshire: an interim interpretation, in R Holgate (ed) *Chiltern archaeology recent work. A handbook for the next decade*. Dunstable: Book Castle, 68–75

Nevell, M (ed), 1999 *Living on the edge of empire: methodology, models and marginality. Late prehistoric and Romano-British rural settlement in North-West England*, Archaeology North West **3**. Manchester: Council for British Archaeology North West, Field Archaeology Centre University of Manchester, Chester Archaeology

Nevell, M, 2001 The edge of empire: late prehistoric and Romano-British settlement in North West England.

A study in marginality, in N J Higham (ed) *Archaeology of the Roman Empire. A tribute to the life and works of Professor Barri Jones*. BAR Int Ser **940**. Oxford: British Archaeological Reports, 59–74

Nevell, M, 2004 The late prehistoric and Romano-British settlement of the Mersey Basin. A study in marginality, *J Chester Archaeol Soc*, **78**, 1–21

Newman, J, 1994 The East Anglian kingdom pilot survey, in M Parker Pearson & R T Schadla-Hall (eds) 1994, 10–15

Newman, J, 2005 Survey in the Deben valley, in M Carver (ed) *Sutton Hoo: a seventh-century princely burial ground and its context*. London: British Museum Press, 477–87

Oosthuizen, S, 1998 Prehistoric fields into medieval furlongs? Evidence from Caxton, south Cambridgeshire, *Proc Cambridge Antiq Soc*, **86**, 145–52

Oosthuizen, S, 2003 The roots of common fields: linking prehistoric and medieval field systems in west Cambridgeshire, *Landscapes*, **4**, 40–64

Oswald, A, 2004 An Iron Age hillfort in an evolving landscape. Analytical field survey on West Hill, Kirknewton, in P Frodsham (ed) 2004, 202–12

Palmer, R, 1984 *Danebury: an Iron Age hillfort in Hampshire. An aerial photographic interpretation of its environs*. London: RCHME

Palmer, R, 1996 Air photo interpretation and the Lincolnshire fenland, *Landscape Hist*, **18**, 5–16

Palmer, S, 2002 *Ling Hall quarry, Church Lawford, Warwickshire, Archaeological excavations 1989–1999*. Warwickshire County Council: Museum Field Services Report

Parker Pearson, M & Schadla-Hall, R T (eds), 1994 *Looking at the land: archaeological landscapes in eastern England*. Leicester: Leicestershire Museums, Arts and Records Service

Parry, S, in press *The Raunds Area Survey*. Oxford: Oxbow Books

Pearce, J, Millett, M & Struck, M (eds), 2000 *Burial in the Roman world*. Oxford: Oxbow Books

Percival, S & Williamson, T M, 2005 Early fields and medieval furlongs: excavations at Creake Road, Burnham Sutton, Norfolk, *Landscapes*, **6**, 1–17

Petch, D F, 1987 The Roman period, in B E Harris & A T Thacker (eds) *A history of the county of Chester volume 1*. London: Victoria County Histories of England, 115–236

Pettit, P, 1995 *Prehistoric Dartmoor*. Newton Abbott: Forest Green

Phillips, C W (ed), 1970 *The fenland in Roman times*. London: Royal Geographical Society

Philpott, R A, 1991 *Burial practices in Roman Britain: a survey of grave treatment and furnishing, AD43–410*, BAR Brit Ser **219**. Oxford: Tempus Reparatum

Pickering, J, 1978 The Jurassic spine. *Curr Archaeol*, **64**, 140–3

Pickering, J, 1979 Aerial archaeology and the prehistoric landscape, *Landscape Hist*, **1**, 10–15

Pickering, J & Hartley, R F, 1985 *Past worlds in a landscape: archaeological crop marks in Leicestershire*. Leicestershire Museums, Art Galleries and Records Service Archaeological Reports **11**. Leicester: Leicestershire Museums, Art Galleries and Records Service

Pope, R, forthcoming *Building, using and abandoning houses in northern Britain c.2400BC–AD500*

Porter, D, 1995 Roman rural settlement. Unpubl report for English Heritage

Potter, T, 1981 The Roman occupation of the central fenland, *Britannia*, **12**, 79–134

Potter, T, 1989 The Roman fenland: a review of recent work, in M Todd (ed) *Research on Roman Britain 1960–89*, Britannia Monograph Series **11**. London: Society for Promotion of Roman Studies, 147–74

Poulton, R, 2004 Iron Age Surrey, in J Cotton, G Crocker & A Graham (eds) *Aspects of archaeology and history in Surrey*. Guildford: Surrey Archaeological Society, 51–64

Powlesland, D, 1998 The West Heslerton assessment, *Internet Archaeology*, **5**

Powlesland, D, 2003 The Heslerton Parish Project: 20 years of archaeological research in the Vale of Pickering, in T G Manby, S Moorhouse & P Ottoway (eds) *The archaeology of Yorkshire. An assessment at the beginning of the 21st century*, Yorkshire Archaeological Society Occasional Paper **3**. Leeds: Yorkshire Archaeological Society, 275–92

Proctor, J, 2002 An Iron Age and Romano-British Settlement at Pegswood, Northumberland, Archaeology in Nothumberland 2002–2003, 15–18. Northumberland County Council

Purcell, N, 1994 The Roman villa and the landscape of production, in T J Cornell & K Lomas (eds) *Urban society in Roman Italy*. London: UCL Press, 151–79

Quinnell, H, 1986 Cornwall during the Iron Age and Roman periods, *Cornish Archaeol*, **25**, 111–34

Quinnell, H, 1994 Becoming marginal? Dartmoor in later prehistory, *Devon Archaeol Soc Proc*, **51**, 75–84

Quinnell, H, 2004 *Trethurgy: excavations at Trethurgy Round, St. Austell: community and status in Roman and post-Roman Cornwall.* Truro: Historic Environment Service, Environment and Heritage, Cornwall County Council

Rackham, O, 1986 *The history of the countryside*. London: Dent

Ramm, H, 1978 *The Parisi*. Gloucester: Sutton

Ray, K, 2001 Iron Age settlements in Herefordshire, *W Midlands Archaeol*, **44**, 77–84

Ray, K & White, P, 2004 *Herefordshire's historic landscape: a characterisation*, Herefordshire Studies in Archaeology **1**. Hereford: Hereford Council

RCHME, 1970 *An inventory of historical monuments in the county of Dorset. Volume 3: central Dorset.* London: HMSO
RCHME, 1972 *An inventory of historical monuments in the county of Dorset. Volume 4: north Dorset.* London: HMSO
RCHME, 1976 *Ancient and historical monuments in the county of Gloucester. Volume 1: Iron Age and Romano-British monuments in the Gloucestershire Cotswolds.* London: HMSO
RCHME, 1995 The Yorkshire Dales Mapping Project. A report for the National Mapping Programme. Unpubl report, RCHME
Reece, R, 1988 *My Roman Britain.* Cirencester: Cotswold Studies
Revell, L, 1999 Constructing Romanitas: Roman public architecture and the archaeology of practice, in P Baker, C Forcey, S Jundi & R Witcher (eds) *TRAC98: proceedings of the eighth annual theoretical archaeology conference Leicester 1998.* Oxford: Oxbow Books, 52–8
Richards, J C, 1978 *The archaeology of the Berkshire downs: an introductory survey.* Reading: Berkshire Archaeological Committee
Richardson, K M, 1951 The excavation of Iron Age villages on Boscombe Down West, *Wiltshire Archaeol Natur Hist Soc Mag*, **54**, 123–68
Riley, D N, 1980 *Early landscape from the air.* Sheffield: Department of Archaeology and Prehistory, University of Sheffield
Riley, H & Wilson-North, R, 2001 *The field archaeology of Exmoor.* Swindon: English Heritage
Rippon, S, 1991 Early planned landscapes in south-east Essex, *Essex Archaeol Hist*, **22**, 46–60
Rippon, S, 1997 *The Severn estuary: landscape evolution and wetland reclamation.* Leicester: Leicester University Press
Rippon, S, 2000 The Romano-British exploitation of coastal wetlands: survey and excavation on the north Somerset Levels, 1993–97, *Britannia*, **31**, 69–200
Robbins, G, 1998 Cropmark remains and domestic space, *Assemblage*, **3**. Available: http://www.shef.ac.uk/assem/previous_issues.html Accessed: 5 April 2007
Roberts, B K & Wrathmell, S, 2000 *An atlas of rural settlement in England.* Swindon: English Heritage
Roberts, I, Burgess, A & Berg, D, 2001 *A new link to the past. The archaeological landscape of the M1–A1 Link Road*, Yorkshire Archaeology Monograph **7**. Leeds: West Yorkshire Archaeology Service
Rodwell, W, 1978 Relict landscapes in Essex, in H C Bowen & P J Fowler (eds) 1978, 89–98
Rogerson, A, Davison, A, Pritchard, D & Silvester, R, 1997 *Barton Bendish and Caldecote: fieldwork in south-west Norfolk*, East Anglian Archaeology **80**. Norwich: Norfolk Archaeology
Rose, P & Johnson, N, 1982 Defended settlement in Cornwall – an illustrated discussion, in D Miles (ed) 1982, 151–207
Rose, P & Preston-Jones A, 1995 Changes in the Cornish countryside AD 400–1100, in D Hooke & S Burnell (ed) *Landscape and settlement in Britain AD 400–1066.* Exeter: Exeter University Press, 51–68
Rudling, D, 1982 Rural settlement in late Iron Age and Roman Sussex, in D Miles (ed) 1982, 269–88
Rudling, D, 2003 Roman rural settlement in Sussex: continuity and change, in D Rudling (ed) *The archaeology of Sussex to AD 2000.* Kings Lynn: Heritage Marketing and Publications, 111–26
Salway, P, 1970 The Roman fenland, in C W Phillips (ed) *The fenland in Roman times.* London: Royal Geographical society, 1–21
Samson, R, 1990a Comment on Eleanor Scott's 'Romano-British villas and the social construction of space', in R Samson (ed) 1990b, 173–80
Samson, R (ed), 1990b *The social archaeology of houses.* Edinburgh: Edinburgh University Press
Schofield, J (ed), 1991 *Interpreting artefact scatters.* Oxford: Oxbow Books
Schrufer-Kolb, I, 2004 *Roman iron production in Britain: technological and socio-economic landscape development along the Jurassic Ridge*, BAR Brit Ser **380**. Oxford: Archaeopress
Scott, E, 1990 Romano-British villas and the social construction of space, in R Samson (ed) 1990b, 149–72
Scott, S, 1995 Symbols of power and nature: the Orpheus mosaics of fourth century Britain and their architectural contexts, in P Rush (ed) *Theoretical Roman archaeology: Second conference proceedings.* Aldershot: Avebury, 105–21
Scott, S, 2000 *Art and society in fourth century Roman Britain.* Oxford: Oxford University Committee for Archaeology
Shennan, S, 1985 *Experiments in the collection and analysis of archaeological survey data: the East Hampshire Survey.* Sheffield: Department of Archaeology and Prehistory, University of Sheffield
Shiel, D, 1995 St Austell north-east distributor road: report on geophysical survey. Unpubl report, GSB
Small, F, 2002 The Lambourn Downs: a report for the National Mapping Programme, Aerial Survey Report AER/13/2002. Swindon: English Heritage
Smith, C, 1977 The valleys of the Tame and the Middle Trent – their populations and ecology during the late first millennium BC, in J Collis (ed) *The Iron Age in Britain: a review.* Sheffield: Department of Archaeology, University of Sheffield, 51–61
Smith, C, 1979 *Fisherwick: the reconstruction of an Iron*

Age landscape, BAR Brit Ser **61**. Oxford: British Archaeological Reports

Smith, J T, 1978 Villas as a key to social structure, in M Todd (ed) 1978, 149–56

Smith, J T, 1987 The social structure of a Roman villa: Marshfield-Ironmongers Piece, *Oxford J Archaeol*, **6**, 243–55

Smith, J T, 1997 *Roman villas: a study in social structure*. London: Routledge

Smith, R J C, Healy, F, Allen, M J, Morris, E L, Barnes, I & Woodward, P J, 1997 *Excavations along the route of the Dorchester by-pass, Dorset, 1986–8*. Salisbury: Wessex Archaeology

Spratt, D, 1989 *Linear earthworks of the Tabular Hills, northeast Yorkshire*. Sheffield: J R Collis

Stevens, C E, 1966 The social and economic aspects of rural settlement, in C Thomas (ed) *Rural settlement in Roman Britain*, CBA Res Rep **7**. London: Council for British Archaeology, 108–28

Still, L & Vyner, B, 1986 Air photographic evidence for later prehistoric settlement in the Tees valley, *Durham Archaeol J*, **2**, 11–24

Still, L, Vyner, B & Bewley, R, 1989 A decade of air survey in Cleveland and the Tees Valley Hinterland and a strategy for air survey in County Durham, *Durham Archaeol J*, **5**, 1–10

Stoertz, C, 1997 *Ancient landscapes of the Yorkshire Wolds. Aerial photographic transcription and analysis*. London: RCHME

Swan, V, 1984 *The pottery kilns of Roman Britain*. London: HMSO

Taylor, J, 1996 Iron Age and Roman landscapes in the East Midlands: a case study in integrated survey. Unpubl PhD thesis, University of Durham

Taylor, J, 1999 Air photography and the Holme-on-Spalding Moor landscape, in P Halkon & M Millett (eds) *Rural settlement and industry: studies in the Iron Age and Roman archaeology of lowland East Yorkshire*, Yorkshire Archaeology Monograph **4**. Leeds: Yorkshire Archaeology Society, 14–41

Taylor, J, 2000a Iron Age and Roman rural settlement in the MPP. Unpubl manuscript report for English Heritage

Taylor, J, 2000b Stonea in its fenland context: moving beyond an imperial estate, *J Roman Archaeology*, **13**, 647–58

Taylor, J, 2001 Rural society in Roman Britain, in S James & M Millett (eds) 2001, 46–59

Taylor, J, 2004 English Heritage Roman Rural Settlement Project: a national overview. Unpubl report, University of Leicester

Thomas, C, 1966 The character and origins of Dumnonia, in C Thomas (ed) *Rural settlement in Roman Britain*, CBA Res Rep **7**. London: Council for British Archaeology, 74–98

Thomas, J, 2005 From 'our place' to 'my place': the origins and development of aggregated settlement in the east midlands. Unpubl MA thesis, University of Leicester

Todd, M (ed), 1978 *Studies in the Romano-British villa*. Leicester: Leicester University Press

Todd, M, 1991 *The Coritani*. Stroud: Sutton

Topping, P, 2004 Hillforts, farms and fields. Excavations on Wether Hill, Ingram 1993–2002, in P Frodsham (ed) 2004,190–201

Upex, S, 2002 Landscape continuity and the fossilization of Roman fields, *Archaeol J*, **159**, 77–108

Van de Noort, R, 2004 *The Humber wetlands: the archaeology of a dynamic landscape*. Bollington: Windgather Press

Van de Noort, R & Ellis, S, 1997 *Wetland heritage of the Humberhead levels: an archaeological survey*. Kingston upon Hull: Humber Wetlands Project, University of Hull

Van de Noort, R & Ellis, S, 1998 *Wetland heritage of the Ancholme and lower Trent valleys: an archaeological survey*. Kingston upon Hull: Humber Wetlands Project, Centre for Wetland Archaeology, University of Hull

van der Veen, M, 1992 *Crop husbandry regimes: an archaeobotanical study of farming in northern England 1000BC–AD500*. Sheffield: Collis Publications

van der Veen, M, & O'Connor, T, 1998 The expansion of agricultural production in late Iron Age and Roman Britain, in J Bailey (ed) *Science in archaeology: an agenda for the future*. Swindon: English Heritage, 127–44

Wainwright, G J & Davies, S M, 1995 *Balksbury Camp, Hampshire: excavations 1973 and 1981*. London: English Heritage

Wait, G, 1985 *Ritual and religion in Iron Age Britain*, BAR Brit Ser **149**, Oxford: British Archaeological Reports

Wallace-Hadrill, A, 1994 *Houses and society in Pompeii and Herculaneum*. Princeton: Princeton University Press

Waller, M, 1994 *The Fenland Project No. 9: Flandrian environmental change in fenland*, East Anglian Archaeology **70**. Cambridge: Fenland Project Committee, Fenland Archaeological Trust

Warner, P, 1996 *The origins of Suffolk*. Manchester: Manchester University Press

Webster, G, 1991 *The Cornovii*. Stroud: Sutton

Webster, J, 1996 Ethnographic barbarity: colonial discourse and 'Celtic warrior societies', in J Webster & N Cooper (eds) *Roman imperialism: post-colonial perspectives*. Leicester: School of Archaeology and Ancient History, University of Leicester, 111–24

Whimster, R, 1981 *Burial practices in Iron Age Britain: a discussion and gazetteer of the evidence c.700BC–*

AD43, BAR Brit Ser **90**. Oxford: British Archaeological Reports

Whimster, R, 1989 *The emerging past*. London: RCHME

White, P, 2003 *The Arrow valley, Herefordshire: archaeology, landscape change and conservation*, Herefordshire Studies in Archaeology Series **2**. Hereford: Herefordshire Archaeology

White, R, 1998 *Wroxeter: life and death of a Roman city*. Stroud: Tempus

Wigley, A, 2007 Pitted histories: early first millennium BC pit alignments in the central Welsh Marches, in C Haselgrove & R Pope (eds) 2007, 119–34

Wilkinson, T J, 1988 *Archaeology and environment in South Essex, rescue archaeology along the Grays by-pass, 1979–80*. Chelmsford: Essex County Council Field Archaeology Unit

Williamson, T M, 1984 The Roman countryside: settlement and agriculture in north west Essex, *Britannia*, **15**, 225–30

Williamson, T M, 1987a Early co-axial field systems on the East Anglian boulder clays, *Proc Prehist Soc*, **53**, 419–31

Williamson, T M, 1987b The development of settlement in north west Essex: the results of recent field survey, *Essex Archaeol Hist*, **17**, 120–32

Williamson, T M, 1988 Settlement, hierarchy and economy in north west Essex, in K Branigan & D Miles (eds) 1988, 73–82

Williamson, T M, 1998 The 'Scole-Dickleburgh field system' revisited, *Landscape Hist*, **20**, 19–28

Williamson, T M, 1993 *The origins of Norfolk*. Manchester: Manchester University Press

Willis, S, 1999 Without and within: aspects of culture and community in the Iron Age of north-eastern England, in B Bevan (ed) *Northern exposure: interpretative devolution and the Iron ages in Britain*. Leicester: School of Archaeological Studies, University of Leicester, 81–110

Willis, S, 2000 The Romanization of pottery assemblages in the east and north-east of England during the first century AD: A comparative analysis, *Britannia*, **27**, 179–221

Willis, S, 2001 An archaeological resource assessment and research agenda for the later Bronze Age and Iron Age (the first millennium BC) in the east midlands. Available: http://www.le.ac.uk/archaeology/research/projects/eastmidsfw/pdfs/emidiron.pdf Accessed: 5 April 2007

Willis, S, 2006 The Later Bronze and Iron Age, in N J Cooper (ed) *The Archaeology of the East Midlands*. Leicester: Leicester Archaeology Monograph **13**, 89–136

Willis, S & Dungworth, D, 1999 *Excavation and fieldwork at Mount Pleasant, Nettleton, Lincolnshire 1998*. Lincoln: Lincolnshire County Council

Wilson, P R (ed), 1989 *The Crambeck Roman pottery industry*. Leeds: Yorkshire Archaeological Society

Witcher, R, 1998 Roman roads: phenomenological perspectives on roads in the landscape, in C Forcey, J Hawthorne & R Witcher (eds) *TRAC97: The seventh theoretical Roman archaeology conference 1997*. Oxford: Oxbow Books, 60–70

Woodiwiss, S (ed), 1992 *Iron Age and Roman salt production and the medieval town of Droitwich: excavations at Old Bowling Green and Friar Street*, CBA Res Rep **81**. London: Council for British Archaeology

Woodward, A, 1991 The landscape survey, in N M Sharples (ed) *Maiden Castle excavations and field survey 1985–86*. London: HBMCE, 9–37

Young, C J, 1977 *The Roman pottery industry of the Oxford region*, BAR Brit Ser **43**. Oxford: British Archaeological Reports

Young, R & Webster, J, forthcoming *Excavations on Bollihope Common 2004*.

Index

Entries in bold refer to the Figures